Modern Critical Interpretations

Modern Critical Interpretations

Alice Walker's
The Color Purple

Edited and with an introduction by
Harold Bloom
Sterling Professor of the Humanities
Yale University

CHELSEA HOUSE PUBLISHERS
Philadelphia

© 2000 by Chelsea House Publishers,
a subsidiary of Haights Cross Communications.

Introduction © 2000 by Harold Bloom

Printed and bound in the United States of America

10 9 8 7 6 5 4 3 2

∞ The paper used in this publication meets the minimum
requirements of the American National Standard for
Permanence of Paper for Printed Library Materials,
Z39.48-1984

Library of Congress Cataloging-in-Publication Data

Alice Walker's The color purple / edited and with an
introduction by Harold Bloom.
        p. cm. — (Modern critical interpretations)
    Includes bibliographical references (p.) and index.
    ISBN 0-7910-5666-X (alk. paper)
    1. Walker, Alice, 1944 – Color purple.
2. Afro-American woman in literature.
I. Bloom, Harold.   II. Series.
PS3573.A425 C6325   2000
813'.54—dc21
                                    99-052024
                                      CIP

Contributing Editor: Erica DaCosta

Contents

Editor's Note

My Introduction stoically considers my own limitations in confronting a novel whose overt ideology is African-American feminism.

Lauren Berlant judges Celie to embrace "a mode of cultural nationalism unable to transmit objective knowledge . . . about the way institutional forms of power" affect both individuals and social relations.

Henry Louis Gates Jr., the best-known of African-American literary critics, considers the inescapable influence of Zora Neale Hurston upon *The Color Purple*, after which the formidable Bell Hooks remarks upon the conservatism of narrative form in the book.

Didactism in Walker's novel is related by Tamar Katz to the prior rhetorical stance of her prime precursor, Hurston, while Carolyn Williams centers upon Walker's "womanist revision of God."

Molly Hite, meditating upon marginality, also returns to Hurston's influence, and to Walker's "reversal" of the "masculine" theory of the anxiety of influence, one that I recognize only with a certain estranged nostalgia in these pages.

The Color Purple is interpreted as social and moral parable by Diane Gabrielsen Scholl, after which it is analyzed as "Womanist Gospel" by Tuzyline Jita Allan.

For Linda Selzer, the book is a sustained critique of racial relations from "within the domestic sphere," while Deborah E. McDowell celebrates *The Color Purple* for creating "a new literary space for a black and female idiom."

In a rather fierce essay, Carla Kaplan insists that "female difference" must not be lulled by the comforts of *The Color Purple*, the implication being that feminist criticism must maintain a polemical stance.

Yvonne Johnson, in the final essay, again returns us to Hurston, another confirmation (at least for me) that the shadow of Hurston is a far more ambivalent phenomenon for Alice Walker than she can either recognize or admit.

Introduction

In my old age, as person and as literary critic, I am resolved to give up all polemic, and to limp off the battlefield, carrying my wounds with me, honorable and otherwise. Since I am (somewhat) at odds with nearly every essayist in this volume, as well as with their illustrious subject, a certain wariness necessarily informs my stance in what follows.

Alice Walker, and her allied critics, tend to idealize the influence-relationship between black women writers, indeed all women writers. Feminist ideology, at least in the academy, holds that rivalry, creative envy, and the sublime contest for the highest place among writers, are all masculine tendencies or anxieties. Either women do not beware other women and never compete with one another (or with their mothers), or else human nature is so purified by feminist discourse that all agonistic elements in literature subside.

Walker, whether in *The Color Purple* or *Meridian*, is very much Zora Neale Hurston's novelistic daughter. No book, she has affirmed, means more to her than *Their Eyes Were Watching God*. Though poignant, this affirmation is a touch redundant, since both Celie and Meridian are palpable revisions of Hurston's Janie. The literary issue then becomes (at least for old Brontosaurus Bloom) what is *added* to the representation of character and personality when we turn from rereading Hurston to rereading Walker. And since we are all mortal, whatever our idealisms or our ideologies, *do* we reread Walker, as I certainly go back to Hurston, or do we yield Walker up, since time is limited?

Walker's most glowing tribute to Hurston has the title: "On refusing to Be Humbled by Second Place in a Contest You Did Not Design." I fear that all of literature is a contest that any new writer did not and could not design. Nietzsche wrote persuasively of "Hesiod's Contest with Homer," and Hemingway memorably boasted of being in training to take on Tolstoy himself. I grant you that Homer, Hesiod, Nietzsche, Tolstoy, and

1

Hemingway were male, but George Eliot, Virginia Woolf, Edith Wharton, Willa Cather, and Iris Murdoch reveal intense agonistic relations between them. Ah, but these were none of them African-American. True. Toni Morrison's superb struggles with precursors involve Faulkner, Woolf, and Ralph Ellison, though Morrison, herself now highly ideological, also denies any share in the anxiety of influence. Perhaps we must wait another generation, and then we will see how younger black women novelists, of comparable gifts, resolve their struggle with Morrison.

The Color Purple, like *Meridian*, closely follows *Their Eyes Were Watching God* by giving us a heroine who has lived more than one revisionist moment in regard to her cultural context. If you *repeat* that moment, as Walker consciously does, then your imaginative gesture will not be one of origination. Hurston, who was anything but an ideologue, who was neither a feminist nor a African-American nationalist, wrote with the freedom of an original. Shadowed always by Hurston's achievement, Walker has shifted the agonistic ground to issues of feminism and political liberation, but at the high cost (at least for me) of speaking in a voice never altogether her own, the voice of Hurston's Janie.

LAUREN BERLANT

Race, Gender, and Nation in The Color Purple

The passion with which native intellectuals defend the
existence of their natural culture may be a source of
amazement; but those who condemn this exaggerated passion
are strangely apt to forget that their own psyche and their own
selves are conveniently sheltered behind a French or German
culture which has given full proof of its existence and which is
uncontested.

—Frantz Fanon, "On National Culture"

Ask anyone up Harlem way
　　Who that guy Bojangles is.
　　They may not know who's President
　　But they'll tell you who Bojangles is.
　　　　　—"Bojangles of Harlem," *Swing Time*

"Dear God, I am fourteen years old. ~~I am~~ I have always been a good girl.
Maybe you can give me a sign letting me know what is happening to me."
The Color Purple begins with the striking out—but not the erasure—of "I
am." Celie's crisis of subjectivity has both textual and historical implications:
her status as a subject is clarified, in the course of the novel, by her

---

From *Critical Inquiry* 14, no. 4 (Summer 1988). © 1988 University of Chicago.

emergence from the enforced privacy of a prayer-letter to God sometime in her fourteenth year, to public speaking, of a sort, during a community celebration on the Fourth of July, during the 1940s. The appearance of the Fourth of July in the novel's final moments appears to be a ratification of Celie's own personal liberation at the nation's mythicopolitical origin, the birth of the American "people." But what Independence Day resolves for the identity of Anglo-Americans it has raised as a question for Afro-Americans: along with narrating Celie's history, *The Color Purple* stages, in its journey to this final day, an instance of black America's struggle to clarify its own national identity from the point of view of American populism.

The Color Purple problematizes tradition-bound origin myths and political discourse in the hope of creating and addressing an Afro-American nation constituted by a rich, complex, and ambiguous culture. But rather than using patriarchal languages and logics of power to describe the emergence of a postpatriarchal Afro-American national consciousness, Celie's narrative radically resituates the subject's national identity within a mode of aesthetic, not political, representation. These discursive modes are not "naturally" separate, but *The Color Purple* deliberately fashions such a separation in its attempt to represent a national culture that operates according to "womanist" values rather than patriarchal forms. While political language is laden with the historical values and associations of patriarchal power, aesthetic discourse here carries with it a utopian force that comes to be associated with the spirit of everyday life relations among women.

Alice Walker has said that her intent with *The Color Purple* was to supplant the typically patriarchal concerns of the historical novel—"the taking of lands, or the births, battles, and deaths of Great Men"—with the scene of "one woman asking another for her underwear." Walker manipulates the horizon of expectations of the historical novel by situating the text within the traditionally confessional, local, privatized concerns of the autobiographical epistolary novel and, from this point of view, expanding to include the broader institutional affiliations and experiences of Afro-American women. This is why the reemergence of nationalism at the end of the novel is puzzling: Celie's New World aesthetic and the celebration of the American revolution seems a contradictory alliance in the postpatriarchal culture set up by the novel.

Unlike *The Color Purple*, Walker's early novel *Meridian* explicitly addresses the *paradoxes* of Afro-American identity. Suffering a "hybrid" affiliation to both sides of the hyphen, the Afro-American citizen learns not of the inalienable rights but of the a priori inferiority and cultural marginality of Afro-Americans—as if the "Afro" in the complex term were a syntactical negation of "American." Meridian, the woman whose political biography is told in the novel, learns of her contested relation to the rights of full American citizens as Celie and many Americans do: in public school, where the ideology of American identity is transmitted as if a part of the very air students inhale. On one important occasion, Meridian participates in an oratorical competition at her high school,

> reciting a speech that extolled the virtues of the Constitution and praised the superiority of The American Way of Life. The audience cared little for what she was saying, and of course they didn't believe any of it, but they were rapt, listening to her speak so passionately and with such sad valor in her eyes.

Suddenly the meaning of what she says pierces Meridian's awareness; she almost faints, simultaneously gaining and losing "consciousness" on comprehending the horrible joke American national ideology has played on her, reproducing itself in her mind like a kind of vague dream or baby talk. On awakening to the hypocrisy behind the discourse of "inalienable rights," Meridian opposes the American assertion that it is a privilege just to be able to utter these phonemes unconsciously. To Meridian, black nationalism must dedicate itself to constructing a political and cultural context in which one might, indeed, enjoy a positive relation to national identity, rather than a negative relation to a race always already marked by its status as a social "problem."

> For she understood, finally, that the respect she owed her life was to continue . . . to live it. . . . And that this existence extended beyond herself to those around her because, in fact, the years in America had created them One Life.

The movement in these phrases from the solipsism of everyday life to the symbolic unity of "One Life" takes place under the symbolic and political force of "years in America." Despite its cruelly oppressive role in the historical formation of racial consciousness, America in this novel remains the sign and utopian paradigm of national identity. Meridian's new selflessness, born of an American-inspired melding of individual self-interest with populist social concerns, serves as a model for the future nation Afro-Americans can construct, founded on a transformation of their atomized historical experience into a mass of resources and a spirit of courage and survival.

Meridian is Walker's most explicitly and narrowly "political" novel. It exposes the gap between the official claims of American democracy and the state's exploitative and repressive practices, and views "personal" relationships as symptoms of the strained political situation. The novel is critical of the sexism within the civil rights movement, for example. Nonetheless *Meridian* subordinates the struggle within gender to the "larger" questions raised by the imminent exhaustion or depletion of the movement itself. Meridian's theory of "One Life" dissolves the barriers of class and education between herself and the black community at large and effectively depoliticizes the struggle within the movement's patriarchal values and practices by locating the "personal" problems of sexism within the nationalist project.

In contrast, *The Color Purple* problematizes nationalism itself, in both its Anglo- and Afro-American incarnations. Most strikingly, the Anglo-American brand of national pride is lampooned. Like Meridian, Celie and Nettie first encounter the concept and the myth of American national identity as a fundamental element of basic literacy disseminated by public schools. But unlike Meridian, Celie is never fooled or impressed by the nation's self-mythification. She reports:

> The way you know who discover America, Nettie say, is think bout cucumbers. That what Columbus sound like. I learned all about Columbus in first grade, but look like he the first thing I forgot. She say Columbus come here in boats call the Neater, the Peter, and the Santomareater. Indians so nice to him he force a bunch of 'em back home with him to wait on the queen.

The Color Purple opens its discourse on the problematics of Afro-American national-historical identity by revealing the manifest irrelevancy of the classic American myth to Celie. Her comic reduction of the American origin tale to a matter of garden-variety phonetics not only indicates the vital importance of oral and folk transmission to less literate communities like the one in which Celie lives, but also suggests the crucial role oral transmission plays in the reproduction of the nation itself, from generation to generation. Elsewhere, for instance, Shug and Celie's rambling discussion of the world during World War II—which ranges among subjects such as the war, U.S. Government theft of land from an "Indian tribe," Hollywood, national and local scandals—represents the haphazard, ad hoc fashion with which the nation disseminates and perpetuates itself among its citizens, even in everyday life.

To maintain power among the people—indeed, to maintain "the people"—America must maintain a presence as accessible and intimate as the familial name and tradition. Celie must gain agency within her immediate, "subjective" environment before she can come to terms with her "impersonal" or institutional relations.

The Color Purple opens with Celie falling through the cracks of a language she can barely use. Her own limited understanding, her technical insecurity, and her plain sense of powerlessness are constructed in contrast to the powerful discourses that share the space with her stuttered utterances. The epigraph of *The Color Purple*, for example, is Stevie Wonder's imperious exhortation, *"Show me how to do like you/Show me how to do it."* Clearly this quotation is a direction as well as a request to the muses, contemporary and historical: *imitatio* is the graphic mode of this novel. Showing me something that is an action you *do* is not only intimately pedagogical, teaching me how to repeat the component gestures of the "doing" that is uniquely like "you"; the epigraph can also be read as the novel's most explicit political directive, deployed to turn individuals into self-conscious and literate users/readers of a cultural semiotic.

For example, Shug is the novel's professor of desire and self-fulfillment, and as such her "example" is not only symbolic but technical, practical. Her first gift of knowledge to Celie is transmitted through a picture Celie and her stepmother see that has fallen out of Mr. _____'s wallet. The answer to Celie's question "What is it?" is "The most beautiful woman I ever saw. . . . I see her there in furs. Her face rouge. Her hair like somethin tail. She grinning. . . ." On the very next page Celie dresses exactly like Shug to keep her father from raping Nettie. Even before Celie possesses technical language about sex, pregnancy, and her body, she "learns" from what Shug "does" in the picture about the standard connection between male sexual desire and the desire to degrade women: "He beat me for dressing trampy but he do it to me anyway." In this regime there is no such thing as "mere" or passive reading: reading is an act of cultural self-assertion, an engagement in the mimesis of social relations.

The crucial intertwining of private and public acts and consciousness signified by the ambiguity of the epigraph's "you" is answered by another ambiguously placed line, hovering above the text proper, also in italics: *"You better not never tell nobody but God. It'd kill your mammy."* This unsigned, double-negative message marks the contested ground on which Celie's negative relation to discourse is established. The disembodied voice pronounces a death threat against Celie's mother, and holds Celie hostage; it is never directly attributed to "Pa," but we learn through linguistic repetition that it must be his. By the end of the third paragraph of Celie's first letter, he repeats the advisory locution "You better" with a similar but different message: "shut up and git used to it."

Lost in a wilderness of unnamed effects, Celie is nonetheless able to resist her silencing by embodying for God's (and the reader's) benefit the generic scene of female humiliation. "Sister Celie" is raised to the level of female exemplum when every woman who sees her tells her, in effect, "You got to fight." Stripped of any right to the privacy of her body, and sentenced to vocal exile, she manages to "speak" in public by becoming a talking book, taking on her body the rape, incest, slave labor, and beating that would otherwise be addressed to other women, her "sisters." Celie's response to these incursions into her autonomy is to enter history for the first time—not really by "asking another woman for her underwear," but by crossing out "I am" and situating herself squarely on the ground of negation.

Celie's particular negation arises not only from the (f)act of rape, effecting her bifurcation into a subject and a subject-made-object-to-itself. Rape here only intensifies the negation that grows from the ongoing patriarchal subjugation of women. Her oppression, as represented early into the novel, circulates around the vulnerabilities that grow from her gender, as constructed within the social space which her "Pa" respectably occupies.

But gender oppression is neither the only nor the main factor operating in the oppressive paternal ideology: behind the story Celie thinks she knows, in which the father's control of the family's "private" resources effectively gives him license to violate "his" women, is a story that reveals not the family's private or internal structure but its social and historical placement. Behind "Pa"'s story, as Celie discovers, is the story of her biological father's lynching and murder.

The Color Purple telegraphs the traumatic transformation of Celie's family history by emphasizing Nettie's generic departure from standard epistolary form to the fairy tale. Nettie writes her, "Once upon a time, there was a well-to-do farmer who owned his property near town. Our town, Celie." Celie's biological father, who, like her mother, is never named in the book (not even by a _____), has been lynched. We receive no eyewitness reports of this event, and no spot or discursive mark verifies the father's life or death. "And so, one night, the man's store was burned down, his smithy destroyed, and the man and his two brothers dragged out of their homes in the middle of the night and hanged." Unlike Celie after her rape, the lynched father cannot speak, act, desire for himself. Moreover, as "Pa" tells Celie, "Lynched people don't git no marker." How does this lynching, and its resistance to representation, transform the cultural politics of this novel, no longer confined to witnessing violence deployed on women by men?

The surprising emergence of racial violence, the murder of three black men by an indeterminate group Nettie calls "the white merchants," induces Celie's second semiotic collapse. The first collapse, which opens the novel, emerges from Celie's confusion about what is "happening" to her in the present tense. Celie's second collapse under the weight of painful knowledge is unconnected to the facts of her contemporary situation: rather, its effects reach back to her origin, and in doing so completely destabilize her identity. This crisis is evident in Celie's almost catatonic announcement—in which, uncharacteristically, all of her verbs are disrupted—"My daddy lynch. My mama crazy. All my little half-brothers and sisters no kin to me. My children not my sister and brother. Pa not pa."

In this revised autobiographical tale, racism succeeds sexism as the cause of social violence in the narrative. The switch from a sexual to a racial code, each of which provides a distinct language and a distinct logic of social relations, releases into the text different kinds of questions about Celie's identity: the new information challenges what Celie (and her readers) mistakenly thought they already knew about the horrific systematic sexual violence that seemed to be the distinguishing mark of family life for women.

For Celie and Nettie's biological father, race functions much as gender functions for the sisters: not as a site of positive identification for the victim, but as an excuse for the oppressor's intricate *style* of cultural persecution. Lynching, in his narrative, has a structural equivalence to Celie's rape, in its violent reduction of the victim to a "biological" sign, an exemplum of subhumanity. This mode of vigilante white justice was a common threat to Southern blacks through the 1930s: Angela Davis, and Frederick Douglass long before her, record the reign of terror propagated by white men ostensibly on behalf of white women's vulnerability to the constant danger of being raped—by black men.

In the narrative of *The Color Purple* the first violation, rape, is succeeded by the second and prior act, lynching: a "logic of equivalence" is installed in the narrative that in effect makes race a synonym for scandalous, transgressive Afro-American sexuality. Both in the conventional link between racial and sexual violence, and in the novel, gender difference takes on the pressure of justifying and representing racial oppression. The (unrepresented) act of lynching effects a transfer at the moment of brutal contact from one (the racial) system of oppression to another (the sexual)—precisely the scandalous code that terrorizes Celie at the beginning of the novel.

This complex substitution of paternal tales effectively frees Celie to reclassify her early experience of sexual violence as a *misunderstanding*. Incest, the collapse of structural taboos that ensure the sexual and economic dissemination of the family, is also a figure for the primal illiteracy with which she has been afflicted. The perversion that marked Celie's entry into consciousness had circumscribed her understanding of the world: fundamentally negated by father and husband, in the church and in the marketplace she would also stay as invisible as possible to avoid provoking further violation. Thus it is understandable that the new tale of paternal origins empowers Celie—because Pa is not pa. Having eliminated the perversion from her memory of being raped by her stepfather, the rapes themselves seem to disappear. Celie then recovers from the guilt and shame that had stood in the way of her "right" to control her body and her pleasure.

But this paternal plot twist also short-circuits whatever legitimate understanding of power's institutional operations Celie might have gained from knowing the complicated motives behind these familial events. If one effect of the second origin tale is to revise Celie's comprehension of the paternal conditions of her production, another simultaneous effect is to repress the scene of history insofar as the extrafamilial elements of social relations are concerned. She understands that people hurt people; but she has no curiosity about the larger situational motives of what appears to be personal behavior.

For instance, the new origin tale reveals yet a third factor driving the transformation of social life and of signification: it reveals the white men's *economic* aim to liquidate the father and his two brothers.

> And as [the father] did so well farming and everything he turned his hand to prospered, he decided to open a store, and try his luck selling dry goods as well. Well, his store did so well that he talked his two brothers into helping him run it. . . . Then the white merchants began to get together and complain that this store was taking all the black business away from them. . . . This would not do.

The store the black men owned took business away from the white men, who then interfered with the free market by lynching their black competitors. Thus class relations, in this instance, are shown to motivate lynching. Lynching was the act of violence white men performed to *racialize*—to invoke the context of black inferiority and subhumanity—the victim; the aura of sexual transgression is also always produced around the lynched by the lynchers, white men guarding the turf of their racial and sexual hegemony.

But Celie never understands it this way, for a number of reasons. First, the language of Nettie's fairy tale encourages the substitution of family discourse for the language of capital relations. Rather than naming names— her own father's, her mother's, her stepfather's—Nettie emphasizes abstract kinship terms like "the man and his two brothers," "the wife," "the widow," "the stranger" to describe their positions in the tale. Because the importance of the story to Celie lies in its transmission within the context of family relations, the tale brackets class issues as if the capitalist economy is generated by the operations of family ideology.

Second, Nettie's fairy tale reflects—without really reflecting on—the historical proximity of racial and sexual oppression to the class struggle that marks Afro-American experience. Yet because her fairy-tale rhetoric emphasizes the personal over the institutional or political components of social relations, the nonbiologized abstraction of class relations virtually disappears from the text.

Third, Celie's disregard of the class issues available in this narrative also serves Walker's desire to effect a shift within the historical novel. The fairy-tale paradigm Nettie provides replaces the "realist" *mise en scène* that had previously governed the novel's representations of intimate familial violence; in so diminishing the centrality of Alfonso's/the stepfather's rapes of Celie, the text abandons its demystification of male behavior in the family to focus on a reconstruction of the "family"—this time under the care of women. This suggests that Celie and Nettie's feminist fairy tale (the "womanist" historical novel) absorbs and transforms the traditional functions of patrifocal-realist mimesis; and that this transformation makes possible the movement of *The Color Purple* into its communal model of utopian representation, in which a partnership of capitalism and sisterhood plays a central role.

In *The Color Purple*, then, the identity crisis that grows from the violence within the family during Celie's childhood is "explained," traced to its origin, in two significantly different ways. The first narrative installs the greed of patriarchal sexual practice in the unflattering mirror of the "private" family; the injustices manifested in the world outside that central core—for example, in Mr. _____'s sadistic treatment of Harpo—appear from the initial point of view to extend, in a vast synchronicity, from the father's private example.

In contrast, the second family fairy tale represents Celie's crisis of self-comprehension—now an inheritance from her mother—as an effect not of sexual abuse but of a relatively noncoagulated set of practices that have escaped full representation within the mainstream culture: class relations filtered through racial animosity, sexual relations resulting from economic domination. Whereas the first representation of family life located evil forces in the most personal of bodies and intentions, the second tale reveals a more general dispersion of responsibility among unnamed and alien subjects and institutions. Still, reflected in the realm of social theatrics that includes but is not contained within the family scene, sexism and racism provide privatizing images for class struggle, making the lynching appear to Celie a personal and "natural"—but not political—event that takes place on "the father's" so-called private body. This set of textual associations, in which class relations become absorbed by personal histories, forms a paradigm in *The Color Purple*: capitalism becomes the sign of "political" history's repression, both in the everyday life consciousness of the subject and in the narrative at large.

Finally, the very *unreality* to the sisters of the new originary fairy tale extends in part from their alienation from the political and historical context within which these acts took place. Neither woman has ever lived outside of the family in the public sphere of American racism. The story of Celie's original parentage marks the first time in her represented life that specifically racist practices come close to hurting her. In *The Color Purple* the burden of operating within a racial social context, which includes working through the oppressive collaboration of racism and sexism, is generally deflected from Celie's tale onto events in the economic and cultural marketplace.

The trial of thinking and making it through the "racial problem" in *The Color Purple* falls mainly to Sofia Butler, the "amazon" who enters Mr. _____'s extended family as Harpo's first wife. The voice of sexual and racial *ressentiment*—for instance, she twice expresses a desire to "kill" her sexual and racial oppressors—Sofia is the first woman Celie knows who refuses to accede to both the patriarchal and the racist demand that the black woman demonstrate her abjection to her oppressors. But the mythic test of Sofia's strength takes place in her refusal to enter the servitude of double discourse demanded of blacks by white culture. She says "Hell no" to the mayor's wife's "complimentary" suggestion that Sofia come to work as her maid; next Sofia answers the mayor's scolding slap of her face with her own powerful punch. For her effort to stay honest in the face of the white demand for black hypocrisy, Sofia gains incarceration in a set of penal institutions that work by a logic similar to that of lynching: to racialize the scene of class struggle in the public sphere and to deploy prejudice against "woman" once behind the walls of the prison and the household. As Sofia tells Celie about her stay in prison: "Every time they ast me to do something, Miss Celie, I act like I'm you. I jump up and do just what they say."

The social coercion of Afro-Americans to participate in a discourse that proclaims their unworthiness is resisted by Sofia, and then performed on Sofia's behalf by Squeak. Squeak's telltale name, in its expression of her distorted, subvocalized voice, describes her original purpose in this text: she enters the narrative as Harpo's dutiful replacement for Sofia, who had refused to allow Harpo to dominate and to beat her.

Squeak knows well how to be properly submissive. But faced with Sofia's crisis Squeak subversively uses her expertise in "proper" feminine self-negating hypocrisy in her supplication for special treatment to the warden of Sofia's prison The warden is conventionally known as her "cousin" since he is the "illegitimate" father of three of Squeak's siblings. This sloppy familial euphemism leads to a comedy of double- and quadruple-talk that includes Squeak asking for (and getting) the *opposite* of what the warden incorrectly *thinks* she wants. (She wants Sofia released from the prison to serve the rest of her sentence as the mayor's maid; she tells the warden that Sofia is not suffering enough in prison, and that to Sofia the most exquisite torture would be being a white woman's maid; he "fornicates" with Squeak and releases Sofia to the mayor's household.)

The warden's "liberties" with Squeak, so different in representational mode than the young Celie's rapes, also serve as the diacritical mark that organizes Squeak's insertion into the "womanist" order. Having exposed herself to sexual, racial, and political abuse in the name of communal solidarity, Squeak assumes the right to her given name, Mary Agnes. She also earns the right to "sing." She wins these privileges by learning to lie and to produce wordplay while seeming to be an unconscious speaker of the enslaved tongue: Squeak attains social mastery in learning to ironize the already-doubled double-talk that marks the discursive situation of the female Afro-American subject in the white patriarchal public sphere.

The degree of discursive self-alienation expressed in the multiple inversions of language that become the violated ground of both rape and humor in *The Color Purple* in part reflects W. E. B. Du Bois' classic observation, in *The Souls of Black Folk*, that his "people" is marked by a "double consciousness." For American blacks, according to Du Bois, irony takes on an almost allegorical charge as the split or "colonized" subject shuttles between subjectivity and his or her cultural, "racial" status as Object. Henry Louis Gates, Jr. has further elaborated on the cultural machinery of Afro-American "double consciousness" by employing Mikhail Bakhtin's reading of class discourses. Gates suggests that colonized discourse is twisted simultaneously in opposite directions: toward an internal polemic and an external irony. Crucially, each of these discursive modes requires the subject's internalized awareness of a hostile audience. This is the context of a priori negation that results in the inevitable production of double consciousness for socially marginalized citizens.

Frantz Fanon complicates the classic mode of the colonized double consciousness by characterizing the body that houses the different modes of self-alienation he feels (Blackness and Objectness) as yet another unsutured site of identity. Rather than reading his fragmentation as the fragmentation of a whole, Fanon observes that the inscription of the white parody of black culture—"I was battered down by tom-toms, cannibalism, intellectual deficiency, fetishism, racial defects, slave-ships, and above all else, above all: 'Sho' good eatin'"—on the colonized black body creates a metonymic paradox. On his body the parts do not stand in for a whole; nor do they add up to a whole. "What else could it be for me but an amputation, an excision, a hemorrhage, that spattered my whole body with black blood? But I did not want this revision, this thematization. All I wanted was to be a man among other men." Body parts erupting blood—not red human blood but the black blood of a race and the indelible ink of cultural textuality—constitute him a priori as a mass of part-objects with no relation to the whole.

Fanon here uses the sensation of dismemberment as an allegory for the effects of racist discourse: the fractured body stands in for the fragmented relation to identity suffered by subjects of a culture who have learned the message of their negation before they had a chance to imagine otherwise. This process of part-identification is different from that of the subject described by post-structuralism, who shuttles between the ruse of self-presence and its dissolution. By definition, the colonized subject is unable to produce even the mirage of his or her own totality. Fanon's catalogue of the society's names for him identifies the surplus naming of the marginalized subject as the crucial incision of history into the subject's self-consciousness.

Fanon speaks within the racist discursive context *already reproducing* the white parody of black culture: this is surely the spirit in which Walker represents Harpo, the black parody of a white man (Harpo Marx) who compensates for his voicelessness with music, whose character is expressed in his "feminine" pathos as well as his pathetic aping of masculine pretensions. The tragic aphonia of Celie's mother and the witty, ironic repartee about "uncle Tomming" by Shug, Squeak, and Sofia reveal the even more complex negotiation required of women who aspire to legitimacy in the face of both sexism and racism. Celie's youthful masquerade as Shug in order to deflect her father's sexual greed can also be read as a complex and contradictory message growing out of this kind of negating context. So what looks like simple irony or sarcasm already contains the negating effects of cultural delegitimation. Blackness does not signify except from inside the negative space prepared for it by the history of white culture's relation to black; the same general idea operates in gender relations as well for the Afro-American woman making her way in the context of a double erasure.

The only relief from such torturous negotiating exists in conversation among women. Speaking as a "woman" among women in *The Color Purple* also involves countering the delegitimating pressure of specifically female marginality by finding expression and refuge in wordplay, in the masterful and courageous deployment of language in irony, in rage, in fun, in lies, in song, and in deadly silences. In the racially and sexually fractured situation, back talk resulted in punishment; among women in a man's world, the back talk produces pleasure.

The singers Shug and Mary Agnes articulate professionally the fact and the privileges (current and imminent) of female speech in the liberatory distinction between words and music in, for example, "Miss Celie's Blues." As Celie says, "it all about some no count man doing her wrong, again. But I don't listen to that part. I look at her [Shug] and I hum along a little with the tune." All the speaking women in the novel learn to turn a phrase in acts of defiance and self-expression. They "fight" for the right to take an *attitude:* style itself, apart from content and reference, becomes the first pure note of female signifying.

Celie first displays the pleasure of speech within a female context in her complex response to Corinne, whom Celie sees in town carrying her stolen child, Olivia. Celie invites Corinne to escape the racist glares of the white men in the marketplace by sitting in her wagon; Corinne expresses her gratitude to Celie with a pun on the word "hospitality." Celie demonstrates the power of the joke: "*Horse*pitality, she say. And I get it and laugh. It feel like to split my face." When Mr. _____ comes out, he realizes immediately that this shared joke, such as it is, threatens his control over the discursive space in which Celie lives. "What you setting here laughing like a fool fer?" he says. Her split face all too graphically refers to the scars she bears, the mask of dumbness she hides behind, and also refers to an object posed, but not yet constituted, the split face that produces plurivocal discourse, not a muted utterance from a victimized shadow.

The implicit context of a priori negation for Afro-Americans that obtains in all American culture undergoes a dramatic shift when Nettie's African letters are read into the record. Nettie's letters from Africa at first seem to provide an indigenous alternative history for black consciousness that reverses its traditional invisibility or debasement in the racist American context. To the missionaries, the mission to convert the Africans to Christianity seems specially authorized by a providential and historical allegiance to all

"Africans." Aware of a potential problem arising from cultural differences between missionaries and the objects of their attention, Samuel articulates the special privilege he, Corinne, and Nettie will enjoy in Africa:

> Samuel . . . reminded us that there is one big advantage we have. We are not white. We are not Europeans. We are black like the Africans themselves. And that we and the Africans will be working for a common goal: the uplift of black people everywhere.

Nettie records with awe how different the world looks to her from the point of view of African/racial dominance: "Something struck in me, in my soul, Celie, like a large bell, and I just vibrated." With amazement she witnesses Americans in Harlem who worship Africa, not America. She reports with pride about an Afro-American church in which God is black. And there's the great text of racial *ressentiment:* in the Olinka origin narrative, white men are secondary productions of African culture expelled into the nakedness and vulnerability of Otherness. The pure pleasure Nettie derives from reading Blackness from a proper and sanctified point of view is the affective origin of the specifically nationalist politics previously repressed in *The Color Purple*: what hope and uplift can Africans all over the world take from their common field of history?

The missionaries' attempt to forge a response to this question produces ambiguous answers. Their version of pan-African consciousness forges a strong sense of world-historical identity within the Afro-American community that in part derives from the greatness of African culture in the centuries before European imperialism. The Afro-American church also sees the spiritual power of the African other-world inhabiting its own driving spirit to convert and to empower the masses of Africans, now disenfranchised from power and progress, economic, cultural, and spiritual.

The white, Western-identified missionaries who sponsor Samuel's particular mission tend, on the other hand, to keep the contemporaneous tribal cultures at arm's length: a white female missionary, for example, "says an African daisy and an English daisy are both flowers, but totally different kinds. The man at the Society says she is successful because she doesn't 'coddle' her charges." The values that lead the missionary society to think it has a progressive message to deliver to the heathen brethren are shown to be well-intentioned, patronizing, misguided, and culturally destructive. While Samuel clearly identifies his destiny with that of the African people, he also unintentionally aims to reproduce the normative social relations of Western culture in the midst of his attempt to reform their spirit.

The primary site of cultural contact between the missionaries and the Africans is pedagogical: the connection between cultural literacy and power established early in the novel is reiterated in the missionaries' retraining of the tribal peoples in the "superior" and Christian practices and materials of Western culture. The issue that brings to the surface the contradictions inherent in the missionaries' creation of a pan-African consciousness is in the sphere of gender relations. Samuel feels compelled to lecture the Olinka women on the virtues of monogamy over polygamy, even though the alliances made among the wives of individual men render the polygamous women far more powerful than Corinne, for example, feels in her ambiguous relation to Nettie. Nettie, in turn, smugly offers to reveal to the Olinka women the movement among women in civilized nations toward liberation from patriarchal oppression in the public and private spheres. But here too the Olinka women see the limitations of Nettie's apparent freedom of movement and knowledge: she is "the missionary's drudge," and "object of pity and contempt." In short, as Samuel later painfully realizes, what passed for racial identification across borders and historical differences was really a system of cultural hegemony disguised as support and uplift.

The event that clarifies how politically useful the missions are to the European imperialists, standing as agents or prophets of spiritual progress, is the coming of the big road. Generous in their estimation of human nature, the Olinka refuse to understand that the theory of property and propriety under which they live is irrelevant to the Western juridical code. Most natives assume (as American white people always do, notes Nettie) that the superpower force that cuts through the jungle builds a road to the tribe, for the tribe; they admire Western technology, viewing it as they view roofleaf, something nature makes in abundance for the well-being of its devoted people.

But Samuel, Corinne, and Nettie are no more sophisticated in their understanding of the ways of "civilized" culture than are the "natives": this is one instance where the pan-national racial identification between American and African blacks proves sadly accurate. Too late, the missionaries realize that their road threatens their mission; desperately, they exhaust their resources trying to protect the tribe. The only survivors are tribal citizens who can read well enough to see their death sentence in Western culture and join the *mbeles*, the underground group of radicalized Olinka.

Samuel could have foreseen the failure of his mission. His life story, the only male autobiographical narrative in *The Color Purple* privileged to replace (temporarily) the reigning female subjectivity, reveals the shallowness with which he understood his own cultural privilege. He tells Nettie of the time in his youth that he encountered W. E. B. Du Bois, whose impatience with the pretensions of missionary culture could have taught Samuel that Pan-Africanism requires material transformations of the techniques of power before a new spirit would have any place to grasp:

> Madame, he said, when Aunt Theodosia finished her story and flashed her famous medal around the room, do you realize King Leopold cut the hands off workers who, in the opinion of his plantation overseers, did not fulfill their rubber quota? Rather than cherish that medal, Madame, you should regard it as a symbol of your unwitting complicity with this despot who worked to death and brutalized and eventually exterminated thousands and thousands of African peoples.

Like the lynched body, the black hand here not only serves as a figure of racial "justice" for whites, but also becomes a kind of rebus for the metonymic "hand" of capitalism, in which the worker is an economic appendage reduced to the (dis)embodiment of his or her alienation. This kind of symbolism was on Du Bois' mind in the period after World War I, when "lying treaties, rivers of rum, murder, assassination, mutilation, rape, and torture have marked the progress of Englishman, German, Frenchman, and Belgian on the Dark Continent." The Pan-African movement, organized by Du Bois to counter the European exploitation of Africa's plentiful resources, took up the question of Belgium in 1919 and 1921 much as these hands "take up" the question of slavery. Du Bois saw in the capitalist infiltration of Africa the origins of world racism against blacks: "'Color' became in the world's thought synonymous with inferiority, 'Negro' lost its capitalization, and Africa was another name for bestiality and barbarism."

The ramifications of the peculiar kind of racism produced by capitalism led Du Bois to try to organize all of the African nations of the world: to create a "people" that would fight for its right to national self-determination, for the (he would say, inevitable) democratization of capital, and for the eradication of the racist representations that have masked the capitalist pilfering of Pan-African resources. But Samuel does not go as far as Du Bois did in attacking the origin of contemporary racism in Western relations of capital, even though Nettie's letters register the information that local traditions of land and cultural ownership are completely subsumed to the absentee ownership of the non-African nations feeding off the continent's wealth. Instead, Samuel sees his failure to understand his unwitting complicity with colonialist practices as a flaw in his theory of spirit. The mission's total powerlessness to prevent the destruction of the culture they had come to "save" provokes Samuel and Nettie to redefine what it means to serve God.

> God is different to us now, after all these years in Africa. More spirit than ever before, and more internal. Most people think he has to look like something or someone—a roofleaf or Christ—but we don't. And not being tied to what God looks like, frees us.

The link between the theory and the practice of "capitalism" and of "religion" or spirit is the key to the novel's reformulation of mainstream Afro-American nationalist politics and consciousness. Having spent the first part of the novel tracing the pernicious effects of the national-patriarchal-capitalist domination of personal and natural resources, Walker opens the second part with Nettie's moving tributes to the fabulous riches of African culture, read as a pan-national phenomenon. Nettie unconsciously quotes "America, the Beautiful" in her report of it: "And we kneeled down right on deck and gave thanks to God for letting us see the land for which our mothers and fathers cried—and lived and died—to see again."

The missionaries' disillusioned removal to the United States signals a transformation of their relation to both African and American nationalism. By viewing America as the place of the new redeemed church shorn of idols, Samuel and Nettie repeat seventeenth-century Puritan religious and civil representations of America as the only site where a sanctified and defetishized church might have a chance for survival. In so embracing the theory of an idol-free America, the missionaries refute their initial intention to enrich their historical affiliation with Africa—Africa seen as a body of land with a distinctive history—and with the problem of Afro-American political disenfranchisement to which Pan-Africanism had been a response. And to replace the cultural and political solution Pan-African nationalism had offered to the missionaries, a religion free from boundaries and margins emerges based on unmediated relations of Being to Being.

The last half of the novel, after Nettie's letters are discovered, traces how the characters' departure from formal alliances—based on race, organized religion, politics—takes the form of a nationalist aesthetic that places essences (human and inhuman) in their proper social relation regardless of apparent material conditions and contradictions. Capitalism, as we shall see, is no longer a hegemonic and mystified mode of exploitation; rather, it becomes an extension of the subject's spiritual *choices*. And the hybrid, fractured status of Afro-American signification reemerges in its earliest form: instead of infusing the African side of the compound term with the positive historical identification usually denied in the American context, the last half of the novel returns "Africa" to the space of disappointment and insufficiency, finally overwhelmed by the power of "America" to give form to the utopian impulse.

Every transformation of belief that marks Samuel and Nettie's return "home" to America has a correlate in a change of Celie's worldview—sexual, social, and spiritual. For Celie, like Nettie, sexual awakening not only transforms her relation to her body and to pleasure in general, but also leads to a major shift in her understanding and mastery of power in the world. It is Shug Avery who saves Celie from being paralyzed by rage at Mr. _____ 's concealment of Nettie's letters; Shug also channels Celie's confusion at the collapse of her original way of understanding the world into a radical revision of that understanding—starting with God, the prime Author and Audience of her tortured inner life.

This shift in Celie's mode of belief reveals to her a world saturated by a sensual beauty that signifies God's work. "Admiration" is Shug's word for worship: Celie's religion, like Nettie's, is transformed from a social, institutional enterprise to an aestheticized and surprisingly solitary sexual practice. Admiring the color purple is equated with what Celie calls "making love to God," an act she performs with the aid of a reefer.

Celie adopts a mode of sensual pleasure and power beyond the body that effectively displaces the injustices that have marked her tenure in the quotidian. She heralds her glorious transformation into self-presence by shedding her scarred historical body as she leaves Mr. _____: "I'm pore, I'm black, I may be ugly and can't cook, *a voice say to everything listening*. But I'm here" (my emphasis). This pure and disembodied voice speaks of its liberation from the disfigured body and enacts, through disembodiment, the utopian scene of self-expression from Celie's point of view. In this scene, the negated, poor, black, female body—created for Mr. _____'s pleasure, profit, and scorn—is replaced by a voice that voids the vulnerability of the bodied historical subject. To Mr. _____'s prophecy that Celie will fail in the world because she has neither talent, beauty, nor courage "to open your mouth to people," Celie performs her triumphant Being—"I'm here"—and asserts the supremacy of speech over the physical, material despotism characteristic of patriarchy. Her new mode of counteropposition also deploys the supernatural power of language, turning Mr. _____'s negativity back on himself: "Until you do right by me, I say, everything you even dream about will fail." The authority of this curse comes from nature: "I give it to him straight, just like it come to me. And it seem to come to me from the trees." Speech here becomes the primary arena of action: the natural world lends not its material resources but a spiritual vitality that can always assert itself while the body is threatened and battered. And writing, as the fact of the letters suggests, is the place where the voice is held in trust for the absent subject who might be seeking a way of countering the patriarchal and racist practices of the social world.

This revision of Celie's point of view frees her from her imprisonment in stoic passivity. But if Celie's body has taken a beating, it also carries the traces of her violently inscribed history: multiple rape, incest, disenfranchisement through a marriage trade made between two men (in which Celie and her cow have equivalent status), as well as through her stepfather's repression of her mother's will, and, finally, sexual, economic, and psychological exploitation and abuse by Mr. _____ and his family. Celie's ascension to speech, a new realm of "bodiless" happiness, does not include coming to terms with these events as she leaves them behind: she is completely reborn, without bearing witness to the scars left in knowledge and memory.

Indeed, in her new domestic regime Celie first occupies her "old" social powerlessness like a natural skin. According to Shug, Celie would have been happy to devote her life to being Shug's maid; but Shug insists that Celie find meaningful work for herself. And the rest, as they say, is history: the letter Celie writes to Nettie describing Shug's capitalization of her production of "perfect pants" is signed "Your Sister, Celie / Folkpants, Unlimited. / Sugar Avery Drive / Memphis, Tennessee." Through Shug, both a sexual and economic provider, Celie gains the *nom du père* of capitalism: a trademark, which becomes a part of Celie's new signature, itself a reflection of Shug's own nominal dissemination on the road map of her culture.

Celie's Folkpants provides such a service for the woman or man who purchases them as well. The simple message Folkpants advertises is that the pants are truly for the "the people," marketed for all genders. The unisexuality of the pants deemphasizes the importance of fashion in the social context in which the pants are worn: following the ethical and aesthetic shift from worshipping the white male God to appreciating the presence of spirit and color, Celie emphasizes fabric, print, and color in their conception and distribution.

A mode of ontological mimesis governs the specifications of each pair of pants, tailoring each to embody the essential person but not his or her physical body: one size, one cut fits all. Each pair of Folkpants is shown to release the wearer into authentic self-expression. At the book's end this semiotic democracy, based on the authenticity of all speaking subjects, reflected in and enacted by their commodity relations, replaces the sexism and racism of "natural" languages of the body and consciousness.

In addition, when grammar enters the realm of the manifest struggle, the essence of the expression reigns over its historical or conventional usage. Darlene, who works in Celie's factory, tries to teach Celie "proper" English:

You say US where most folks say WE, she say, and peoples think you dumb. Colored peoples think you a hick and white folks be amuse.

What I care? I ast. I'm happy.

Shug settles the argument by asserting that Celie can "talk in sign language for all I care": in Shug's revisionary semiotic, the medium of transmission is proclaimed as transparent while "the message" is everything. She embraces an aesthetic of live performance: a mode of discourse that can only be activated in the performance of a speech act between a living speaker and a co-present receiver. As a result, all speech acts become intersubjective and are therefore authentic within the speech context created by the confluence of subjectivities. Shug here produces the "theory" of the everyday life language practiced by Celie: the populist elements of such an ethic are vital to the formation of the Folkpants industry.

The vestments of "the people" quickly become the ligaments of a new family as the workshop where the Folkpants are made moves from Shug's house to the house of Celie's birth. Celie's return to this house, however, is not represented as a confrontation with long-buried memories of sexual violation or personal danger. On this go-round, the house comes with yet a new prehistoric origin myth, in which the Mother has protected her daughters from the deadliest penetration of patriarchy by preserving her property for the girls. The wicked stepfather, trespassing on their property as he has on Celie's body, had wrested it from the sisters; his death sets them free from their exile and they return, one at a time.

This move does more than to bring them back to the Mother: it also provides closure to the narrative genealogy of racism and class struggle inscribed in Celie's family history. Celie now situates herself firmly in her family's entrepreneurial tradition; she runs her business from the store tragically occupied by her stepfather, and her father before him. Where her father and uncles were lynched for presuming the rights of full American citizens to participate in a free market, and where her stepfather survived by doing business exclusively for and with whites, Celie's business is as perfectly biracial as it is unisexual, employing both Sofia and a white worker to sell her goods so that *everyone* will be well served.

Thus it would seem that capitalism, figured as a small (but infinitely expandable) family-style business, provides for the socially marginalized characters in *The Color Purple* the motivating drive for forging a positive relation to social life. The family-as-business has the power and the resources to absorb adversity while providing the ground for social relations based on cooperation rather than on coercion. Not socialist-style cooperation, of course—Shug, Celie's financial backer, specifically orders her to hire "women . . . to cut and sew, while you sit back and design."

To join the closely knit family of female capitalists, one must simply identify with the "female world of love and ritual" that includes the everyday working relations among women that center on the home. A woman can assert her allegiance to other women simply by joining the business: for men who admit a childhood/natural desire to engage in the housekeeping practices of their mothers (Harpo, Mr._____), the franchise is conferred.

United around these activities, Celie's new family emerges from the gender and racial fractures that had threatened to destroy it. Yet it is finally not family discourse that organizes the life of the redeemed community: the last event of the novel, after Nettie and the children's return to Celie, not only fulfills the familial model of utopian capitalism that dominates the last third of the narrative, but also reinstates nationalist discourse as the proper context for Celie's autobiography.

"Dear God. Dear stars, dear trees, dear sky, dear peoples. Dear Everything. Dear God." With this lyric, the end of *The Color Purple* proclaims the ascendancy of a new mode of national and personal identity. In a letter Celie addresses not to the God who is everything but to the everything that incorporates godly spirit, she writes of the fulfillment of the womanist promise, as the community turns toward the future in expectation of more profit, pleasure, and satisfaction from their labor and from each other. Shug speaks of retiring. "Albert"/ Mr._____ prattles about the new shirt he's made. Celie speaks about "how things doing generally" while she compulsively stitches "up a bunch of scraps, try to see what [she] can make." As in the rest of the novel, the idiom of Celie's victory is deliberately apolitical: while she might have used the new formation of the utopian community as an opportunity for meta-commentary about the revolutionary conditions of its productions, Celie continues to favor the materials of the common language in the construction of the new social space.

And yet is precisely at this protonationalist moment, when the changes sought within the family have been realized in the woman-identified community and extended to the outside world through the garment business, that *The Color Purple* turns back toward the kinds of explications of social life that Celie has previously rejected. In the novel's final pages, conventional mythopoetic political discourse about American culture, about "the births, battles, and deaths of Great Men" previously exiled from the text's concerns and representations, surfaces for adoption. In so doing, this radically revised and "womanized" historical novel calls into question its own carefully established social and textual metamorphosis.

Celie's rapprochement with Mr. _____, for example, is significantly sealed when he personally places a letter in her hand—not from Nettie, but from America: the Department of Defense telegram notifying Celie of Nettie's apparent death. But this gesture comments more on the symbolic relations of patriarchal to state forms than it does on changes in the experiences or consciousness of the characters. The redemption of America is linked with the redemption of Mr. _____, forecasting the novel's imminent refranchising of patriarchal modes of analysis and representation.

On this occasion we also witness Celie's startling use of the narrowly "political" language which, I have argued, has been absent from her practice throughout the rest of the novel. Celie's fear of Nettie's death suggests to her that, in this time of crisis, America confers on American blacks the cultural status of lynched subjects like Celie's father: "Plus," she says, "colored don't count to those people." There is nothing contradictory or insidious in this particular observation of Celie's, but it too heralds the revalorization of a mode of heretofore exiled cultural analysis.

The final day of the narrative telegraphs the novel's turn to American nationalism at its most blatant and filiopietistic: it is July 4, Independence Day. It is the first and only day narrated in the novel that takes place after Nettie's return to the fold. It is uniquely positioned to provide textual commentary about the relation between its limited set of "characters" and the operation of dominant and contested cultures that has marked Afro-American experience.

The dialogue that constitutes explicit comment on the subject of the holiday ranges from personal "complaint" to epic recognition:

> Why us always have family reunion on July 4th, says Henrietta, mouth poke out, full of complaint. It so hot.
> White people busy celebrating independence from England July 4th, say Harpo, so most black folks don't have to work. Us can spend the day celebrating each other.
> Ah, Harpo, say Mary Agnes, . . . I didn't know you knowed history.

We didn't know that Harpo knew history either: he never seemed to need to know it. With the single, special exception of Sofia's fifteen minutes of freedom on Christmas while indentured to the mayor's wife, at no other time in the novel has work on the farm or anywhere else within the black community depended on or referred to the demands of white American hegemonic culture for its work timetable or its mode of leisure. Mary Agnes' surprise at Harpo is appropriate, for this consciousness of "history" is imported specially for the novel's closing moments.

But what does the rearticulation of Celie's family within a specifically American scene do to the politics of history in *The Color Purple*? In this late moment, Celie's early assertion of her autonomy from American national identity is silently answered by the next generation's commentary: Harpo's "history" suggests instead that Afro-American culture exists confidently in the interstices of Anglo-American historical time. He characterizes the relation between Anglo- and Afro-American culture as structured around an opposition and a hierarchy that discriminates racially, and yet implies that blacks have all the room they need for full cultural self-articulation.

Possibly this shift represents a historical change—a change in the modes of cultural reproduction. Whereas the home life Celie experienced as a child and a young woman mainly involved the black community, the life she leads with Shug overlaps the circulation of blues culture throughout both black and white urban communities. Perhaps, as a result of her wider experience, a traditionally national language was the only discourse available to describe this variegated cultural landscape. If this multiracial cultural articulation, commonly known as the American "melting pot," is the main motive behind the resurgence of American consciousness, then the final images of *The Color Purple* might be said to abandon the project of specifically representing an Afro-American national culture for a less racially delimited, more pluralist model.

But if the image of the reconstituted family in the text's final letter suggests the American melting pot, it also represents the clearly Jeffersonian cast of Celie's family. Rural, abstracted from the mainly urban scene of consumption, this "matrician" homestead remains the symbolic and actual seat of the production of Folkpants. Folkpants, in turn (no doubt soon to be joined by a line of Folkshirts designed by Mr. _____), retain their capacity to express the consumer's unique and unmarked soul, along with embodying the ideal conditions of social relations.

From this point of view, the novel's resuscitation of American national discourse can be explained by the way Celie's "family," in the final instance, can be said to mark its own separate, specifically Afro-American recolonization of American time, American property, and mythic American self-help ideology by casually ironizing it. Harpo's droll analysis of the reason behind their July Fourth gathering minimizes the melting-pot aspect of American Independence Day, reducing the holiday to a racial and not a national celebration. Mary Agnes' uncontested depiction of Harpo's statement as history might suggest that this final event is meant to illuminate the real poverty of a politically established Anglo-American national identity when set next to that of the Afro-American community that has fought on all grounds for the right to have everything—life, dignity, love, family, nation.

But to enter, as the novel does, into a mode of political analysis that employs the ideological myths of hegemonic culture to define Afro-American culture raises questions about the oppositional status of the novel. Such an alliance severely problematizes the critique of conventional historical "memory" and cultural self-transmission that Walker intended to make in this "historical novel." It implicitly represents American racism as a condition of Afro-American self-celebration.

The novel's apparent amnesia about the conditions of its own production is symbolized in the denial or reversal of age heralded in the novel's and Celie's closing sentence: "Matter of fact, I think this the youngest us ever felt." As if deliberately replacing her very first utterance, "I am fourteen years old," with an assertion of victorious subjectivity and a control over the context in which she speaks, Celie commits herself to the production of a new age but ascribes no value to the influence of the past on the subject or on the culture.

Such a model for the reformulation of Afro-American national identity threatens to lose certain historical events in the rush to create the perfect relations of a perfect moment. That the text might use the repression of certain kinds of memory as a strategy for representing its new, utopian mode of production was signaled in the narrative repression of the class element in Celie's father's lynching. The profit motive killed her father and, indirectly, her mother; it made Celie vulnerable to her stepfather's sexual imperialism and almost resulted in her disenfranchisement from her property. But the novel's progressive saturation with capitalism and its fruits, along with its insistence on the significance of the product in the consumer's self-knowledge and self-expression, marks the relative cleansing of violence from its class and capital relations. The Afro-American nationalism imaged in the new familial system can be said to use the American tradition of autonomy through property to imagine the new social epoch.

The Color Purple's strategy of inversion, represented in its elevation of female experience over great patriarchal events, had indeed aimed to critique the unjust practices of racism and sexism that violate the subject's complexity, reducing her to a generic biological sign. But the model of personal and national identity with which the novel leaves us uses fairy-tale explanations of social relations to represent itself: this fairy tale embraces America for providing the Afro-American nation with the right and the opportunity to own land, to participate in the free market, and to profit from it. In the novel's own terms, American capitalism thus has contradictory effects. On one hand, capitalism veils its operations by employing racism, using the pseudonatural discourse of race to reduce the economic competitor to a subhuman object. In Celie's parental history, *The Color Purple* portrays the system of representation characteristic of capital relations that *creates* the situation of nationlessness for Afro-Americans.

But the novel also represents the mythic spirit of American capitalism as the vehicle for the production of an Afro-American utopia. Folkpants, Unlimited is an industry dedicated to the reproduction and consumption of a certain system of representation central to the version of Afro-American "cultural nationalism" enacted by *The Color Purple*. But Folkpants, Unlimited also participates in the profit motive: the image of the commodity as the subject's most perfect self-expression is the classic fantasy bribe of capitalism. The illogic of a textual system in which the very force that disenfranchises Afro-Americans provides the material for their national reconstruction is neither "solved" by the novel nor raised as a paradox. The system simply stands suspended in the heat of the family reunion on Independence Day.

What saves Celie and Nettie from disenfranchisement is their lifelong determination to learn, to become literate: Nettie's sense that knowledge was the only route to freedom from the repressive family scene gave her the confidence to escape, to seek "employment" with Samuel's family, to record the alternative and positive truth of Pan-African identity, to face the truth about her own history, to write it down, and to send it to Celie, against all odds. Writing was not only the repository of personal and national hope; it became a record of lies and violences that ultimately produced truth.

The Color Purple nonetheless ultimately rejects writing for an ethic of voice—from Shug's advocacy of self-present, performative discourse to Walker's own postscriptural description of herself as the book's "medium." The fantasy of the novel is that these voices might be preserved as pure "text," cleansed of the residues of historical oppression. Celie herself embraces a mode of cultural nationalism unable to transmit objective knowledge—knowledge that does not derive from experience and intimacy—about the way institutional forms of power devolve on "private" individuals, alone and in their various social relations. Such an emphasis on individual essence, in a false opposition to institutional history, seems inadequate to the construction of any national consciousness, especially one developing in a hostile, negating context. Mythic American political discourse is precisely unable to account for the uneven devolvement of legitimacy on citizens obfuscated within the nation's rhetoric of identity. And if *The Color Purple* clearly represents anything, it is the unreliability of "text" under the historical pressure to interpret, to predict, and to determine the cultural politics of the colonized signifier.

HENRY LOUIS GATES JR.

Color Me Zora:
Alice Walker's (Re)Writing of the Speakerly Text

O, write my name, O write my name:
        O write my name . . .
Write my name when-a you get home . . .
Yes, write my name in the book of life . . .
The Angels in the heav'n going-to write my name.
                        Spiritual Underground Railroad

My spirit leans in joyousness tow'rd thine,
My gifted spirit, as with gladdened heart
My vision flies along thy "speaking pages."
            Ada, "A Young Woman of Color," 1836

I am only a pen in His hand.
                             Rebecca Cox Jackson

I'm just a link in a chain.
                 Aretha Franklin, "Chain of Fools"

For just over two hundred years, the concern to depict the quest of the black speaking subject to find his or her voice has been a repeated topos of

---

From *The Signifying Monkey: A Theory of Afro-American Literary Criticism* by Henry Louis Gates Jr.
© 1988 Henry Louis Gates Jr.

the black tradition, and perhaps has been its most central trope. As theme, as revised trope, as a double-voiced narrative strategy, the representation of characters and texts finding a voice has functioned as a sign both of the formal unity of the Afro-American literary tradition and of the integrity of the black subjects depicted in this literature.

Esu's double voice and the language of Signifyin(g) have served throughout this book as unifying metaphors, indigenous to the tradition, both for patterns of revision from text to text and for modes of figuration at work within the text. The Anglo-African narrators published between 1770 and 1815 placed themselves in a line of descent through the successive revision of one trope, of a sacred text that refuses to speak to its would-be black auditor. In *Their Eyes Were Watching God*, Zora Neale Hurston depicts her protagonist's ultimate moment of self-awareness in her ability to name her own divided consciousness. As an element of theme and as a highly accomplished rhetorical strategy that depends for its effect on the bivocality of free indirect discourse, this voicing of a divided consciousness (another topos of the tradition) has been transformed in Ishmael Reed's *Mumbo Jumbo* into a remarkably self-reflexive representation of the ironies of writing a text in which two foregrounded voices compete with each other for control of narration itself. Whereas the development of the tradition to the publication of *Their Eyes Were Watching God* seems to have been preoccupied with the mimetic possibilities of the speaking voice, black fiction after *Their Eyes* would seem even more concerned to explore the implications of doubled voices upon strategies of writing.

Strategies as effective as Hurston's innovative use of free indirect discourse and Reed's bifurcated narrative voice lead one to wonder how a rhetorical strategy could possibly extend, or Signify upon, the notions of voice at play in these major texts of the black tradition. How could a text possibly trope the extended strategies of voicing which we have seen to be in evidence in *Their Eyes* and in *Mumbo Jumbo*? To Signify upon both Hurston's and Reed's strategies of narration would seem to demand a form of the novel that, at once, breaks with tradition yet revises the most salient features through which I have been defining the formal unity of this tradition.

Just as Hurston's and Reed's texts present seemingly immovable obstacles to an equally telling revision of the tradition's trope of voicing, so too does *Invisible Man*, the tradition's text of blackness and, in my opinion, its most profound achievement in the novel. The first-person narration of *Invisible Man*, the valorization of oral narration in *Their Eyes*, and the italicized interface of showing and telling in *Mumbo Jumbo*, taken together, would seem to leave rather little space in which narrative innovation could even possibly be attempted. Alice Walker's revisions of *Their Eyes Were Watching God* and of Rebecca Cox Jackson's *Gifts of Power*, however, have defined an entirely new mode of representation of the black quest to make the text speak.

To begin to account for the Signifyin(g) revisions at work in Walker's *The Color Purple*, it is useful to recall the dream of literacy figured in John Jea's autobiography. In Chapter 4, I maintained that Jea's odd revision of the scene of the Talking Book served to erase the figurative potential of this trope for the slave narrators who followed him. After Jea, slave narrators refigured a repeated scene of instruction in terms of reading and writing rather than in terms of making the text speak. While these two tropes are obviously related, it seems equally obvious that the latter represents a key reworking of the former, in terms more conducive to the directly polemical role in which the slave narratives were engaged in an antebellum America seemingly preoccupied with the future of human slavery.

While the trope of the Talking Book disappeared from the male slave narratives after Jea literalized it it is refigured in the mystical writings of Rebecca Cox Jackson, an Afro-American visionary and Shaker eldress who was a contemporary of Jea's. Jackson was a free black woman who lived between 1795 and 1871. She was a fascinating religious leader and feminist, who founded a Shaker sisterhood in Philadelphia in 1857, after a difficult struggle with her family, with her initial religious denomination, and even with the Shakers. Her extensive autobiographical writings (1830–1864) were collected and edited by Jean McMahon Humez, published in 1981, and reviewed by Alice Walker in that same year. The reconstitution of Jackson's texts is one of the major scholarly achievements in Afro-American literature, both because of the richness of her texts and because the writings of black women in antebellum America are painfully scarce, especially when compared to the large body of writings by black men.

Jackson, like her contemporary black ex-slave writers, gives a prominent place in her texts to her own literacy training. Hers is a divinely inspired literacy training even more remarkable than Jea's. Writing between 1830 and 1832, just fifteen-odd years after Jea, Jackson—with or without Jea's text in mind—refigures Jea's divine scene of instruction. Jackson's refiguration of this supernatural event, however, is cast within a sexual opposition between male and female. Whereas her antecedents used the trope to define the initial sense of difference between slave and free, African and European, Jackson's revision charts the liberation of a (black) woman from a (black) man over the letter of the text. I bracket *black* because, as we shall see, Jackson freed herself of her brother's domination of her literacy and her ability to interpret, but supplanted him with a mythical white male interpreter.

Jackson, recalling Jea, writes, "After I received the blessing of God, I had a great desire to read the Bible." Lamenting the fact that "I am the only child of my mother that had not learning," she seeks out her brother to "give me one hour's lesson at night after supper or before we went to bed." Her brother, a prominent clergyman in the Bethel African Methodist Episcopal Church, was often "so tired when he came home that he had not [the] power so to do," a situation, Jackson tells us, which would "grieve" her. But the situation that grieved Jackson even more was her brother's penchant to "rewrite" her words, to revise her dictation, one supposes, to make them more "presentable." Jackson takes great care to describe her frustration in the fight with her brother to control her flow of words:

> So I went to get my brother to write my letters and to read them. . . . I told him what to put in. Then I asked him to read. He did. I said, "Thee has put in more than I told thee." This he done several times. I then said, "I don't want thee to *word* my letter. I only want thee to *write* it." Then he said, "Sister, thee is the hardest one I ever wrote for!" These words, together with the manner that he had wrote my letter, pierced my soul like a sword. . . . I could not keep from crying.

This scene is an uncanny prefigurement of the battle over her public speaking voice that Janie wages with Joe Starks in *Their Eyes Were Watching God*, as we have seen in Chapter 5. Jackson's brother, "tired" from his arduous work for the Lord, cannot be relied on to train his sister to read. When she compromises by asking him to serve as her amanuensis, he "words" her letters, as Jackson puts it, rather than simply translating her words (in their correct order, as narrated) from spoken to written form. This contest over her wording is not merely the anxiety the author experiences when edited or rewritten; rather, we eventually learn that Rebecca's rather individual mode of belief not only comes to threaten the minister-brother but also leads ultimately to a severance of the kinship bond. The brother-sister conflict over the "word" of the letter, then, prefigures an even more profound conflict over the word and letter of God's will.

God, however, takes sides. He comforts the grieving Rebecca with a divine message: "And these words were spoken in my heart, 'Be faithful, and the time shall come when you can write.' These words were spoken in my heart as though a tender father spoke them. My tears were gone in a moment." God was as good as his promise. Just as he had done for his servant, John Jea, the Lord taught Jackson how to read:

> One day I was sitting finishing a dress in haste and in prayer. [Jackson sustained herself by dressmaking.] This word

was spoken in my mind, "Who learned the first man on earth?" "Why, God." "He is unchangeable, and if He learned the first man to read, He can learn you." I laid down my dress, picked up my Bible, ran upstairs, opened it, and kneeled down with it pressed to my breast, prayed earnestly to Almighty God if it was consisting to His holy will, to learn me to read His holy word. And when I looked on the word, I began to read. And when I found I was reading, I was frightened—then I could not read one word. I closed my eyes again in prayer and then opened my eyes, began to read. So I done, until I read the chapter. . . . So I tried, took my Bible daily and praying and read until I could read anywhere. The first chapter that I read I never could know it after that day. I only knowed it was in James, but what chapter I can never tell.

When confronted with the news, Jackson's incredulous husband challenged her claim: "Woman, you are agoing crazy!" Jackson, undaunted, read to him. "Down I sat and read through. And it was in James. So Samuel praised the Lord with me." Similarly, her brother accused her merely of memorizing passages overheard being read by his children: "Once thee has heard the children read, till thee has got it by heart." Once convinced by Jackson's husband, Jackson tell us with an air of triumph, "He sat down very sorrowful."

When challenged by her doubting brother, Jackson tell us, "I did not speak," allowing her husband, Samuel, to speak in her defense. At the end of her long description of this miracle of literacy, this "gift of power," she summarizes the event as "this unspeakable gift of Almighty God to me." It is this double representation of unspeakability which connects Jackson's miracle of literacy to Alice Walker's strategies of narration in *The Color Purple*.

Despite the parallel in Jackson's mini-narrative of her fight to control her words and Janie's fight to control hers (resolved, for Jackson, by the divine discourse of God, and for Janie by the black vernacular discourse of Signifyin(g)), we know that Hurston did not have access to Jackson's texts. Walker, however, makes much of this scene in her essay on Jackson, underscoring the fact that "Jackson *was* taught to read and write by the spirit within her." When Walker dedicates *The Color Purple* "To the Spirit," it is to this spirit which taught Rebecca Jackson to read. It is the representation of the unfolding of this gift of the "spirit within her," an "unspeakable gift," through which Walker represents the thoroughly dynamic development of her protagonist's consciousness, within the "unspeakable" medium of an epistolary novel comprised of letters written but never said, indeed written but never read. Celie's only reader, and Rebecca's only literacy teacher, is God.

Rather than representing the name of God as unspeakable, Walker represents Celie's words, her letters addressed to "God," as unspeakable. God is Celie's silent auditor, the addressee of most of her letters, written but never sent. This device, as Robert Stepto has suggested to me, is an echo of the first line of W. E. B. Du Bois's well-known "After-Thought" to *The Souls of Black Folk*: "Hear my cry, O God the Reader." But more important to our analysis of Walker's revisions of *Their Eyes Were Watching God*, Celie's written voice to God, her reader, tropes the written yet never uttered voice of free indirect discourse which is the predominant vehicle of narrative commentary in Hurston's novel.

As I have attempted to show in Chapter 5, Hurston draws upon free indirect discourse as a written voice masked as a speakerly voice, as an "oral hieroglyphic," as Hurston put it. Celie's voice in *The Color Purple*, on the other hand, is a spoken or mimetic voice, cast in dialect, yet marked as a written one—a mimetic voice masking as a diegetic voice, but also a diegetic voice masking as a mimetic one. If mimeses is a showing of the fact of telling, then Celie's letters are visual representations that attempt to tell the fact of showing. Whereas Hurston represents Janie's discovery of her voice as the enunciation of her own doubled self through a free indirect "narrative of division," Walker represents Celie's growth of self-consciousness as an act of writing. Janie and her narrator speak themselves into being; Celie, in her letters, writes herself into being. Walker Signifies upon Hurston by troping the concept of voice that unfolds in *Their Eyes Were Watching God*. Whereas Janie's movement from object to subject begins with her failure to recognize an image of her colored self in a photograph, precisely at a point in her childhood when she is known merely as "Alphabet" (a figure for all names and none), Celie's ultimate movement of self-negation is her self-description in her first letter to God: "~~I am.~~" Celie, like Janie, is an absence, an erased presence, an empty set. Celie, moreover, writes in "Janie's voice," in a level of diction and within an idiom similar to that which Janie speaks. Celie, on the other hand, never speaks; rather, she writes her speaking voice and that of everyone who speaks to her.

This remarkably self-conscious Signifyin(g) strategy places *The Color Purple* in a direct line of descent from *Their Eyes Were Watching God*, in an act of literary bonding quite unlike anything that has ever happened within the Afro-American tradition. Walker, we well know, has written at length about her relationship to Zora Neale Hurston. I have always found it difficult to identify this bond textually, by which I mean that I have not found Hurston's presence in Walker's texts. In *The Color Purple*, however, Walker rewrites

Hurston's narrative strategy, in an act of ancestral bonding that is especially rare in black letters, since, as we saw in Chapter 3, black writers have tended to trace their origins to white male parents.

Walker, in effect, has written a letter of love to her authority figure, Hurston. While I am not aware of another epistolary novel in the Afro-American tradition, there is ample precedent in the tradition for the publication of letters. Ignatius Sancho's *Letters* were published at London in 1782. As we saw in Chapter 3, Phillis Wheatley's letters to Arbour Tanner were so well known by 1830 that they could be parodied in a broadside. Even the device of locating Celie's sister in Africa, writing letters home to her troubled sister, has a precedent in the tradition in Amanda Berry Smith's diarylike entries about her African missionary work, published in her *Autobiography* (1893). But we do not have, before *The Color Purple*, an example of the epistolary novel in the black tradition of which I am aware.

Why does Walker turn to the novel of letters to revise *Their Eyes Were Watching God*? As a way of concluding this study of voices in texts, and texts that somehow talk to other texts, I would like to discuss some of the implications of Walker's Signification upon Hurston's text by examining, if only briefly, a few of the more startling aspects of the rhetorical strategies at work in *The Color Purple* and its use of the epistolary form of narration.

The Color Purple is comprised of letters written by two sisters, Celie and Nettie. Celie addresses her letters first to God and then to Nettie, while Nettie, off in the wilds of Africa as a missionary, writes her letters to Celie—letters intercepted by Celie's husband, stashed away in a trunk, and finally read by Celie and Shug Avery, her friend, companion, and lover. Nettie's unreceived letters to Celie appear, suddenly, almost at the center of the text and continue in what we might think of as the text's middle passage with interruptions of three letters of Celie's addressed to God. Then Celie's addressee is Nettie, until she writes her final letter, which is addressed to God (twice) and to the stars, trees, the sky, to "peoples," and to "Everything." While I do not wish to diminish the importance of the novel's plot or its several echoes of moments in Hurston's novel, I am more interested here in suggesting the formal relationship that obtains between the strategies of narration of *Their Eyes* and of *The Color Purple*. Like Janie, Celie is married to a man who would imprison her, indeed brutalize her. Unlike Janie, however, Celie is liberated by her love for Shug Avery, the "bodaciously" strong singer with whom she shares the love that Janie shared with Tea Cake. It is Shug Avery, I shall argue, who stands in this text as Walker's figure for Hurston herself. Perhaps it will suffice to note that this is Celie's text, a text of becoming as is *Their Eyes*, but a becoming with a signal difference.

The most obvious difference between the two texts is that Celie writes herself into being, before our very eyes. Whereas Janie's moment of consciousness is figured as a ritual speech act, for Celie it is the written voice which is her vehicle for self-expression and self-revelation. We read the letters of the text, as it were, over Celie's shoulder, just as we overhear Janie telling her story to Phoeby as they sit on Janie's back porch. Whereas Janie and the narrator do most of Janie's speaking (in an idiomatic free indirect discourse), in *The Color Purple* two of the novel's three principle characters do all of the writing. Celie is her own author, in a manner that Janie could not possibly be, given the third-person form of narration of *Their Eyes*. To remind the reader that we are rereading letters, the lower border of each page of *The Color Purple* is demarcated by a solid black line, an imitation of how the border of a photoduplicated letter might look if bound in hardcover.

What is the text's motivation for the writing of letters? Nettie writes to Celie because she is far away in Africa. Celie writes to God for reasons that Nettie recapitulates in one of her letters:

> I remember one time you said your life made you feel so ashamed you couldn't even talk about it to God, you had to write it, bad as you thought your writing was. Well, now I know what you meant. And whether God will read letters or no, I know you will go on writing them; which is guidance enough for me. Anyway, when I don't write to you I feel as bad as I do when I don't pray, locked up in myself and choking on my own heart. I am so *lonely, Celie.*

The italicized comment that opens the novel—*"You better not tell nobody but God. It'd kill your mammy."*—which we assume has been uttered by Celie's stepfather, is responded to literally by Celie. Celie writes to God for the same reason that Nettie writes to Celie, so that each may read the text of her life, almost exactly or simultaneously as events unfold.

This is the text's justification of its own representation of writing. But what are Walker's motivations? As I suggested above, Celie writes herself into being as a text, a text we are privileged to read over her shoulder. Whereas we are free to wonder aloud about the ironies of self-presentation in a double-voiced free indirect discourse, the epistolary strategy eliminates this aspect of reader response from the start. Celie writes her own story, and writes everyone else's tale in the text except Nettie's. Celie writes her text, and is a text, standing in discrete and episodic letters, which we, like voyeurs, hurriedly read before the addressees (God and Nettie) interrupt our stolen pleasures. Celie is a text in the same way in which Langston Hughes wrote (in *The Big Sea*) that Hurston was a book—"a perfect book of entertainment in herself." We read Celie reading her world and writing it into being, in one subtle discursive act. There is no battle of voices here, as we saw in *Their Eyes*, between a disembodied narrator and a protagonist; Celie speaks—or writes—for Celie and, of course, to survive for Nettie, then for Shug, and finally for Celie.

Ironically, one of the well-known effects of the epistolary narrative is to underscore the illusion of the real, but also of the spontaneous. The form allows for a maximum of identification with a character, precisely because the devices of empathy and distance, standard in third-person narration, no longer obtain. There is no apparent proprietary consciousness in the epistle, so readers must supply any coherence of interpretation of the text themselves. Samuel Richardson understood this well:

> It is impossible that readers the most attentive, can always enter into the views of the writer of a piece, written, as hoped, to Nature and the moment. A species of writing, too, that may be called new; and every one putting him and herself into the character they read, and judging of it by their own sensations.

Celie recounts events, seemingly as they unfold; her readers decide their meaning. Her readers piece together a text from the fragmented letters which Celie never mails and which Celie, almost all at once, receives. But Walker escapes the lack of control over how we read Celie precisely by calling before us a writing style of such innocence with which only the most hardened would not initially sympathize, then eventually *empathize*. By showing Celie as the most utterly dynamic of characters, who comes to know her world and to trust her readings of her world, and by enabling Celie to compel from us compassion for the brutalities she is forced to suffer, followed triumphantly by Celie's assertion of control (experiential control that we learn of through her ever-increasing written control of her letters), Walker manipulates our responses to Celie without even once revealing a voice in the text that Celie or Nettie does not narrate or repeat or edit.

How is this different from first-person narration in a fluid, or linear, narrative? Again, a remarkably self-conscious Richardson tells us in *Clarissa*:

> Such a sweetness of temper, so much patience and resignation, as she seems to be mistress of: yet writing of and in the midst of *present* distresses! How *much more* lively and affecting, for that reason, must her style be; her mind tortured by the pangs

of uncertainty (the events then hidden in the womb of fate) *than* the dry, narrative, unanimated style of persons, relating difficulties and dangers surmounted; the relator perfectly at ease; and if himself unmoved by his own story, not likely greatly to affect the reader!

Unlike the framed tales of Janie in *Their Eyes* or of the nameless protagonist of *Invisible Man*, the reader of a novel of letters does not, indeed cannot, know the outcome of Celie's tale until its writing ceases. The two voices that narrate Ishmael Reed's "anti-detective" novel, for instance, are troped in *The Color Purple* almost by a pun that turns upon this fact: whereas a topos of *Mumbo Jumbo* is a supraforce searching for its text, for its "writing," as Reed puts it, Celie emerges as a force, as a presence, by writing all-too-short letters which, taken together, her readers weave or stitch together as both the text of *The Color Purple* and the autobiographical text of Celie's life and times, her bondage and her freedom. Celie charts her growth of consciousness day to day, or letter to letter. By the end of the novel, we know that Celie, like Reed's silent character, "jes' grew." Celie, moreover, "jes' grew" by writing her text of herself. Whereas Reed's Jes Grew disappears, at the end of *The Color Purple* we are holding Celie's text of herself in our hands. It is we who complete or close the circle or chain of Jes Grew Carriers, in an act of closure that Jes Grew's enemies disrupt in *Mumbo Jumbo*. When Nettie inevitably gets around to asking Celie how she managed to change so much, Celie quite probably could respond, "I jes' grew, I 'spose," precisely because the tyranny of the narrative present can only be overthrown by a linear reading of her letters, from first to last. Celie does not recapitulate her growth, as does Ellison's narrator or Hurston's Janie; only her readers have the leisure to reread Celie's text of development, the text of her becoming. Celie exists letter to letter; her readers supply the coherence necessary to speak of a precisely chartable growth, one measured by comparing or compiling all of the fragments of experience and feeling that Celie has selected to write.

Let us consider this matter of what I have called the tyranny of the narrative present. Celie, as narrator or author, presents herself to us, letter to letter, in a continuous written present. The time of writing is Celie's narrative present. We see this even more clearly when Celie introduces Nettie's first letter, the first letter that Celie and Shug recover from the attic trunk:

Dear God,
    This the letter I been holding in my hand.

The text of Nettie's letter follows, as an embedded narrative. This narrative present is comprised of (indeed, *can* be compromised of) only one event: the process of writing itself. All other events in *The Color Purple* are in the narrative past: no matter how near to the event Celie's account might be, the event is past, and it is this past about which Celie is writing.

We can see this clearly in Celie's first letter. The letter's first paragraph both underscores the moment of writing and provides a frame for the past events that Celie is about to share with her addressee, God:

> Dear God,
>   I am fourteen years old. ~~I am~~ I have always been a good girl.

Celie places her present self ("I am") under erasure, a device that reminds us that she is writing, and searching for her voice by selecting, then rejecting, word choice or word order, but also that there is some reason why Celie was once "a good girl" but no longer feels that she can make this claim before God. Because "a good girl" connotes the avoidance of sex, especially at the age of fourteen, we expect her fall from grace to be a fall of sensual pleasure. Celie tells us that we were right in this suspicion, but also wrong: there has been no pleasure involved in her "fall." Her account of the recent past explains:

> Last spring after little Lucious come I heard them fussing. He was pulling on her arm. She say It too soon, Fonso, I ain't well. Finally he leave her alone. A week go by, he pulling on her arm again. She says Naw, I ain't gonna. Can't you see I'm already half dead, an all of these chilren.
>
>   She went to visit her sister doctor over Macon. Left me to see after the others. He never had a kine word to say to me. Just say You gonna do what your mammy wouldn't. First he put his thing up gainst my hip and sort of wiggle it around. Then he grab hold my titties. Then he push his thing inside my pussy. When that hurt, I cry. He start to choke me, saying You better shut up and git used to it.
>
>   But I don't never git used to it. And now I feels sick every time I be the one to cook. My mama she fuss at me an look at me. She happy, cause he good to her *now*. But too sick to last long. (emphasis added)

Celie has been raped by the man she knows as her father. Her tale of woe has begun. Celie's first letter commences in a narrative present, shifts to a narrative past, then, in the letter's penultimate sentence, returns to a narrative present signified by "now." Prophetically, she even predicts the future, her mother's imminent death. In the narrative past, Celie develops, in fact controls, the representation of character and event. In the narrative present, Celie reveals to us that hers is the proprietary consciousness that we encounter in third-person narration, rendered in an epistle in a first-person narrative present. Celie, as author of her letters to God, might not be able to know what course events shall take, but the past belongs to her, salient detail by salient detail. We only know of Celie's life and times by her recounting of their significance and meaning, rendered in Celie's own word order. In this epistolary novel, the narrator of Celie's tale is identical with the author of Celie's letters. Because there is no gap here, as we saw in *Their Eyes* between the text's narrator and Janie, there would seem to be no need to bridge this gap through free indirect discourse.

This, however, is not the case in *The Color Purple*. While the gap between past and present is not obliterated, the gap between who sees and who speaks *is* obliterated by Celie's curious method of reporting discourse. The epistolary form's necessary shift between the narrative present and the narrative past creates the very space in which free indirect discourse dwells in Celie's narrative. It is in her representation of free indirect discourse that Walker undertakes her most remarkable revision of *Their Eyes Were Watching God*.

The Color Purple is replete with free indirect discourse. The double-voiced discourse of *Their Eyes* returns in the text of Celie's letters. Celie, as I have said, is the narrator and author of her letters. The narrator's voice, accordingly, is the voice of the protagonist. This protagonist, moreover, is divided into two parts: Celie, the character whose past actions we see represented in letters (an active but initially dominated and undereducated adolescent), and that other Celie, who—despite her use of written dialect—we soon understand is a remarkably reflective and sensitive teller, or writer, of a tale, or her own tale. Because of the curious interplay of the narrative past (in which Celie is a character) and a narrative present (in which Celie is the author), Celie emerges as both the subject and object of narration. The subject-object split, or reconciliation, which we have seen in Hurston's use of free indirect discourse, in *The Color Purple* appears as the central rhetorical device by which Celie's self-consciousness is represented, in her own capacity to write a progressively better-structured story of herself.

Whereas Hurston represents Janie's emergent self in the shifting level of diction in the narrator's commentary and in the black-speech-informed indirect discourse, Walker represents Celie's dynamism in her ability to control her own narrative voice (that is, her own style of writing), but also in her remarkable ability to control all other voices spoken to Celie, which we encounter only in Celie's representation of them. Celie represents these voices, this spoken discourse, through the rhetorical device of free indirect discourse. It is Celie's voice that is always a presence whenever anyone in her world is represented as having spoken. We can, therefore, never be certain whether a would-be report, or mimesis, of dialogue is Celie's or the character's whose words we are overhearing or, more precisely, reading over Celie's shoulder.

Let me be clear: no one speaks in this novel. Rather, two sisters correspond to each other, through letters which one never receives (Celie's) and which the other receives almost all at once (Nettie's). There is not true mimeses, then, in *The Color Purple*, only diegesis. But, through Celie's mode of apparently reporting speech, underscored dramatically by her written dialect voice of narration, we logically assume that we are being shown discourse, when all along we never actually are. Celie only tells us what people have said to her. She never shows us their words in direct quotation. Precisely because her written dialect voice is identical in diction and idiom to the supposedly spoken words that pepper her letters, we believe that we are overhearing people speak, just as Celie did when the words were in fact uttered. We are not, however; indeed, we can never be certain whether or not Celie is showing us a telling or telling us a showing, as awkward as this sounds. In the speeches of her characters, Celie's voice and a character's merge into one, almost exactly as we saw happen in *Their Eyes* when Janie and her narrator speak in the merged voice of free indirect discourse. In these passages from *The Color Purple*, the distinction between mimesis and diegesis is apparently obliterated: the opposition between them has collapsed.

This innovation, it seems to me, is Walker's most brilliant stroke, her most telling Signifyin(g) move on Hurston's text. Let us examine just a few scores of examples. The first is Celie's account of Mr. _____'s sisters, named Carrie and Kate, as one of Walker's Signifyin(g) gestures toward Jean Toomer's *Cane*, where Carrie Kate appears as a central character in "Kabnis." (Walker, incidentally, loves *Cane* almost as much as she does *Their Eyes*, as she writes in "Zora Neale Hurston: A Cautionary Tale and a Partisan View.") Celie's depiction of Carrie and Kate's discourse follows:

> Well that's no excuse, say the first one, Her name Carrie, other one name Kate. When a woman marry she spose to keep a decent house and a clean family. Why, wasn't nothing to come

here in the winter time and all these children have colds, they
have flue, they have direar, they have newmonya, they have
worms, they have the chill and fever. They hungry. They hair
ain't comb. They too nasty to touch.

Who is speaking in these passages: Carrie and Kate, or Celie, or all three?
All three are speaking, or, more properly, no one is speaking, because Celie
has merged whatever was actually said with her own voice and has written it
out for us in a narrative form that aspires to the spoken but never represents
or reports anyone else's speech but Celie's on one hand, and Celie-cum-
characters' on the other. Celie is in control of her narration, even to the point
of controlling everyone else's speech, which her readers cannot encounter
without hearing their words merged with Celie's.

 We can see Celie's free indirect discourse in another example, which
reveals how sophisticated an editor Celie becomes, precisely as she grows in
self-awareness. Celie is introducing, or framing, one of Nettie's letters, in a
narrative present:

> It's hot, here, Celie, she writes. Hotter than July. Hotter than
> August and July. Hot like cooking dinner on a big stove in a
> little kitchen in August and July. Hot.

Who said, or wrote, these words, words which echo both the Southern
expression "a cold day in August" and Stevie Wonder's album *Hotter Than
July*? Stevie Wonder? Nettie? Celie? All three, and no one. These are Celie's
words, merged with Nettie's, in a written imitation of the merged voices of
free indirect discourse, an exceptionally rare form in that here even the
illusion of mimesis is dispelled.

 I could cite several more examples, but one more shall suffice. This
moving scene appears just as Celie and Shug are beginning to cement their
bond, a bond that bespeaks a sisterly, and later a sexual, bonding:

> Shug saying Celie. Miss Celie. And I look up where she at.
> She say my name again. She say this song I'm bout to sing
> is call Miss Celie's song. Cause she scratched it out of my head
> when I was sick. . . .
> First time somebody made something and name it after me.

Once again, Celie's voice and Shug's are merged together into one, one we
think is Shug's but which can only be Celie-and-Shug's, simultaneous,
inseparable, bonded.

What are we to make of Walker's remarkable innovation in Hurston's free indirect discourse? We can assume safely that one of Hurston's purposes in the narrative strategies at play in *Their Eyes* was to show James Weldon Johnson and Countee Cullen, and just about everyone else in the New Negro Renaissance that dialect not only was not limited to two stops—humor and pathos—but was fully capable of being used as a literary language even to write a novel. Dialect, black English vernacular and its idiom, as a literary device was not merely a figure of spoken speech; rather, for Hurston, it was a storehouse of figures. As if in a coda to the writing of *Their Eyes*, Hurston even published a short story entirely in the vernacular, entitled "Story in Harlem Slang" (1942), complete with a "Glossary." Yet, just as Johnson has edited or interpreted the language of the black vernacular in his rendition of the "Seven Sermons in Verse" that comprise *God's Trombones* (1927), so too had Hurston merged dialect and standard English in the commentary in *Their Eyes*. Hurston showed the tradition just how dialect could blend with standard English to create a new voice, a voice exactly as black as it is white. (Johnson, of course, had "translated" from the vernacular into standard English.) Walker's Signifyin(g) riff on Hurston was to seize upon the device of free indirect discourse as practiced in *Their Eyes* but to avoid standard English almost totally in Celie's narration. Walker has written a novel in dialect, in the black vernacular. The initial impression that we have of Celie's naiveté slowly reveals how one can write an entire novel in dialect. This, we must realize, is as important a troping of *Their Eyes* as is the page-by-page representation of Celie's writing her own tale. If Hurston's writing aspired to the speakerly, then Walker's apparently speaking characters turn out to have been written.

There are other parallels between the two texts which provide evidence of their Signifyin(g) relationship. Whereas Janie's sign of self-awareness is represented as her ability to tell Phoeby her own version of events, Walker matches this gesture by having Celie first write her own texts, discover her sister's purloined letters, arrange them with Shug in "some kind of order," as Shug says to Celie, then read them so that a second narrative unfolds which both completes and implicitly comments on Celie's narrative which has preceded it by 106 of the text's pages. This newly recovered narrative is a parallel text. This initial cache of unreceived letters functions as a framed tale within Celie's tale, as do Nettie's subsequently received letters, recapitulating events and providing key details absent from Celie's story. Nettie's letters are written in standard English, not only to contrast her character to Celie's but also to provide some relief from Celie's language. But even this narrative Celie controls, by ordering their reading but especially by introducing them, within her letters, with her own commentary. Nettie's letters function as a second narrative of the past, echoing the shift from present to past that we see within the time shifts of Celie's letters. But Nettie's discovered letters are *The Color Purple*'s structural revision of Janie's bracketed tale. We recognize a new Celie once Nettie's letters have been read. Celie's last letter to God reads:

> Dear God,
>   That's it, say Shug. Pack your stuff. You coming back to Tennessee with me.
>   But I feels daze.
>   My daddy lynch. My mama crazy. All my little half-brothers and sisters no kin to me. My children not my sister and brother. Pa not pa.
>   You must be sleep.

Order has been restored, the incest taboo has not been violated, Celie is confused but free and moving.

Janie's Signifyin(g) declaration of independence read in the starkest of terms to her husband, Joe, in *Their Eyes* is repeated in *The Color Purple*. As Celie is about to leave with Shug, this exchange occurs between her and her husband:

> Celie is coming with us, say Shug.
>   Mr. _____'s head swivel back straight. Say what? he ast.
>   Celie is coming to Memphis with me.
>   Over my dead body, Mr. _____ say, . . . what wrong now?
>   You a lowdown dog is what's wrong, I say. It's time to leave you and enter into the Creation. And your dead body just the welcome mat I need.
>   Say what? he ast. Shock.
>   All round the table folkses mouths be dropping open. . . .
>   Mr. _____ start to sputter. ButButButButBut. Sound like some kind of motor.

This marvelous exchange refigures that between Janie and Joe. Celie's newly found voice makes "folkses mouths" drop open, and Mr. _____'s voice inarticulate and dehumanized, "like some kind of motor." A bit later, Celie continues, in triumph, to curse her oppressor:

> Any more letters come? I ast.
> He say, What?
> You heard me, I say. Any more letters from Nettie come?

> If they did, he say, I wouldn't give 'em to you. You two of a kind, he say. A man try to be nice to you, you fly in his face.
>
> I curse you, I say.
>
> What that mean? he say.
>
> I say, Until you do right by me, everything you touch will crumble.

This quasi-Hoodoo curse reads like one of Hurston's recipes for revenge that she published in her classic work on Vaudou, entitled *Tell My Horse* (1938). Significantly, these exchanges—Celie's first open defiance of her husband, Albert—are repeated or written in Celie's first two letters addressed to Nettie rather than God. Celie's husband's desperate response follows:

> He laugh. Who you think you is? he say. You can't curse nobody. Look at you. You black, you pore, you ugly, you a woman. Goddam, he say, you nothing at all.

But Albert no longer has the power of the word over Celie, just as in Hurston Joe cannot recoup from Janie's Signifyin(g) on his manhood in public. This exchange continues:

> Until you do right by me, I say, everything you even dream about will fail. I give it to him straight, just like it come to me. And it seem to come to me from the trees.
>
> Whoever heard of such a thing, say Mr. _____. I probably didn't whup your ass enough.
>
> Every lick you hit me you will suffer twice, I say. Then I say, You better stop talking because all I'm telling you ain't coming just from me. Look like when I open my mouth the air rush in and shape words.
>
> Shit, he say. I should have lock you up. Just let you out to work.
>
> The jail you plan for me is the one in which you will rot, I say. . . .
>
> I'll fix her wagon! Say Mr. _____, and spring toward me.
>
> A dust devil flew up on the porch between us, fill my mouth with dirt. The dirt say, Anything you do to me, already done to you.
>
> Then I feel Shug shake me. Celie, she say. And I come to myself.
>
> I'm pore, I'm black. I may be ugly and can't cook, a voice

say to everything listening. But I'm here.
    Amen, say Shug. Amen, amen.

Celie has at last issued her liberating (and liberated) call, while her friend
Shug, like any black audience, provides the proper ritual response to a
masterful performance: "Amen, say Shug. Amen, amen." Celie speaks herself
free, as did Janie, but in a speaking we know only by its writing, in a letter to
Nettie. Celie has conquered her foe, Albert, and the silences in her self, by
representing an act of speech in the written word, in which she turns Albert's
harsh curses back on him, masterfully.

Just as this scene of instruction echoes Janie's, so too is *The Color Purple*
full of other thematic echoes of *Their Eyes Were Watching God*. Houses
confine in *The Color Purple* just as they do in *Their Eyes*, but Celie, Nettie,
Shug, and Janie all find a form of freedom in houses in which there are no
men: Nettie's hut in Africa, Shug's mansion in Tennessee, and Janie's empty
home in Eatonville. The home that Nettie and Celie inherit will include
men, but men respectful of the inherent strength and equality of women.
Celie and Nettie own this home, and the possession of property seems to
preclude the domination of men.

Shug would seem to be a refugee from *Their Eyes*. It is Shug who
teaches Celie that God is not an "old white man," that God is nature and love
and even sex, that God is a sublime feeling:

> Here's the thing, say Shug. The thing I believe. God is
> inside you and inside everybody else. You come into the world
> with God. But only them that search for it inside find it. And
> sometimes it just manifest itself even if you not looking, or
> don't know what you looking for. Trouble do it for most folks,
> I think. Sorrow, lord. Feeling like shit.
>   It? I ast.
>   Yeah, It. God ain't a he or a she, but a It.
>   But what do it look like? I ast.
>   Don't look like nothing, she say. It ain't a picture show. It
> ain't something you can look at apart from anything else,
> including yourself. I believe God is everything, say Shug.
> Everything that is or ever was or ever will be. And when you
> can feel that, and be happy to feel that, you've found It.

But it is also Shug who teaches Celie about Janie's lyrical language of the
trees, a language of nature in which God speaks in the same metaphors in

which he spoke to Janie, a divine utterance which led Janie to enjoy her first orgasm, an experience that Shug tells Celie is God's ultimate sign of presence:

> She say, My first step from the old white man was trees. Then air. Then birds. Then other people. But one day when I was sitting quiet and feeling like a motherless child, which I was, it come to me: that feeling of being part of everything, not separate at all. I knew that if I cut a tree, my arm would bleed. And I laughed and I cried and I run all round the house. I knew just what it was. In fact, when it happen, you can't miss it. It sort of like you know what, she say, grinning and rubbing high up on my thigh.
>
> *Shug!* I say.
>
> Oh, she say. God love all them feelings. That's some of the best stuff God did. And when you know God loves 'em you enjoys 'em a lot more. You can just relax, go with everything that's going, and praise God by liking what you like.
>
> God don't think it dirty? I ast.

God don't think it dirty? I ast. And if we miss Shug's connection with Janie, Walker first describes Shug in terms in which she has described Hurston:

> She do more then that. She git a picture. The first one of a real person I ever seen. She say Mr. _____ was taking something out his billfold to show Pa an it fell out an slid under the table. Shug Avery was a woman. The most beautiful woman I ever saw. She more pretty than my mama. She bout ten thousand times more prettier than me. I see her there in furs. Her face rouge. Her hair somethin tail. She grinning with her foot up on somebody motocar. Her eyes serious tho. Sad some.

Compare that description with Walker's description of Hurston:

> [She] loved to wear hats, tilted over one eye, and pants and boots. (I have a photograph of [Hurston] in pants, boots, and broadbrim that was given to me by her brother, Everette. She has her foot up on the running board of a car—presumably hers, and bright red—and looks racy.)

There are several other echoes, to which I shall allude only briefly. Celie's voice, when she first speaks out against the will of Mr. _____, "seems to come to me from the trees" just as Janie's inner voice manifests itself under the pear tree. Celie, like Janie, describes herself as a "motherless child." Key metaphors repeat: Hurston's figure of nature mirroring Janie's emotions— "the rose of the world breathing out smell"—becomes Shug and Celie's scene in which Shug teaches Celie to masturbate, using a mirror to watch herself:

> I stand there with the mirror.
> She say, What, too shame even to go off and look at yourself? And you look so cute too, she say, laughing. All dressed up for Harpo's, smelling good and everything, but scared to look at your own pussy. . . .
> I lie back on the bed and haul up my dress. Yank down my bloomers. Stick the looking glass tween my legs. Ugh. All that hair. Then my pussy lips be black. Then inside look like a wet rose.
> It a lot prettier than you thought, ain't it? she say from the door.

Later, in her first letter to Nettie, Celie uses the figure of the rose again in a simile: "Shug a beautiful something, let me tell you. She frown a little, look out cross the yard, lean back in her chair, look like a big rose."

In the same way that Walker's extends to the literal Hurston's figure of the rose of the world breathing out smell, she also erases the figurative aspect of Janie's metaphor for her narration to Phoeby ("mah tongue is in mah friend's mouf") by making Shug and Celie literal "kissin-friends," or lovers. That which is implicit in Hurston's figures Walkers makes explicit. Walker, in addition, often reverses Hurston's tropes: whereas *Their Eyes* accounts for the orgasm Janie experiences under the pear tree by saying, in free indirect discourse, "So this was a marriage!", Celie writes that when Mr. _____ beats her, she turns herself into a tree:

> He beat me like he beat the children. Cept he don't never hardly beat them. He say, Celie, git the belt. The children be outside the room peeking through the cracks. It all I can do not to cry. I make myself wood. I say to myself, Celie, you a tree. That's how come I know trees fear man.

Their Eyes' circular narration, in which the end is the beginning and the beginning the end, *The Color Purple* tropes with a linear narration. There are several other examples of these Signifyin(g) riffs.

Walker has Signified upon Hurston in what must stand to be the most loving revision, and claim to title, that we have seen in the tradition. Walker has turned to a black antecedent text to claim literary ancestry, or motherhood, not only for content but for structure. Walker's turn to Hurston for form (and to, of all things, the topoi of medieval romance known as "The Incestuous Father" and "The Exchanged Letter" for plot structure), openly disrupts the pattern of revision (white form, black content) that we have discussed in Chapter 3. Even Walker's representation of Celie's writing in dialect echoes Hurston's definition of an "oral hieroglyphic," and her ironic use of speakerly language which no person can ever speak, because it exists only in a written text. This, too, Walker tropes, by a trick of figuration, one so clever that only Esu's female principle could have inspired it: people who speak dialect *think* that they are saying standard English words; when they write the words that they speak as "dis" and "dat," therefore, they spell "this" and "that." Walker, like Hurston, masters the illusion of the black vernacular by its writing, in a masterful exemplification of the black trope of Stylin' out.

Walker's revision of Hurston stands at the end of a chain of narration. Walker's text, like those by Toni Morrison, James Baldwin, Ann Petry, Paule Marshall, Leon Forrest, Ernest Gaines, John Wideman, and others, afford subsequent writers tropes and topoi to be revised. Endings, then, imply beginnings. Increasingly, however, after Walker and Reed, black authors could even more explicitly turn to black antecedent texts for both form and content. The tradition of Afro-American literature, a tradition of grounded repetition and difference, is characterized by its urge to start over, to begin again, but always to begin on a well-structured foundation. Our narrators, our Signifiers, are links in an extended ebony chain of discourse, which we, as critics, protect and explicate. As Martin Buber puts the relation in *The Legend of Baal-Shem:*

> I have told it anew as one who was born later. I bear in me the blood and spirit of those who created it, and out of my blood and spirit it has become new. I stand in the chain of narrators, a link between links; I tell once again the old stories, and if they sound new it is because the new already lay dormant in them when they were told for the first time.

While the principal silent second text is *Their Eyes Were Watching God,* Walker's critique of Celie's initial conception of God, and especially its anthropomorphism, revises a key figure in Rebecca Cox Jackson's narrative and perhaps surfaces as a parable for the so-called noncanonical critic.

Just after Celie and Shug have discovered, arranged, and read Nettie's purloined letters, Celie writes this to Nettie:

> Dear Nettie,
>   I don't write to God no more, I write to you.
>   What happen to God? ast Shug.
>   Who that? I say.
>   . . . what God do for me? I ast.
>   She say, Celie! Like she shock. He gave you life, good health, and a good woman that love you to death.
>   Yeah, I say, and he give me a lynched daddy, a crazy mama, a low-down dog of a step pa and a sister I probably won't ever see again. Anyhow, I say, the God I been praying and writing to is a man. And act just like all the other mens I know. Trifling, forgitful, and lowdown.

A few pages later, Shug describes to Celie the necessity of escaping the boundaries caused by the anthropomorphism of God and calls this concept that of "the old white man." This, Celie confesses, is difficult: "Well, us talk and talk bout God, but I'm still adrift. Trying to chase that old white man out of my head." Shug responds that the problem is not only "the old white man," but all men:

> Still, it is like Shug say, You have got to git man off your eyeball, before you can see anything a'tall.
>   Man corrup everything, say Shug. He on your box of grits, in your hand, and all over the road. He try to make you think he everywhere. Soon as you think he everywhere, you think he God. But he ain't. Whenever you trying to pray, and man plop himself on the other end of it, tell him to git lost, say Shug. Conjure up flowers, wind, water, a big rock.

This passage, most certainly, constitutes an important feminist critique of the complex fiction of male domination. But it also recalls a curious scene in Rebecca Cox Jackson's text. Indeed, Walker's text Signifies upon it. Earlier, I discussed Jackson's supernatural mastery of literacy. Jackson was careful to show that God's gracious act of instruction freed her from the domination and determination of her words (their order, their meaning) by her minister-brother, who by rearranging her words sought to control their sense. Jackson indeed became free, and freely interprets the Word of God in her own, often idiosyncratic way. But is Jackson's a truly liberating gesture, a fundamental gesture of a nascent feminism?

Jackson substitutes a mystical "white man," the image of whom Shug and Celie seek to dispel, for the interpretive role of the male, the relation of truth to understanding, of sound and sense. Jackson's account is strikingly vivid:

> A white man took me by my right hand and led me on the north side of the room, where sat a square table. On it lay a book open. And he said to me, "Thou shalt be instructed in this book, from Genesis to Revelations." And then he took me on the west side, where stood a table. And it looked like the first. And said, "Yea, thou shall be instructed from the beginning of creation to the end of time." And then he took me on the east side of the room also, where stood a table and book like the two first, and said, "I will instruct thee—yea, thou shall be instructed from the beginning of all things to the end of all things. Yea, thou shall be well instructed. I will instruct."
>
> When Samuel handed me to this man at my own back door, he turned away. I never saw him any more. When this man took me by the hand, his hand was soft like down. He was dressed all in light drab. He was bareheaded. His countenance was serene and solemn and divine. There was a father and a brother's countenance to be seen in his face.
>
> And then I awoke, and I saw him as plain as I did in my dream. And after that he taught me daily. And when I would be reading and come to a hard word, I would see him standing at my side and he would teach me the word right. And often, when I would be in meditation and looking into things which was hard to understand, I would find him by me, teaching and giving me understanding. And oh, his labor and care which he had with me often caused me to weep bitterly, when I would see my great ignorance and the great trouble he had to make me understand eternal things. For I was so buried in the depth of the tradition of my forefathers, that it did seem as I never could be dug up.

Jackson opposes the "white man" who would "teach me the right word," he who would stand "by me, teaching and giving me understanding," with the delineation of understanding imposed by her brother and, curiously enough, by "the depth of the traditions of my forefathers." So oppressive was the latter that, she admits, "it did seem as if I never could be dug up."

Shug and Celie's conception of God Signifies upon these passages from Jackson. Jackson's "white man" and Celie's, the speaking interpreter and the silent reader, are identical until Celie, with Shug's help, manages to "git man off your eyeball." Whereas Jackson suffocates under the burden of tradition, "buried in the depth" as she puts it, Walker's text points to a bold new model for a self-defined, or internally defined, notion of tradition, one black and female. The first step toward such an end, she tells us, was to eliminate the "white man" to whom we turn for "teaching" and the "giving [of] understanding." This parable of interpretation is Walker's boldest claim about the nature and function of the black tradition and its interpretation. To turn away from, to step outside the white hermeneutical circle and into the black is the challenge issued by Walker's critique of Jackson's vision.

BELL HOOKS

Writing the Subject: Reading The Color Purple

*T**he Color Purple* broadens the scope of literary discourse, asserting its primacy in the realm of academic thought while simultaneously stirring the reflective consciousness of a mass audience. Unlike most novels by any writer it is read across race, class, gender, and cultural boundaries. It is truly a popular work—a book of the people—a work that has many different meanings for many different readers. Often the meanings are not interesting, contained as they are within a critical discourse that does not resist the urge to simplify, to overshadow, to make this work by a contemporary African-American writer mere sociological treatise on black life or radical feminist tract. To say even as some critics do that it is a modern day "slave narrative" or to simply place the work within the literary tradition of epistolary sentimental novels is also a way to contain, restrict, control. Categorizing in this way implies that the text neither demands nor challenges, rather, that it can be adequately and fully discussed within an accepted critical discourse, one that remains firmly within the boundaries of conservative academic aesthetic intentionality. While such discourse may illuminate aspects of the novel, it also obscures, suppresses, silences. Michel Foucault's comments on discourse in *The History of Sexuality* serve as a useful reminder that critical vision need not be fixed or static, that "discourse can be both an instrument

From *Alice Walker*, edited by Harold Bloom. © 1988 Bell Hooks.

and an effect of power, but also a hindrance, a stumbling block, a point of resistance and a starting point for an opposing strategy."

To critically approach *The Color Purple* from an oppositional perspective, it is useful to identify gaps—spaces between the text and conventional critical points of departure. That the novel's form is epistolary is most obvious, so apparent even that it is possible to overlook the fact that it begins not with a letter but an opening statement, a threatening command—speaker unidentified. "You better not never tell nobody but God. It'd kill your mammy." Straightaway Celie's letter writing to God is placed in a context of domination; she is obeying orders. Her very first letter reveals that the secret that can be told to no one but God has to do with sexuality, with sexual morality, with a male parent's sexual abuse of a female child. In form and content the declared subject carries traces of the sentimental novel with its focus on female characters and most importantly the female as potential victim of exploitative male sexual desire, but this serves only as a background for deviation, for subversion.

Significantly, *The Color Purple* is a narrative of "sexual confession." Statements like: "First he put his thing up against my hip and sort of wiggle it around. Then he grabs hold my titties. Then he put his thing inside my pussy," refer solely to sexual encounters. Throughout *The Color Purple*, sexuality is graphically and explicitly discussed. Though a key narrative pattern in the novel, it is usually ignored. As readers approaching this novel in the context of a white supremacist patriarchal society wherein black women have been and continue to be stereotyped as sexually loose, a black woman writer imagining a black female character who writes about sexuality in letters to God, using graphic and explicit language, may not seem unusual or even interesting, particularly since graphic descriptions of sexual encounters conform to a current trend in women's writing. But this is most unlikely, as it is the culture's fascination with sexual autobiography that has led to a burgeoning of fiction and true-life stories focusing on sexual encounters. This trend is especially evident in popular women-centered novels. Attracting mass audiences in similar ways as their nineteenth-century female predecessors, these new works captivate readers not by covert reference to sexual matters but by explicit exposure and revelation. They completely invert the values of the Victorian novel. While the nineteenth-century protagonist as innocent had no language with which to speak sexual desire, the contemporary heroine of the woman-centered novel is not only the speaking sex, the desiring sex; she is talking sex.

Celie's life is presented in reference to her sexual history. Rosalind Coward's witty essay, "The True Story of How I Became My Own Person," in her collection *Female Desires*, warns against the reproduction of an ideology where female identity is constructed solely in relationship to sexuality, where sexual experience becomes the way in which a woman learns self-knowledge.

> There's a danger that such structures reproduce the Victorian ideology that sexuality is somehow outside social relationships. The idea that a woman could become her own person just through sexual experiences and the discovery of sexual needs and dislikes again establishes sexual relations as somehow separate from social structures.

Walker reproduces this ideology in *The Color Purple*. Patriarchy is exposed and denounced as a social structure supporting and condoning male domination of women, specifically represented as black male domination of black females, yet it does not influence and control sexual desire and sexual expression. While Mr. _____, dominating male authority figure, can become enraged at the possibility that his wife will be present at a jukejoint, he has no difficulty accepting her sexual desire for another female. Homophobia does not exist in the novel. Celie's sexual desire for women and her sexual encounter with Shug is never a controversial issue even though it is the catalyst for her resistance to male domination, for her coming to power. Walker makes the powerful suggestion that sexual desire can disrupt and subvert oppressive social structure because it does not necessarily conform to social prescription, yet this realization is undermined by the refusal to acknowledge it as threatening—dangerous.

Sexual desire, initially evoked in the novel as a subversive transformative force, one that enables folk to break radically with convention (Mr. _____'s passion for Shug transcends marriage vows; Celie's acceptance and fulfillment of her desire for a female leads her to reject heterosexuality; Shug's free-floating lust shared with many partners, each different from the other, challenges the notion of monogamous coupling) is suppressed and finally absent—a means to an end but not an end in itself. Celie may realize she desires women, express that longing in a passionate encounter with Shug, but just as the signifier lesbian does not exist to name and affirm her experience, no social reality exists so that she can express that desire in ongoing sexual practice. She is seduced and betrayed. Seduced by the promise of an erotic vocation wherein sexual fulfillment is deemed essential to self-recovery and self-realization, she must deny the primacy of this sexual awakening and the pain of sexual rejection.

Ironically, Shug's rejection serves as a catalyst enabling Celie and Albert to renew and transform their heterosexual bonding. Walker upholds the promise of an intact heterosexual bond with a relational scenario wherein the point of intimate connection between coupled male and female is not the acting out of mutual sexual desire for one another, but the displacement of that desire onto a shared object—in this case Shug. Given such a revised framework for the establishment of heterosexual bonds, sex between Shug and Celie does not threaten male-female bonding or affirm the possibility that women can be fulfilled in a life that does not include intimate relationships with men. As Mariana Valverde emphasizes in *Sex, Power, and Pleasure*:

> Lesbianism is thus robbed of its radical potential because it is portrayed as compatible with heterosexuality, or rather as part of heterosexuality itself. The contradictions that our society creates between hetero- and homosexuality are wished away and social oppression is ignored.

Wedded by their mutual desire for Shug, their shared rejection, Celie and Albert are joined in a sustained committed relationship. Reunited, they stand together, "two old fools left over from love, keeping each other company under the stars."

Shug, whose very name suggests that she has the power to generate excitement without the ability to provide substantive nourishment, must also give up sexual pleasure. Betrayed by the sexual desire that has been the source of her power, Shug's lust for a young man is not depicted as an expression of sexual liberation, of longing for a new and different sexual pleasure, instead it is a disempowering force, one that exposes her vulnerability and weakness. Placed within a stereotypical heterosexist framework wherein woman is denied access to ongoing sexual pleasure which she seeks and initiates, as the novel progresses Shug is depicted as an aging female seducer who fears the loss of her ability to use sex as a means to attract and control men, as a way to power. Until this turning point, sex has been for Shug a necessary and vital source of pleasure. As object of intense sexual desire, she has had power to shape and influence the actions of others but always in the direction of a higher good.

Ultimately, Walker constructs an ideal world of true love and commitment where there is no erotic tension—where there is no sexual desire or sexual pleasure. Just as the reader's perception of Shug is dramatically altered towards the end of the novel, so is the way we see and understand Celie's sexual history; her sexual confession changes when it is revealed that she has not been raped by her real father. The tragedy and trauma of incest, so graphically and poignantly portrayed, both in terms of the incest-rape and Celie's sexual healing which begins when she tells Shug what happened, is trivialized as the novel progresses. Presented in retrospect as though it was all an absurd drama, the horror of Celie's early sexual experience and the pleasure of her sexual awakening assume the quality of spectacle, of exaggerated show. A curious tale told in part as a strategy to engage and excite the reader's imagination before attention is diverted towards more important revelations. Given the fascination in this culture with sex and violence, with race and sex, with sexual deviance, a fascination which is recognized and represented most often in pornography, Walker's subject has immediate appeal. Readers are placed in the position of voyeurs who witness Celie's torment as victim of incest-rape, as victim of sexual violence in a sadistic master-slave relationship; who watch her sexual exploration of her body and experience vicarious pleasure at her sexual awakening as she experiences her first sexual encounter with Shug. Ironically, pornographic fiction consumed by a mass audience is a genre which has always included narratives describing women engaged in sexual acts with one another, observed by powerful others—usually men. Walker subverts this pattern. As readers we represent the powerful other. Her intent is not to titillate sexually, but to arouse disgust, outrage, and anger at male sexual exploitation of females and to encourage appreciation and acceptance of same-sex female sexual pleasure.

To achieve this end, which is fundamentally anti–male domination, Walker relies on similar narrative strategies and preoccupations as those utilized in the pornographic narrative. Annette Kuhn's essay on representation and sexuality which focuses on pornography's "Lawless seeing" points to the connection between pornographic fiction and other simple narratives:

> in pornographic stories, literary as well as visual, characters are never very strongly developed or psychologically rounded human beings. They perform function, they take on roles already fixed within the commonplace fantasies that porn constructs—the sexually active woman, the Peeping Tom, the plumber out on his rounds. In porn, characters are what they do, and given a minimal amount of familiarity with the genre, the reader needs little by way of explanation in order to understand what is going on. Pornography has a good deal in common with other simple forms of narrative, stories in which characters are no more than what they do and the reader has some general idea, as soon as the story begins, of who is going to do what to whom and with what outcome. . . . In many respects, pornographic stories work like fairy tales.

Characters are very much what they do in *The Color Purple*. Mr. _____ is brute, Lucious the rapist, Harpo the buffoon, Celie the sexual victim, Shug the sexual temptress. Many of the characters perform roles that correspond with racial stereotypes. The image of "the black male rapist" resonates in both racial and sexual stereotypes; Walker's characterization cannot be viewed in a vacuum, as though it does not participate in these discourses which have been primarily used to reinforce domination, both racial and sexual.

Pornography participates in and promotes a discourse that exploits and aesthetisizes domination. Kuhn asserts that pornography insists on sexual difference, that sexual violence in master-slave scenarios reduces this difference to relations of power. Feminists who focus almost exclusively on male violence against women as the central signifier of male domination also view sexual difference as solely a relation of power. Within pornography, Kuhn states, there is

> an obsession with the otherness of femininity, which in common with many forms of otherness seems to contain a threat to the onlooker. Curiosity turns to terror, investigation to torture, the final affirmation of the objecthood of the other. The feminine here represents a threat to the masculine, a threat which demands containment. Sexually violent pornography of this kind concretises this wish for containment in representations which address the spectator as masculine and place the masculine on the side of container of the threat. It insists that sexuality and power are inseparable.

Walker inverts this paradigm. Presuming a female spectator (women and specifically white women from privileged classes are the primary audience for women-centered novels), she constructs a fiction in which it is the masculine threat, represented by black masculinity, that must be contained, controlled, and ultimately transformed. Her most radical re-visioning of the oppressive patriarchal social order is her insistence on the transformation of Mr. _____. He moves from male oppressor to enlightened being, willingly surrendering his attachment to the phallocentric social order reinforced by the sexual oppression of women. His transformation begins when Celie threatens his existence, when her curse disempowers him. Since sexuality and power are so closely linked to politics of domination, Mr. _____ must be completely desexualized as part of the transformative process.

Unable to reconcile sexuality and power, Walker replaces the longing for sexual pleasure with an erotic metaphysics animated by a vision of the unity of all things, by the convergence of erotic and mystical experience.

This is ritually enacted as Shug initiates Celie into a spiritual awakening wherein belief in God as white male authority figure, who gives orders and punishes, is supplanted by the vision of a loving God who wants believer to celebrate life, to experience pleasure, a God who is annoyed, "if you walk by the color purple in a field somewhere but don't notice it." In *The Color Purple* Christianity and patriarchy are oppressive social structures which promote anhedonia. Celie and Albert, as oppressed and oppressor, must as part of their personal transformation learn to feel pleasure and develop a capacity to experience happiness. Concurrently, Nettie and Samuel, laboring as missionaries in Africa, develop a critical consciousness that allows them to see the connections between Western cultural imperialism and Christianity; and this enables them to see God in a new way. Nettie writes to Celie, "God is different to us now, after all these years in Africa, more spirit than even before, and more internal." Though critical of religious beliefs which reinforce sexist and racist domination, Shug insists on the primacy of a spiritual life, constructing a vision of spirituality which echoes the teachings of religious mystics who speak of healing alienation through recognition of the unity in all life.

Spiritual quest is connected with the effort of characters in *The Color Purple* to be more fully self-realized. This effort merges in an unproblematic way with a materialist ethic which links acquisition of goods with the capacity to experience emotional well-being. Traditionally mystical experience is informed by radical critique and renunciation of materialism. Walker positively links the two. Even though her pronounced critique of patriarchy includes an implicit indictment of perverse individualism which encourages exploitation (Albert is transformed in part by his rejection of isolation and self-sufficiency for connection and interdependency), Celie's shift from underclass victim to capitalist entrepreneur has only positive signification. Albert, in his role as oppressor, forces Celie and Harpo to work in the fields, exploiting their labor for his gain. Their exploitation as workers must cease before domination ends and transformation begins. Yet Celie's progression from exploited black woman, as woman, as sexual victim, is aided by her entrance into the economy as property owner, manager of a small business, storekeeper—in short, capitalist entrepreneur. No attention is accorded aspects of this enterprise that might reinforce domination: attention is focused on how useful Celie's pants are for family and friends; on the way Sofia as worker in her store will treat black customers with respect and consideration. Embedded in the construction of sexual difference as it is characterized in *The Color Purple* is the implicit assumption that women are innately less inclined to oppress and dominate than men; that women are not easily corrupted.

Rewarded with economic prosperity for her patient endurance of suffering, Celie never fully develops capacities for sustained self-assertion. Placed on a moral pedestal which allows no one to see her as a threat, she is always a potential victim. By contrast, Sofia's self-affirmation, her refusal to see herself as victim, is not rewarded. She is constantly punished. Sadly, as readers witness Celie's triumph, her successful effort to resist male domination which takes place solely in a private familial context, we also bear witness to Sofia's tragic fate, as she resists sexist and racist oppression in private and public spheres. Unlike Celie or Shug, she is regarded as a serious threat to the social order and is violently attacked, brutalized, and subdued. Always a revolutionary, Sofia has never been victimized or complicit in her own oppression. Tortured and persecuted by the State, treated as though she is a political prisoner, Sofia's spirit is systematically crushed. Unlike Celie, she cannot easily escape and there is no love strong enough to engender her self-recovery. Her suffering cannot be easily mitigated, as it would require radical transformation of society. Given all the spectacular changes in *The Color Purple*, it is not without grave and serious import that the character who most radically challenges sexism and racism is a tragic figure who is only partially rescued—restored to only a semblance of sanity. Like the lobotomized Native American Indian in *One Flew Over the Cuckoo's Nest*, Sofia's courageous spirit evokes affirmation, even as her fate strikes fear and trepidation in the hearts and minds of those who would actively resist oppression.

Described as a large woman with a powerful presence, Sofia's vacant position in the kinship network is assumed by Squeak, a thin petite woman, who gains presence only when she acts to free Sofia, passively enduring rape to fulfill her mission. This rape of a black woman by a white man does not have grievous traumatic negative consequences, even though it acts to reinforce sexist domination of females and racist exploitation. Instead, it is a catalyst for positive change—Sofia's release, Squeak asserting her identity as Mary Agnes. Such a benevolent portrayal of the consequences of rape contrasts sharply with the images of black male rapists, images which highlight the violence and brutality of their acts. That the text graphically emphasizes the horror and pain of black male sexist exploitation of black females while de-emphasizing the horror and pain of racist exploitation of black women by white men that involves sexual violence is an unresolved contradiction if Walker's intent is to expose the evils of sexual domination. These contrasting depictions of rape dangerously risk reinforcing racist stereotypes that perpetuate the notion that black men are more capable of brutal sexist domination than other groups of men.

Throughout *The Color Purple* exposures of the evils of patriarchal domination are undercut by the suggestion that this form of domination is not necessarily linked to race and class exploitation. Celie and Albert are able to eradicate sexism in their relationship. The threat of masculine domination ceases when Albert forgoes phallic privilege and serves as a helpmate to Celie, assuming a "feminine" presence. However, the phallocentric social order which exists outside the domain of private relationships remains intact. As symbolic representation of masculine otherness, the phallus continues to assert a powerful presence via the making of pants that both women and men will wear. This is not a radical re-visioning of gender. It is a vision of inclusion that enables women to access power via symbolic phallic representation. As French feminist Antoinette Fougue reminds us:

> Inversion does not facilitate the passage to another kind of structure. The difference between the sexes is not whether or not one does or doesn't have a penis, it is whether or not one is an integral part of a phallic masculine economy.

Within *The Color Purple* the economy Celie enters as entrepreneur and landowner is almost completely divorced from structures of domination. Immersed in the ethics of a narcissistic new-age spiritualism wherein economic prosperity indicates that one is chosen—blessed, Celie never reflects critically on the changes in her status. She writes to Nettie, "I am so happy. I got love. I got work. I got money, friends and time."

Indeed the magic of *The Color Purple* is that it is so much a book of our times, imaginatively evoking the promise of a world in which one can have it all; a world in which sexual exploitation can be easily overcome; a world of unlimited access to material well-being; a world where the evils of racism are tempered by the positive gestures of concerned and caring white folks; a world where sexual boundaries can be transgressed at will without negative consequences; a world where spiritual salvation is the lot of the elect. This illusory magic is sustained by Walker's literary technique, the skillful combining of social realism and fantasy, the fairy tale and the fictionalized autobiographical narrative.

As the fictive autobiography of an oppressed black woman's journey from sexual slavery to freedom, *The Color Purple* parodies those primary texts of autobiographical writing which have shaped and influenced the direction of African-American fiction—the "slave narrative." With the publication of slave autobiographies, oppressed African-American slaves moved from object to subject, from silence into speech, creating a revolutionary literature—one that changed the nature and direction of African-American history; that laid the groundwork for the development of a distinct African-American literary tradition. Slave autobiographies worked to convey as accurately as possible the true story of slavery as experienced and interpreted by slaves, without apology or exaggeration. The emphasis on truth had a twofold purpose, the presentation of reliable sources, and, most importantly, the creation of a radical discourse on slavery that served as a corrective and a challenge to the dominant culture's hegemonic perspective. Although Walker conceived of *The Color Purple* as a historical novel, her emphasis is less on historical accuracy and more on an insistence that history has more to do with the interpersonal details of everyday life at a given historical moment than with significant dates, events, or important persons. Relying on historical referents only insofar as they lend an aura of credibility to that which is improbable and even fantastic, Walker mocks the notion of historical truth, suggesting that it is subordinate to myth, that the mythic has far more impact on consciousness. This is most evident in the letters from Africa. Historical documents, letters, journals, articles, provide autobiographical testimony of the experience and attitudes of nineteenth-century black missionaries in Africa, yet Walker is not as concerned with a correspondence between the basic historical fact that black missionaries did travel to Africa than providing the reader with a fictive account of those travels that is plausible. Walker uses the basic historical fact as a frame to enhance the social realism of her text while superimposing a decidedly contemporary perspective. Historical accuracy is altered to serve didactic purposes—to teach the reader history not as it was but as it should have been.

A revolutionary literature has as its central goal the education for critical consciousness, creating awareness of the forces that oppress and recognition of the way those forces might be transformed. One important aspect of the slave narrative as revolutionary text was the insistence that the plight of the individual narrator be linked to the oppressed plight of all black people so as to arouse support for organized political effort for social changes. Walker appropriates this form to legitimize and render authentic Celie's quest without reflecting this radical agenda. Celie's plight is not representative; it is not linked to collective effort to effect radical social change. While she is a victim of male domination, Shug is not. While she has allowed patriarchal ideology to inform her sense of self, Sofia has not. By de-emphasizing the collective plight of black people, or even black women, and focusing on the individual's quest for freedom as separate and distinct, Walker makes a crucial break with that revolutionary African-American literary tradition which informs her earlier work, placing this novel outside that framework. Parodying the slave narrative's focus on racial oppression, Walker's emphasis on sexual oppression acts to delegitimize the historical specificity and power of this form. Appropriating the slave narrative in this way, she invalidates both the historical context and the racial agenda. Furthermore, by linking this form to the sentimental novel as though they served similar functions, Walker strips the slave narrative of its revolutionary ideological intent and content, connecting it to Eurocentric bourgeois literary traditions in such a way as to suggest it was merely derivative and in no way distinct.

Slave narratives are a powerful record of the particular unique struggle of African-American people to write history—to make literature—to be self-defining people. Unlike Celie, the slave who recorded her or his story was not following the oppressors' orders, was not working within a context of domination. Fundamentally, this writing was a challenge, a resistance affirming that the movement of the oppressed from silence into speech is a liberatory gesture. Literacy is upheld in the slave narrative as essential to the practice of freedom. Celie writes not as a gesture of affirmation or liberation but as a gesture of shame. Nettie recalls, "I remember one time you said your life made you feel so ashamed you couldn't even talk about it to God. You had to write it." Writing then is not a process which enables Celie to make herself subject, it allows distance, objectification. She does not understand writing as an act of power, or self-legitimation. She is empowered not by the written word but by the spoken word—by telling her story to Shug. Later, after she has made the shift from object to subject she ceases to write to God and addresses Nettie, which is an act of self-affirmation.

Taken at face value, Celie's letter writing appears to be a simple matter-of-fact gesture when it is really one of the most fantastical happenings in *The Color Purple*. Oppressed, exploited as laborer in the field, as worker in the domestic household, as sexual servant, Celie finds time to write—this is truly incredible. There is no description of Celie with pen in hand, no discussion of where and when she writes. She must remain invisible so as not to expose this essential contradiction—that as dehumanized object she projects a self in the act of writing even as she records her inability to be self-defining. Celie as writer is a fiction. Walker, as writing subject, oversees her creation, constructing a narrative that purports to be a space where the voice of an oppressed black female can be heard even though the valorization of writing and the use of the epistolary form suppress and silence that voice.

Writing in a manner that reads as though she is speaking, talking in the voice of a black folk idiom, Celie, as poor and exploited black female, appears to enter a discourse from which she has been excluded—the act of writing, the production of story as commodity. In actuality, her voice remains that of appropriated other—interpreted—translated—represented as authentic unspoiled innocent. Walker provides Celie a writing self, one that serves as a perfect foil for her creator. Continually asserting her authorial presence in *The Color Purple*, she speaks through characters sharing her thoughts and values. Masquerading as just plain folks, Celie, Nettie, Shug, and Albert are the mediums for the presentation of her didactic voice. Through fictive recognition and acknowledgment, Walker pays tribute to the impact of black folk experience as a force that channels and shapes her imaginative work, yet her insistent authorial presence detracts from this representation.

Traces of traditional African-American folk expression as manifest in language and modes of story-telling are evident in Celie's letters, though they cannot be fully voiced and expressed in the epistolary form. There they are contained and subsumed. Commenting on the use of the epistolary form in *Seduction and Betrayal: Women and Literature*, Elizabeth Hardwick suggests,

> A letter is not a dialogue or even an omniscient exposition. It is a fabric of surfaces, a mask, a form as well suited to affectations as to the affection. The letter is, by its natural shape, self-justifying; it is one's own evidence, deposition, a self-serving testimony. In a letter the writer holds all the cards, controls everything.

That Celie and Nettie's letters are basically self-serving is evident when it is revealed that there has never been a true correspondence. And if readers are to assume that Celie is barely able to read and write as her letters suggest, she would not have been able to comprehend Nettie's words. Not only is the inner life of the characters modified by the use of the epistolary form, but the absence of correspondence restricts information, and enables the letters to serve both the interest of the writers, and the interests of an embedded didactic narrative. Functioning as a screen, the letters keep the reader at a distance, creating the illusion of intimacy where there is none. The reader is always voyeur, outsider looking in, passively awaiting the latest news.

Celie and Nettie's letters testify, we as readers bear witness. They are an explanation of being, which asserts that understanding the self is the precondition for transformation, for radical change. Narrating aspects of their personal history, they engage in an ongoing process of demythologizing that makes new awareness and change possible. They recollect to recover and restore. They seek to affirm and sustain the initial bond of care and connection experienced with one another in their oppressive male-dominated family. Since the mother is bonded with the father, supporting and protecting his interests, mothers and daughters within this fictive patriarchy suffer a wound of separation and abandonment; they have no context for unity. Mothers prove their allegiance to fathers by betraying daughters; it is only a vision of sisterhood that makes woman bonding possible. By eschewing the identity of Mother, black women in *The Color Purple*, like Shug and Sofia, rebelliously place themselves outside the context of patriarchal family norms, revisioning mothering so that it becomes a task any willing female can perform, irrespective of whether or not she has given birth. Displacing motherhood as central signifier for female being, and emphasizing sisterhood, Walker posits a relational basis for self-definition that valorizes and affirms woman bonding. It is the recognition of self in the other, of unity, and not self in relationship to the production of children that enables women to connect with one another.

The values expressed in woman bonding—mutuality, respect, shared power, and unconditional love—become guiding principles shaping the new community in *The Color Purple* which includes everyone, women and men, family and kin. Reconstructed black males, Harpo and Albert are active participants expanding the circle of care. Together this extended kin network affirms the primacy of a revitalized spirituality in which everything that exists is informed by godliness, in which love as a force that affirms connection and intersubjective communion makes an erotic metaphysic possible. Forgiveness and compassion enable individuals who were estranged and alienated to nurture one another's growth. The message conveyed in the novel that relationships no matter how seriously impaired can be restored is compelling. Distinct from the promise of a happy ending, it allows for the recognition of conflict and pain, for the possibility of reconciliation.

Radical didactic messages add depth and complexity to *The Color Purple* without resolving the contradictions between radicalism—the vision of revolutionary transformation, and conservatism—the perpetuation of bourgeois ideology. When the novel concludes, Celie has everything her oppressor has wanted and more—relationships with chosen loved ones; land ownership; material wealth; control over the labor of others. She is happy. In a *Newsweek* interview, Walker makes the revealing statement, "I liberated Celie from her own history. I wanted her to be happy." Happiness is not subject to re-vision, radicalization. The terms are familiar, absence of conflict, pain, and struggle; a fantasy of every desire fulfilled. Given these terms, Walker creates a fiction wherein an oppressed black woman can experience self-recovery without a dialectical process; without collective political effort; without radical change in society. To make Celie happy she creates a fiction where struggle—the arduous and painful process by which the oppressed work for liberation—has no place. This fantasy of change without effort is a dangerous one for both oppressed and oppressor. It is a brand of false consciousness that keeps everyone in place and oppressive structures intact. It is just this distortion of reality that Walker warns against in her essay "If the Present Looks Like the Past":

> In any case, the duty of the writer is not to be tricked, seduced,
> or goaded into verifying by imitation or even rebuttal other

people's fantasies. In an oppressive society it may well be that all fantasies indulged in by the oppressor are destructive to the oppressed. To become involved in them in any way at all is, at the very least, to lose time defining yourself.

For the oppressed and oppressor the process of liberation—individual self-realization and revolutionary transformation of society—requires confrontation with reality, the letting go of fantasy. Speaking of his loathing for fantasy Gabriel García Márquez explains:

> I believe the imagination is just an instrument for producing reality and that the source of creation is always, in the last instance, reality. Fantasy, in the sense of pure and simple Walt Disney-style invention without any basis in reality is the most loathsome thing of all. . . . Children don't like fantasy either. What they do like is imagination. The difference between the one and the other is the same as between a human being and a ventriloquist's dummy.

The tragedy embedded in the various happy endings in *The Color Purple* can be located at that point where fantasy triumphs over imagination, where creative power is suppressed. While this diminishes the overall aesthetic power of *The Color Purple*, it does not render meaningless those crucial moments in the text where the imagination works to liberate, to challenge, to make the new—real and possible. These moments affirm the integrity of artistic vision, restore and renew.

TAMAR KATZ

"Show Me How to Do Like You": Didacticism and Epistolary Form in The Color Purple

Show me how to do like you
Show me how to do it.
　　　　　　　　—STEVIE WONDER

Beginning with its epigraph, Alice Walker marks off *The Color Purple's* territory and purpose: it is a novel that intends to teach its readers, and it is also a novel about how that instruction might take place. *The Color Purple's* central character, Celie, serves as an example of the ideal learning process. Poor, oppressed, miserable, she learns to shed the yoke of patriarchal oppression in its many forms—in marriage, in love, in economics, in religion. As readers we are, in a sense, to learn from Celie how it is done by seeing it done.

　　The Color Purple is an epistolary novel: a series of letters from Celie to God, Nettie to Celie, Celie to Nettie, and finally Celie to God, the stars, trees, sky, peoples, Everything. Through its epistolary structure *The Color Purple* establishes two juxtaposed structures of instruction—direct address, or persuasion, and indirect: the use of the example or the document. The relation between these two structures inside the boundaries of the novel echoes and reenacts the inherently destabilized project of the novel as a whole, indeed of any overtly didactic fiction. *The Color Purple* must adopt a

From *Alice Walker*, edited by Harold Bloom. © 1988 Tamar Katz.

stance toward its readers that combines the strength of persuasive address with the authority traditionally ceded to nonpersuasive, "disinterested" writing. And by making explicit the problems of address in, and within, the novel's formal structure, Walker brings to light not just this epistemological dilemma underlying didactic fiction, but the specific dilemma of the marginal writer.

Walker thematicizes the issue of instruction most clearly in a section of the novel found by many readers, ironically, to be jarring and disjunctive: Nettie's letters from Africa. These letters, however, set up a model of teaching and learning that provides a foil for the central plot of Celie's education.

Throughout *The Color Purple*, Nettie is associated with teaching. Her stepfather, early on, claims he wants to "make a schoolteacher out of her," and after Celie is kept home from school, Nettie teaches her about Christopher Columbus and his boats "the Neater, the Peter, and the Santomareater." Later, when Nettie joins Corrine and Samuel in missionary work, she speaks explicitly of their life together as a process of instruction:

> Although I work for Corrine and Samuel and look after the children, I don't feel like a maid. I guess this is because they teach me, and I teach the children and there's no beginning or end to teaching and learning and working—it all runs together.

But *The Color Purple* associates Nettie with a purely formal kind of instruction, one that is drastically undercut throughout. Nettie's stepfather's claim that he wants to make her a teacher masks his real intention; he wishes to keep her at home in order to rape her as he has raped Celie. As models of primer understanding and rote memory, Nettie's lessons to Celie about Columbus bear only the most ironic relation to the conditions of Celie's life. And Nettie's entire story of her missionary work with the Olinka takes the form of a gradual disenchantment with the formal Christian ideals she was taught and must herself teach. Corrine comes to distrust her and treat her with less than the Christian charity she has preached. The Olinka are not interested in being taught by missionaries—they feel no need for this instruction. As Samuel notes bitterly, "it isn't resentment, exactly. It really is indifference. Sometimes I feel our position is like that of flies on an elephant's hide." Ultimately, the education the missionaries offer—an education in the name of a white, male God whose existence the novel itself finally denies—is powerless to help the Olinka defend themselves against the invasion of the road and the rubber plantation.

The model of education associated with Nettie in *The Color Purple* has a parallel in a form of instruction directed at Celie continuously. Other characters try to improve her, in the most direct way. "You got to fight them, Celie," Mr. _____'s sister says. "You got to fight them for yourself." Nettie's very first letter repeats this theme: "You got to fight and get away from Albert. He ain't no good." But such direct instruction is rarely effective in the novel, and often furthers white or patriarchal systems of oppression—as in the missionary imposition of the impractical Mother Hubbard dress, or Darlene's attempts to teach Celie to speak "standard" English. And of course the most insidious direct instruction of all opens the entire novel: "You better not never tell nobody but God. It'd kill your mammy."

But for all these failed, misguided, or insidious models of instruction, *The Color Purple* remains, above all, a type of *Bildungsroman*—a novel about the instruction of Celie and her coming to consciousness. Accordingly, I wish to turn away from the novel's internal thematicization of instruction, and toward an investigation of the same issues as they occur in its formal structure. For through epistolary form, *The Color Purple* also presents an alternative model of instruction, a model based not on direct address, but indirect, not on the didactic lecture, but the didactic example. This model, on its own and in its intersection and juxtaposition with direct address, makes clear the patterns in which Celie and the reader learn.

We can trace the literary roots of *The Color Purple*'s instructional model to a form traditionally allied with the didactic—the epistolary novel as the genre flowered in eighteenth-century England—and in particular to the work of Samuel Richardson. Richardson came to write epistolary fiction with the explicit intent to teach; before either *Pamela* or *Clarissa*, he published, in 1741, a letter manual. This volume provided exemplary letters for all manner of relevant topics. Richardson elucidated what he felt to be its edifying purpose in its full title:

> *Letters Written to and for Particular Friends on the Most Important Occasions Directing not only the Requisite Style and Forms to be Observed in Writing FAMILIAR LETTERS; But How to Think and Act Justly and Prudently in the Common Concerns of Human Life.*

The didactic potential of this letter manual calls attention to a similar potential in the epistolary novel as a closely related form. And one source of didactic power for both was their proximity to real life. For epistolary novels especially, the connection to a nonfictional form reinforced their moral power and relevance to their readers' lives.

But if the epistolary novel has often been used for didactic purposes, it possesses as well certain problems inherent in its structure, problems that have to be struggled with in any attempt at conclusive didactic effect. As Terry Eagleton points out in *The Rape of Clarissa*, epistolary fiction tends in two opposite directions at once—toward structural openness and doctrinal closure. Since the form leaves no room for an authorial voice to make its moral points independently, it must rely on more indirect means. Richardson recognized this problem as well: "It is impossible that readers the most attentive, can always enter into the views of the writer of a piece, written, as hoped, to Nature and the moment." For Richardson, the answer (or the attempt at one) lay in the constant revising of his work according to comments sent him by friends and critics.

But, just as epistolary fiction dramatizes the acts of writing and reading, it also dramatizes this very dilemma of uncertain reception—both within epistolary structure (on the level of the characters as readers) as well as without (on the level of a work's author and public).

As distinguished from autobiography or diary fiction, epistolary fiction focuses specifically on the relation of letter writer to letter reader. The problems usually get cast from the reverse of Richardson's perspective: not how to ensure your meaning is taken correctly, but how to ensure the letter you're reading is reliable. Since both the style and content of letters are shaped by the expectation of a particular reader, every letter is not simply a true record of feeling, but a directed, persuasive action. (Novels of seduction like *Clarissa* unfold the perils of just such a situation.) The problem, worded from either perspective, inside or outside the novel's frame, is essentially the same. In Richardson's *Pamela*—and still further in *The Color Purple*—epistolary structure not only poses the problem but offers its own attempt at a solution.

Richardson offers in *Pamela* a possible test for the truth of any epistolary message. Mr. B_____, who has been making repeated attempts on Pamela's virtue, forces her to surrender her copies of the letters in which she has reported to her parents the story of his advances and her distress. While B_____ has never believed Pamela's protestations of virtue *to him*, he is moved to belief by the incontrovertible evidence of her letters. Her letters, in fact, can be treated as *evidence* because they are not directed to him, and thus they are not an attempt to persuade him.

It has been suggested that as readers of epistolary fiction we are placed in the position of B_____, not as the recipient of a novel's letters, but as voyeurs. However, in specifically didactic epistolary fiction, I would argue, this schema is simultaneously both true and untrue. The reader of didactic fiction occupies a double stance. He or she *is* the recipient of a directed message—a novel in this case, not a letter. But the peculiarity of epistolary fiction (and this accounts perhaps for its particular affinity with the didactic) is that it summons the documentary authority vested in a letter directed to someone other than the reader.

And now, to return to *The Color Purple*, I think it might become clearer how Richardson and the epistolary tradition (with certain changes rung on it) serve Walker in both the instruction of Celie and the instruction of the reader.

The Color Purple highlights the doubleness of the reader's stance in the significant manner in which in truncates traditional epistolary form. For Walker has given us a series of letters that almost never reach their addressees, a series of letter writers with absent, unhearing, or impotent readers. Celie writes to a God who is either "sleep" or nonexistent (at least in the form in which she addresses him). Nettie writes letters that, at first, don't reach Celie, then reach her all at once (and so end up serving as a related tale, but not, in effect, as direct communication). Celie's letters to Nettie are returned to her unopened. In fact, most of the novel's epistolary exchanges are nonfunctional in the traditionally understood sense of communication between writer and reader. Walker emphasizes, even ironizes, this lack of function, as both Celie and Nettie exhort their readers to act in impossible or idealized ways. "I am fourteen years old," Celie writes in her opening letter to God. "I have always been a good girl. Maybe you can give me a sign letting me know what is happening to me." And we recall that Nettie's first letter to Celie begins, "You've got to fight and get away from Albert." These letters serve only to remind us that the expected connection of writer to reader has failed to take place.

These letters lack their expected functions and qualities in other ways as well. Celie's letters to God, for instance, are oddly incorporeal. In a literary genre traditionally obsessed with the privacy necessary for letter writing, and the material conditions necessary for that privacy—the locked room, the hiding place, the constant threat of violation hovering over both—*The Color Purple* presents us with a letter writer who possesses neither the time nor the privacy to write, and whose own letters are never hidden or uncovered.

Nettie's letters to Celie follow a more conventional plot pattern—Mr. _____ intercepts them and hides them. Yet in this too, traditional plot functions are cut short and bear little narrative fruit. Although Mr. _____ hides Nettie's letters, he does not bother to read or even to open all of them. And Celie's discovery of the hidden letters does not bring about any significant action (she just hates Mr. _____ more than she did before). What this particular twist on epistolary convention does effect, however, is a repositioning of Celie that is especially interesting in light of all the missing addressees in the novel. When Celie reads Nettie's letters, she reads them as

Mr. _____ (or Mr. B _____, in *Pamela*) would have read them. She "overhears" correspondence directed at herself. She must split herself, act as addressee and voyeur simultaneously. And in this, as a reader of a miniature epistolary novel embedded in the larger epistolary novel that is *The Color Purple*, Celie stands in for the reader of didactic epistolary fiction in general.

(It would be possible, though I don't intend to pursue it much further here, to extend this model of intercepted documents or overheard discourse to Walker's thematic representation of the way in which Celie and the other characters in the novel learn and come to consciousness [*within* the frame of the letters]. They all witness scenes: Celie watches Sofia with Harpo, Shug with Mr. _____; Nettie observes the Olinka among themselves and with the roadbuilders. It remains unclear from whom, exactly, Mr. _____ learns— quite possibly he does so from sending Celie the rest of her sister's letters, thus enabling her to continue "overhearing" her own correspondence.)

A reader of *The Color Purple*, then, learns (or receives instruction) by assuming Celie's ambivalent position within the novel, outside it. He or she learns by watching Celie as a double example. Celie exists as a form of "documentary" proof from whom we can draw edifying conclusions, convincing us as an example of woman's oppression and liberation because she does not direct her confidences to us. In fact, even the direction of her letters adds to her authority as an example. We trust Celie because of her "innocence," as Henry Louis Gates, Jr. has put it. This innocence exists not only in her ignorance of her own pregnancy and in her use of the vernacular; it is established the moment she addresses her initial plea to God. And Celie also exists as an example of how we should behave—and learn—as readers. In her reading of Nettie's letters, and in her reading of other characters as examples around her, she shows us how to learn from both written and social documents.

I have spoken so far mostly of Celie as an addressee or a voyeur—the recipient and interpreter of messages. But as Gates points out, the progress of *The Color Purple* can easily be seen as the process of Celie's writing herself into being and consciousness, of her growing power and control as a writer. And it is to Celie's role as writer that I now wish to turn, in the context of some of the problems of direction and reliability already mapped out. Celie, in her innocence and in the context of her address to God, is an ostensibly reliable reporter of events. Her stepfather further confirms her authority for an outside reader by preempting the possibility of taking the cynical view— claiming it for himself and imposing it on Mr. _____. "She near twenty," he says. "And another thing—she tell lies." This claim for Celie's unreliability— and particularly the danger that she might attempt to convince *us*—undercuts its own position. Her stepfather's statement, we can clearly see, in *its* discursive context, intends to persuade and to mislead. And this claim, when juxtaposed to the opening injunction, "You better not never tell nobody but God," strengthens the truth value of Celie's story, when and because it is told to God.

The idea of Celie's absolute reliability, however, is at odds in more subtle ways with her development as a writer. While we take Celie's written words to be essentially "true," in the way an uncovered document might be true, we also watch the character Celie as she gains control over the reporting of actions. The idea of an absolute division between the two becomes increasingly difficult to maintain. The collapse of this division (which Gates discusses at length) occurs in Walker's use and revision of free indirect discourse, especially as it comes to her through Zora Neale Hurston's *Their Eyes Were Watching God*. With Celie's *written* free indirect discourse, it becomes impossible to sort out whether we're reading the actual reported words of another character (that is, whether we're seeing discourse of a documentary nature), because all words are but ultimately written by Celie.

It is possible to discuss this collapse of division in terms of showing and telling. Such a collapse, when translated into these terms, demonstrates the added relevance of *The Color Purple*'s epigraph to its project. The Stevie Wonder quote, "Show me how to do like you. Show me how to do it," aptly summarizes not only this central theme of the novel, but its inherent self-contradiction—one that exists as two separate poles at once collapsed and distinct. The Wonder quote parallels a hypothetical reader's request for an ideal, reliable source of instruction (a showing—a document or example, in the terms the novel establishes). Both Celie and Walker would seem to move toward a model of instruction that operates simply by showing, by the authority of the example. But both character and author present their examples in the shape of their own words; they both *tell* whatever they show.

Barbara Johnson, in her article "Thresholds of Difference: Structures of Address in Zora Neale Hurston," discusses a related issue as it occurs in Hurston's work. She shows how the enactment of this paradox has special resonance in black women's writing, where the status of the example is a particularly problematic one. The question of difference between writer and literary (or anthropological) example holds a special charge because it underlines and undercuts the traditional division of whites/men as writers and blacks/women as written about.

The breakdown of this division in Hurston's work appears most clearly and parallels *The Color Purple* most strongly in *Mules and Men*. Here Hurston sets out to "report" black folktales much as Walker in a sense "reports" Celie and Nettie's letters, or as Celie herself "reports" dialogue. The same slide that we have seen between Celie as addressee and Celie as voyeur, or between Celie/Walker as reporter of evidence and Celie/Walker as shaper of a message, occurs in Hurston's introduction. Johnson explains:

> Hurston began as an outsider, a scientific narrative voice that refers to "these people" in the third person, as a group whose inner lives are difficult to penetrate. Then, suddenly, she leaps into the picture she has just painted, including herself in a "we" that addresses a "you"—the white reader, the new implied outsider. The structure of address changes from description to direct address. From that point on it is impossible to tell whether Hurston the narrator is *describing* a strategy or *employing* one.

Hurston's rhetorical stance throughout *Mules and Men* (and elsewhere in her writings, as Johnson shows) highlights and enacts the peculiarly marginal and shifting position of the black woman writer. The "outsider" role in which Hurston begins—the scientific reporter—is traditionally that of a white male, traditionally that of the insider who establishes the black object of study as a "they." Hurston here reverses the terms—turns the insider into an outsider and turns the black object of study into a black subject—the "we" of the passage. In so doing, she not only reverses the terms, she problematizes and undermines the opposition on which they are built.

The Color Purple enacts the same destabilization. Walker's subject matter (that is, her object) is the life of a black woman—so far traditional subject-object divisions remain intact. But Walker questions the otherness of that object (Celie) by maintaining her in the position of a readable document or example, while simultaneously repositioning her in the roles of both author and reader.

As a black, female writer, Alice Walker is herself dangerously subject to a shift in position—but in reverse. While Celie is made to slide from example to author, Walker, like Hurston, can often be seen to slip all too readily from author to example. Hurston, at the time of the Harlem Renaissance, sometimes became what Langston Hughes described as "a perfect book of entertainment." Walker, in the hands of the mass media of the 1980s, often slips back to the status of example herself. In interviews, articles, calendars, Walker is treated as exemplary—not just as a black feminist writer but as *the* black feminist writer. This is true to a large extent because, as Trudier Harris acutely observes, "the media, by its very racist nature, seems able to focus on only one black writer at a time." This societal reinscription of Walker back into her "place"—as exemplar and object—ironically alerts us again to the formal and epistemological issues raised in *The Color Purple*, and their political implications. For while Celie can be said to shift from example to author (from object to subject), she also embodies—as does Walker—the ever-present political threat of this transition's reversal. What Walker risks creating, and becoming, is an exemplary subject. The dangers inherent in this position are made clear once again in the novel's epigraph: Showing someone how to do *like you* is equivalent to showing them how to do *it*. The example, ever again, reasserts its nature as object.

The Color Purple enacts this problem on all levels—structural and thematic. What the novel intends to teach us on a thematic level—the nature of patriarchal oppression, the nature of learning and enlightenment—relies on Celie, and in part Walker, as examples. But what *The Color Purple* also intends both to teach and show us through its epistolary structure, is the constant, and inevitable, transgression and reassertion of the boundaries and risks of what we know as the example.

CAROLYN WILLIAMS

"Trying To Do Without God": *The Revision of Epistolary Address in* The Color Purple

In her first letter to God, Celie recounts her rape at the hands of her Pa. Celie is fourteen at the time, and she prays to God for "a sign letting [her] know what is happening to [her]." But the sign for which she prays is not forthcoming. That first letter initiates the story of Celie's unrelenting victimization, until little by little she manages—through identification with other women—to find her strength and identity. The epistolary form of Alice Walker's *The Color Purple* highlights this aspect of its content, since the letters themselves figure crucially in the plot. Toward the middle of the novel, Celie discovers that her husband, Mr. _____, has been hiding the letters from her sister, Nettie, and allowing Celie to believe that her sister is dead. Through Nettie's restored letters, Celie eventually learns that the man who raped her—thus motivating her correspondence with God—was not her Pa after all, but her stepfather. Her last letter to God at this point reveals the amazed disgust she feels upon realizing that her chosen correspondent could hardly have been paying attention to her letters at all:

> Dear God,
>   That's it, say Shug. Pack your stuff. You coming back to Tennessee with me.

From *Writing the Female Voice: Essays on Epistolary Literature*, edited by Elizabeth C. Goldsmith. © 1989 Elizabeth C. Goldsmith.

> But I feels daze.
>
> My daddy lynch. My mama crazy. All my little half-brothers and sisters no kin to me. My children not my sister and brother. Pa not pa.
>
> You must be sleep.

Surely the most striking feature of the novel's particular epistolary form involves the shift in address that occurs at this point, as Celie turns away from her first correspondent and begins instead to address her sister. In her second letter to Nettie, Celie offers an explanation of her turn away from God as addressee. True to the womanist philosophy of the novel, Celie's explanation involves the race and class as well as the gender associated with a God who does not listen to "poor colored women."

> Dear Nettie,
>
> I don't write to God no more, I write to you.
>
> What happen to God? ast Shug.
>
> Who that? I say. . . .
>
> Anyhow, I say, the God I been praying and writing to is a man. And act just like all the other mens I know. Trifling, forgitful and lowdown.
>
> She say, Miss Celie, You better hush. God might hear you.
>
> Let 'im hear me, I say. If he ever listened to poor colored women the world would be a different place, I can tell you.
>
> She talk and she talk, trying to budge me way from blasphemy. But I blaspheme much as I want to.
>
> All my life I never care what people thought bout nothing I did, I say. But deep in my heart I care about God. What he going to think. And come to find out, he don't think. Just sit up there glorying in being deef, I reckon. But it ain't easy, trying to do without God. Even if you know he ain't there, trying to do without him is a strain.

In the remainder of this critical letter, Shug offers Celie a revised understanding of what "God" might be; and by the end of the novel, Celie has managed to put Shug's revised notion of God into practice. On the level of form as well as explicit content, this epistolary text performs the work of "trying to do without God," and by the end, that work is no longer such a "strain." The shift in Celie's address from God to Nettie, divinity to humanity, figurative to real family, "father" to sister, male to female, white to black, turns the novel in a new direction, toward the affirmative "Amen" of its closure.

Though Celie does not understand this until much later, the God whom she initially addresses is identified with men from the start. The choice of God as addressee, for example, is not made by Celie herself but is urged by the man she calls Pa. His suggestion that God is the only "safe" confidant involves an explicit prohibition of the mother, as well as an implicit bond between the abusive human father and his God. This is clear in the italicized epigraph to the first letter, which suggests that Celie's text opens under the auspices of a voice other than her own: *"You better not never tell nobody but God. It'd kill your mammy."* Celie follows this advice when she "protects" her mother from knowing the identity of her first child's father, and thereby, of course, she also protects the abusive father. "She ast me bout the first one Whose is it? I say God's. I don't know no other man or what else to say." This refusal to identify the real father has the ironic effect of identifying that father with God; and this ironic association further serves Celie to explain to her mother when the child disappears. "Finally she ast Where is it? I say God took it." Here "God" serves Celie as a mask for that other "he," who gives her children and then takes them away.

Recognizing the bitter irony of Pa's recommendation of God as correspondent depends on seeing Celie's simultaneous exclusion from and implication within the male network of power relations. She attempts to protect her mother from death by collaborating with the father's lies, but her mother dies anyway, and Celie then realizes that her death came as a result of the very lies she herself had helped to tell. "Trying to believe his story kilt her." Celie's mother, weakened through repeated pregnancy, had never provided her daughter with a strong support against her Pa. But with her mother gone, Celie herself is left in the position of surrogate mother to her sister, Nettie, and Nettie becomes her primary female relation. She hopes to protect Nettie from her own fate. "I see him looking at my little sister. She scared. But I say I'll take care of you. With God help." Her desire to protect her sister motivates Celie's marriage to Mr. _____, insofar as her motives figure at all in what is basically an arrangement of convenience between father and husband. Mr. _____ turns out to be a fit successor to Pa, and Celie's plan to protect Nettie from Pa only puts her in danger from Mr. _____, who, like Pa, has his eye on Nettie. When she refuses his sexual advances, he sends her away and revenges himself on the sisters by plotting to keep Celie from receiving Nettie's letters. In other words, he takes Celie's sister away from her, completing the process that Pa began of isolating Celie from the other women in her family.

Her isolation is the precondition of Celie's continued correspondence with God. The novel's epistolary form, in other words, is the most fundamental representation of a concern with women isolated from one another within the patriarchal network, a concern that is also elaborately thematized within the novel. Because of Pa and Mr. _____, there is no one safe to talk to, and the emblem of Celie's solitude becomes her choice of God as epistolary addressee. When parted from her sister by Mr. _____, she covers her isolation by turning to God and to writing. "But I just say, Never mine, never mine, long as I can spell G-o-d I got somebody along." Thus very early in the novel the functional analogy is established between God and the sister in the role of possible confidant. Here, "spelling G-o-d" is clearly meant to fill the gap left by the absence of the sister, as the first letter to God clearly substitutes for telling the mother. This formal substitution will be reversed later in the novel in the pivotal shift in address from God to Nettie. But until that moment signals Celie's decisive rejection of God as addressee, the ironic result is her correspondence with a confidant who only reinforces her passivity toward the male power structure.

The inadequacy of God as a confidant is underscored later in the novel when Squeak recounts the story of her rape by her uncle, the prison warden. Shug encourages her to unburden herself to her family by making fun of the only alternative: "If you can't tell us, who you gon tell, God?" Early in the story, however, Celie is caught up in just this mystification. Even then, the voices of other women—Nettie, Kate, Sofia—try to break through the mystified submission to her husband which Celie rationalizes with reference to God. "Well, sometime Mr. _____ git on me pretty hard. I have to talk to Old Maker. But he my husband. I shrug my shoulders. This life soon be over, I say. Heaven last all ways." Sofia replies: "You ought to bash Mr. _____ head open, she say. Think bout heaven later." But since her sister is absent and presumed dead, Celie can think of rebellion only as futile, speech as impossibly dangerous. Her passivity and silence depend upon the absence of her sister and the lesson she reads in that absence. "I don't say nothing. I think bout Nettie, dead. She fight, she run away. What good it do? I don't fight. I stay where I'm told. But I'm alive." Writing—as opposed to speech— seems safe, seems even the sign of ongoing life. Within this context, epistolarity itself must be seen to represent both the resignation of Celie's silence and its implicit strength: her silent refusal to lose her identity, despite her isolation.

According to the logic of epistolarity, all the while Celie addresses God in letters, God too is absent—not necessarily and definitively "deef," as Celie later complains, but distant and uncertain of response. Janet Altman has theorized the play of absence and presence that characterizes "epistolary mediation" in general. Within this context, the wit of *The Color Purple* implicitly draws attention to a similarity between epistolary desire and prayer; both represent attempts, through language, to conjure presence from absence. In addressing God, Celie prays to read a sign of his presence in order to feel her own more clearly; if he were to answer her prayers, she would know herself, would know "what is happening to [her]." Of course, God never answers, and the epistolary relation remains incomplete. For Celie, the practice of addressing God simply reaffirms her solitude; she is essentially writing to herself. *The Color Purple* is thus an example of an epistolary novel with close affinities to the journal, diary, or autobiographical confession. As in those genres, here the practice of introspective letter writing records the disciplined process of increasing self-knowledge. In this case, however, self-revelation is at first referred to a principle of absolute exteriority—God—which is always paradoxically close to sheer interiority, and prayer always an exercise in attempted self-possession. The effect of this epistolary address is also similar to that of the poetic strategy of apostrophe or prosopopoeia, however, in which the lyric address of something absent, inanimate, or dead conjures the illusion of presence and voice but at the same time has the uncanny effect of reflecting absence back upon the lyric "I." This feature of epistolary address, in other words, cuts across and complicates the fiction of increasing self-knowledge and self-presence, which is the generic mark of autobiography.

When she receives no letters, Celie must conclude that Nettie is not merely absent but dead, especially since the sisters have made a pact explicitly establishing letters as the sign of their ongoing life. Parting from her sister, Celie demands correspondence. "I say Write. She say, nothing but death can keep me from it. She never write." Absence, the necessary precondition of any epistolary exchange, is here given its most ominous significance. Nettie's presumed death rationalizes Celie's continued address to God, and at the same time it provides the narrative opportunity for resurrection. When her letters do finally appear in the text, they appear suddenly, in a group that presents a more or less complete record of Nettie's life since the two sisters parted. The last letter in the group explains that "Pa is not our Pa," allowing Celie to revise her own personal history and forcing her to realize that God has never been adequate to her correspondence. Thus Nettie's figurative (and epistolary) reappearance from the dead gives Celie a new life as well. The first letter Celie writes to Nettie rather than to God tells of a day "like it be round Easter," when she revisits their childhood home, now transformed, with flowering trees all around.

The figurative resurrection that takes place in Celie's life is of course made possible through her love for Shug. This is most obvious on the level of plot and theme, but it is true on the level of narrative form as well, for Shug is the route through which Nettie's letters are restored. They begin appearing two pages after Celie and Shug make love for the first time. In terms of plot, this is fully rationalized—after Celie tells her about Nettie, Shug figures out where the letters are—but in textual terms it seems like magic, as if the act of love has conjured Nettie's voice. The plot structure demonstrates the axiom that sexuality conjures the sister, for when each one falls in love—Celie with Shug and Nettie with Samuel—she tells her beloved all about her sister. It is this chiasmic confidence—Celie's talking about Nettie with Shug while Nettie talks about Celie with Samuel—that causes the parallel but divided plots of the two sisters to come together again. Shug produces Nettie's letters, the last of which reveals to Celie that "Pa not pa." Through Shug, Nettie is restored; and through Nettie, Celie's children return, purged of an incestuous origin (though never of rape).

Celie's turn toward women overturns her earlier implication in the patriarchal network, and the revision in her epistolary address is the most graphic reminder of this shift. However, the sudden, pivotal shift in address is but the decisive register of an internal process of transformation, which begins before it and continues long beyond it. The awakening of Celie's sexuality begins the process of replacing God with the sister as addressee. Long before they become lovers, she feels for Shug's body a reverence that reminds her of prayer. "I wash her body, it feel like I'm praying. My hands tremble and my breath short." But her sexual correspondence with Shug accomplishes what prayer could never do; it derives from and leads back to her increasing self-possession. Just before making love with Shug for the first time, Celie tells of her rape by Pa. For the first time, she experiences the comforting and responsive love of an attentive listener. This enables her to mourn her past life, to achieve the catharsis of tears, and to gain the intensified comprehension of her story afforded by the retrospective reenactment with another of her past losses.

Finally, the sexual correspondence with Shug metaphorically restores the familial—and definitively feminine—relations whose removal constituted the crisis of the novel's opening. While she combs out Shug's hair, for example, Celie is reminded of her mother and her daughter through the intimacy of this bodily attention. In one of the last letters to God she muses on what making love with Shug is like—"little like sleeping with mama . . . little like sleeping with Nettie," but different from both. This maternal network is drawn very close during Celie and Shug's first sexual encounter. "Then I feels something real soft and wet on my breast, feel like one of my little lost babies mouth. Way after while, I act like a little lost baby too." In the moment of ecstasy, Celie finds within herself the capacity to enact her greatest loss and its restoration. Sexuality in this novel represents the principle of transference, substitution, and internalization. As Celie learns to love Shug, she finds her mother, sister, and lost babies within. No longer isolated, and full of her remembered relations, Celie begins to experience a sense of wholeness. "Dear God, Now I know Nettie alive I begin to strut a little bit." At the end of the first letter addressed not to God but to Nettie, Celie reports Shug's summary of this compensatory vision. "Shug say, Us each other's peoples now, and kiss me."

Celie's sense of wholeness is not complete until she manages to recognize both "God" and the absent sister within herself. "Trying to do without God," in other words, paradoxically involves an act of self-possession, of internalization, which cannot take place as long as she addresses God and thereby reinscribes an absence. Only after turning to address her sister as correspondent, and then almost immediately, Celie begins the work of radically redefining and internalizing God. Her "blasphemy" in rejecting God as addressee inspires Shug to put her through a catechism. She forces Celie to recognize that her God has been a white man, imprinted in her imagination by the pictures in "the white folks' white bible. . . . You mad cause he don't seem to listen to your prayers. Humph! Do the mayor listen to anything colored say?" After making the point that "God" is a culturally conditioned concept, Shug pursues a strategy of negativity, first rejecting race, then gender, as defining attributes of her God. "God ain't a he or a she, but a It." Finally her iconoclasm goes far beyond Celie's "blasphemy" as she insists that God cannot be envisioned at all. God is absolutely interior, a matter of responsiveness, affirmation, love. Since It is inside, It includes Everything.

> Here's the thing, say Shug. The thing I believe. God is inside you and inside everybody else. You come into the world with God. But only them that search for it inside find it. . . . Don't look like nothing, she say. It ain't a picture show. It ain't something you can look at apart from anything else, including yourself. I believe God is everything, say Shug. Everything that is or ever was or ever will be. And when you can feel that, and be happy to feel that, you've found It.

The impersonal pronoun "It," which names Shug's "God," as well as the internal sensation of being a part of everything else, is close to the euphemistic usage of "It" to refer to the sexual act; this association is explicit in Shug's remark that "when it happen you can't miss it. It sort of like you know what, she say, grinning and rubbing high up on my thigh." In Shug's theology, sexual pleasure is the best metaphor for the state of ecstatic affirmation that characterizes God-as-Everything, for "Everything want to be loved." In fact, the title of the novel comes from this second letter to Nettie, suggesting the crucial importance of Shug's theology of love, admiration, and appreciation. "I think it pisses God off if you walk by the color purple in a field somewhere and don't notice it."

Unfortunately, the state of total responsiveness and affirmation is not easy to achieve, for the work of negation must constantly go on, in order to purge the world of the associations "man" has made.

> Man corrupt everything, say Shug. He on your box of grits, in your head, and all over the radio. He try to make you think he everywhere. Soon as you think he everywhere, you think he God. But he ain't. Whenever you trying to pray, and man plop himself on the other end of it, tell him to git lost, say Shug.

"But this hard work, let me tell you," Celie comments. "He been there so long, he don't want to budge." In fact, this "hard work" is the work of this text. The narrative work of internalizing divinity is a familiar feature of a certain Protestant tradition in the English novel, a tradition in which *The Color Purple* still participates. But the way that work gets done is of course particular to each narrative form. In *The Color Purple* the epistolary form enacts the effort to negate the corruption man has wrought upon "everything" and to address a female principle of totality and familiarity instead. The "Amen" that ends this crucial letter suggests again that Celie is finally really praying only when she begins writing to Nettie. The functional analogy established earlier between God and the sister is now fulfilled at the moment of its reversal, as the sister replaces God in the role of confidant. Addressing the sister instead is the route of detaching the concept of "God" from patriarchal oppression and allowing "It" to embrace "Everything." Paradoxically, the internalization of God accomplishes this massive externalization as "Everything." This revised divinity is no longer absent or distant, but close and familiar. "To do without God," then, is paradoxically to have "It" always readily available.

Meanwhile, through her experiences in Africa, Nettie too recognizes that "God" is a relative, culturally bound concept, for the Olinka have projected "roofleaf" as their divinity. Through the painful process of witnessing the colonization of the Olinka, she is forced to realize how powerless her own God really is. She too must come to the conclusion that divinity is internal, and therefore unrepresentable.

God is different to us now, after all these years in Africa. More spirit than ever before, and more internal. Most people think he has to look like something or someone—a roofleaf or Christ—but we don't. And not being tied to what God looks like, frees us.

Since Celie's letters to Nettie are never received, only the reader can see how thoroughly the two correspondents "answer" each other. The parallel plots of the two sisters' radically different lives work out elaborately parallel experiences of racism and sexism. Through their work in the world, both Nettie and Celie accomplish the transformation, internalization, possession, and negation of God. But at the same time, each sister must achieve a similar sort of faith in relation to the other; the sister, too, must be internalized. Here again, the process of internalization depends upon absence. In the case of Celie's communications to Nettie as well as to God, the epistolary relation must remain unfulfilled in order for this crucial fiction of internalization to be enacted. In a sense, then, the epistolary form of *The Color Purple* is ironic throughout. A full epistolary exchange is never established, either with God or with Nettie, and the most profound motives of the narrative depend upon this fact. Meanwhile, the hope and faith that epistolary desire *might* be internally fulfilled sustain the epistolarity of the second half of the novel.

As correspondent, Nettie's position in relation to Celie is like Celie's position in relation to God: radical solitude prompts the address, and neither letter writer gets an answer. Nettie knows that Mr. _____ is diverting the letters and that Celie has probably never heard from her. "I know you think I am dead," she explains, in the first letter from her produced in the text. Despite the lack of response, however, Nettie continues to write to her sister.

> I remember one time you said your life made you feel so ashamed you couldn't even talk about it to God, you had to write it, bad as you thought your writing was. Well, now I know what you meant. And whether God will read letters or no, I know you will go on writing them; which is guidance enough for me. Anyway, when I don't write to you I feel as bad as I do when I don't pray, locked up in myself and choking on my own heart. I am so *lonely*, Celie.

Nettie takes up the practice of writing from Celie and reflects back to Celie a theoretical understanding of what that practice means. She has already learned what Celie, too, will learn: the figurative equivalence of prayer and

epistolary address to the sister. Finally, she expresses through this
equivalence the sense that re-externalizing the internal is the dynamic of
conjuring presence, companionship, and correspondence.

> But always, no matter what I'm doing, I am writing to you.
> Dear Celie, I say in my head in the middle of Vespers, the
> middle of the night, while cooking, Dear, dear Celie. And I
> imagine that you really do get my letters and that you are
> writing me back: Dear Nettie, this is what life is like for me.

In this figurative sense, the faithful continuity of Nettie's invocation keeps
Celie alive to her, though after thirty years of this unfulfilled
correspondence, she begins to imagine that Celie might be dead. But Samuel
counsels her at this point to trust in God and to have faith of another,
analogous sort as well, "to have faith in the sturdiness of [her] sister's soul."

In the second half of the novel, after receiving Nettie's letters, Celie too
learns to keep this faith "in the sturdiness of [her] sister's soul." A second
time she is threatened with Nettie's death, when Mr. _____ gives her the
telegram from the Department of Defense saying that Nettie's returning ship
has been sunk by German mines off the coast of Gibraltar. "They think you
all drowned. Plus, the same day, all the letters I wrote to you over the years
come back unopen." The return of Celie's unopened letters is an apt emblem
of her sister's possible death, as the sudden appearance of Nettie's letters
testified to her resurrection. At this point it seems that Celie's second
correspondence will be as fruitless as her first. But her refusal this time to
believe in Nettie's death is a mark of exactly how far she has come into her
own. She, like Nettie, has learned to internalize her sister's presence.

> And I don't believe you dead. How can you be dead if I still feel
> you? Maybe, like God, you changed into something different
> that I'll have to speak to in a different way, but you not dead to
> me Nettie. And never will be. Sometime when I git tired of
> talking to myself I talk to you.

Celie's explicit association of faith in her sister with the transformation of
God emphasizes the parallel dynamic at work. And again, the thematic point
is reinforced by the narrative form, which wittily exploits the temporal
disjunction, or lag time, involved in any epistolary relation. Celie's faith in
the sturdiness of her sister's soul is supported by a figure of her abiding
presence, the evidence of her letters. "And no matter how much the telegram

said you must be drown, I still git letters from you."

Once more Celie must practice internalization as a compensatory technique, when Shug leaves with Germaine; and this final movement recapitulates and concludes this line of development in the novel. "Feel like I felt when Nettie left," writes Celie when Shug leaves earlier in the novel, emphasizing the association of Shug with her sister. After a time, Celie establishes an epistolary relation with Shug, and through this relation Celie learns both to do without Shug and at the same time to have her always within. No sooner has Celie accomplished the internal restoration of their relation than it is re-externalized—that is to say, rewarded in the plot—by Shug's appearance.

> And then, just when I know I can live content without Shug,
> . . . Shug write me she coming home.
> Now. Is this life or not?
> *I be so calm.*
> If she come, I be happy. If she don't, I be content.
> And then I figure this the lesson I was suppose to learn.

The extravagant magic of the plot's resolution may seem more fundamentally grounded if we have appreciated "this lesson" of epistolarity, its fictive trick of conjuring presence. Celie's internalized recreations of "Everything" and everyone eventually issue in their external appearances in the plot. The work of internalization done, Celie is complete; her solitude has become a company, and the narrative represents this achievement in the dramatized reunion of the family. After Shug returns, Nettie again turns out to be alive. The male characters, who were expunged from the narrative's good graces during its period of separatism, are redeemed and given reformed characters. Celie's children are no longer lost but grown up and joined by their African counterpart. The parallel and divided plots of the two sisters are reunited. Time is figuratively reversed, and everyone feels young again. And epistolary address ceases altogether, for Celie's correspondent has returned.

The closure of the epistolary form turns again on Celie's pivotal revision of address. Since she can no longer address Nettie, Celie returns to her earlier addressee, now thoroughly transformed, both internalized (as Spirit) and externalized (as Everything). "Dear God. Dear stars, dear trees, dear sky, dear peoples. Dear Everything. Dear God." This last letter closes with "Amen," Celie's characteristic signature ever since the second letter to Nettie, the one in which she describes her transformation of God. Nettie has begged Celie to "Pray for us," and the novel's last word is the close of that prayer. It is also the "Amen" of enthusiastic response to "Everything"—as in a church service or revival meeting one answers the arrival of the Spirit with the tribute of a loud "Amen."

This epistolary novel is framed at its outer edges by epigraphs that break the fiction of presence and refer us to its author. We find, on the last page of the text: "I thank everybody in this book for coming. / A.W., author and medium." Alice Walker closes the book as if it had been one long letter to the reader and this were her signature. The usual effects of epistolarity are set in motion again at the edges of the text in order to assert authorial presence and at the same time to deny it. As "author" she claims the novel as artifice, an aesthetic form created by her own letter-writing hand; but as "medium" she refers authority to a power external to herself, who speaks through her. The conception of the artist as mediating the voice of a higher power is but one step removed from the conception of the artist as analogous to or a surrogate for God; both conceptions are traditional in romantic literature where, as feminist critics have pointed out, they operate to reserve authorial power in the male line.

Here Walker's womanist revision of God has consequences for her vision of narrative authority as well. Through correspondence with the sister, the notion of God has been detached from the patriarchal chain of authorization, with the result that, when the female artist refers to her power as a "medium," she makes a claim at once more humble and at the same time more vast than the traditional male claim. She defers to Everything, and as a consequence her voice is multitudinous, democratic, and responsive; she speaks for Everything, and as a result everyone speaks through her. The authority of her voice is grounded in its paradoxical assertion of deferral. She claims to have transcribed Celie's voice, to have listened carefully, to have responded. Walker's closing signature returns us to the opening epigraph of the novel, in which she introduces this epistolary fiction of presence with a gesture of deferring her own. Her dedication strikingly conflates life outside and inside the text; and it invites the reader to consider epistolarity as a paradigm for all creation. "*To the Spirit:* / Without whose assistance / Neither this book / Nor I / Would have been / Written."

Romance, Marginality, Matrilineage: The Color Purple

The publication of *The Color Purple* transformed Alice Walker from an indubitably serious black writer whose fiction belonged to a tradition of gritty, if occasionally "magical," realism into a popular novelist, with all the perquisites and drawbacks attendant on that position. Unlike either *The Third Life of Grange Copeland* (1970) or *Meridian* (1976), *The Color Purple* gained immediate and widespread public acceptance, winning both the Pulitzer Prize and the American Book Award for 1982–1983. At the same time, however, it generated immediate and widespread critical unease over what appeared to be manifest flaws in its composition. Robert Towers, writing in the *New York Review of Books*, concluded on the evidence of *The Color Purple* that "Alice Walker still has a lot to learn about plotting and structuring what is clearly intended to be a realistic novel." His opinion was shared by many reviewers, who pointed out variously that in the last third of the book the narrator-protagonist Celie and her friends are propelled toward a fairy-tale happy ending with more velocity than credibility; that the letters from Nettie, with their disconcertingly literate depictions of life in an African village, intrude into the middle of the main action with little apparent motivation or warrant; and that the device of the letters to God is especially unrealistic inasmuch as it foregoes the concretizing details that have traditionally given the epistolary form its peculiar verisimilitude: the

From *The Other Side of the Story: Structures and Strategies of Contemporary Feminist Narrative* by Molly Hite. © 1989 Cornell University.

secret writing place, the cache, the ruses to enable posting letters, and especially the letters received in return.

Indeed, the violations of realist convention are so flagrant that they might well call into question whether *The Color Purple* "is clearly intended to be a realistic novel," especially as there are indications that at least some of the aspects of the novel discounted by reviewers as flaws may constitute its links to modes of writing other than Anglo-American nineteenth-century realism. For example, Henry Louis Gates, Jr., has recently located the letters to God within an Afro-American tradition deriving from slave narrative, a tradition in which the act of writing is linked to a powerful deity who "speaks" through scripture and bestows literacy as an act of grace. For Gates, concern with finding a voice, which he sees as the defining feature of Afro-American literature, becomes the context for the allusive affinities between Celie's letters and the "free indirect 'narrative of division'" that characterizes the acknowledged predecessor of *The Color Purple*, Zora Neale Hurston's 1937 novel *Their Eyes Were Watching God*.

Gates's paradigm suggests how misleading it may be to assume that mainstream realist criteria are appropriate for evaluating *The Color Purple*. But the Afro-American preoccupation with voice as a primary element unifying both the speaking subject and the text as a whole does not deal with many of the more disquieting structural features of Walker's novel. For instance, while the letters from Nettie clearly illustrate Nettie's parallel acquisition of her own voice, a process that enables her to arrive at conclusions very like Celie's under very different circumstances, the Afro-American tradition sheds little light on the central *place* these letters occupy in the narrative or on why the plot takes this sudden jump into geographically and culturally removed surroundings. And Gates's subtle explication of the ramifications of "voice" once Walker has reconstrued the term to designate a *written* discourse does not address the problematic ending, in which the disparate members of Celie's extended family come together as if drawn by a cosmic magnet—and as if in defiance of the most minimal demands of narrative probability.

The example of *Their Eyes Were Watching God* tends to compound these problems rather than provide a precedent that helps explain them, for Hurston's most famous novel has also been judged flawed, and for many of the same reasons. To a certain extent, placing *Their Eyes* in the context of an Afro-American tradition that Hurston herself did much to document reveals how central the act of storytelling is in this book, to the point where Janie's discovery and use of her narrative voice emerges as the major action. This context helps explain the tendency of the story *about* storytelling to usurp the ostensible main plot of Janie's quest for happiness with a man—for example, the apparent disproportionate emphasis given to the digressive "co-talking'" of such minor characters as Hicks and Coker in Eatonville or to the rhetoric of the "skin games" played by Ed Dockery, Bootyny, and Sop-de-Bottom on the muck and the exuberant fabulation that takes over chapter 6 so completely that the story of the mule "freed" at Janie's instigation turns completely away from realism and becomes a beast fable, with buzzards as parson and congregation chanting a parodic litany over the carrion.

But once again the Afro-American paradigm leaves untouched some of the most problematic structural elements of this novel, elements that according to many critics constitute lapses or flaws in its composition. Dianne Sadoff makes the case most persuasively, and most sympathetically inasmuch as she discerns "marks, fissures, and traces of 'inferiorization'" that amount to "scars of disguise or concealment because [Hurston] is black and female—doubly alienated from a white and patriarchal mainstream literature." Sadoff views *Their Eyes Were Watching God* as a celebration of heterosexual love that is undercut by Hurston's own ambivalence over the compatibility of marriage and the creative "voice" that produces fiction. The ambivalence is figured most acutely in the misogynistic attitudes and behavior that Hurston tacitly ascribes to Janie's third husband and great love, Tea Cake, and in the action of the scene where, according to the covert logic of the narrative, if not the overt logic of explication, Janie murders Tea Cake, just as she has murdered her previous husband, Jody Starks. As Sadoff observes, "Hurston has motivated her narrative, perhaps unconsciously, to act out her rage against male domination and to free Janie, a figure for herself, from all men."

In making the "marks" and "scars" that she perceives in Hurston's novel the inevitable consequence of Hurston's doubly marginalized social position, Sadoff employs a version of the Gilbert and Gubar "anxiety of authorship" model pioneered in *The Madwoman in the Attic*. In the process, however, she underscores problems with this model's presumption that apparent inconsistencies in the narrative are due to unintended eruptions of repressed biographical material into the text. While Sadoff is more thorough and more sympathetic in her treatment of *Their Eyes Were Watching God* than, say, Robert Towers is in his treatment of *The Color Purple*, she presumes, as Towers does, that the author has inadvertently written something other than what she intended, and that what the author intended was an unironic and unambiguous realism, in Hurston's case the realism of the heterosexual romance plot that structured so many European and American novels about women in the eighteenth and nineteenth centuries. Neither critic entertains the possibility that certain ostensible violations may be calculated subversions of conventions that the authors regarded as permeated with white, masculinist values or that other ostensible violations may arise from the fact that the authors were writing not realism, but romance—perhaps in part because, unlike the genre of realism, the genre of romance is recognized as highly conventional, so that its ideological implications are easier both to underscore and to undermine.

Romance is a term with a wide range of applications, especially when contrasted to *realism*, but it also has a more delimited technical sense that turns out to be surprisingly relevant to *The Color Purple* and illuminates certain analogous aspects of *Their Eyes Were Watching God*. Such late plays of Shakespeare as *The Tempest* and, especially, *The Winter's Tale*, which draw on pastoral for a number of their governing premises but go on to use these premises as means to develop a tragicomic plot, have striking affinities with the narrative strategies created by Walker and Hurston. Shakespearean romance can in certain respects serve as a structural paradigm for these two novels without necessarily standing in a relationship of direct influence to them or absorbing them into its own network of assumptions about how the world is structured and how human beings fit into this world. Indeed, the romance paradigm seems most important in this context precisely because it formally encodes a system of hierarchical relations that have ideological repercussions, and because this recognizably conventional system of hierarchical relations is also the ideology of racism and patriarchy, which the two novels expose and, ultimately, invert.

I

In his introduction the New Arden edition of *The Tempest*, Frank Kermode advances "pastoral tragi-comedy" as a more precise, if more cumbersome, designation for the late plays of Shakespeare more commonly termed romances. The phrase is useful insofar as it invokes the tradition of pastoral and thus a set of conventions celebrating a rural, "natural" community often explicitly identified with the nonwhite inhabitants of Africa or the New World and constituted in implicit opposition to a dominant urban community. *The Color Purple* is clearly pastoral in these respects, for in it Walker makes a group of black farmers the central social unit and uses this community as a vantage point from which to deliver a blistering critique of the surrounding white culture. The denunciation is sometimes overt, as when Sofia fulminates: "They have the nerve to try to make us think slavery fell through because of us. . . . Like us didn't have sense enough to handle it. All the time breaking hoe handles and letting the mules loose in the wheat. But how anything they build can last a day is a wonder to me. They backward. . . . Clumsy, and unlucky." More frequently, however, the white society figures as profoundly unnecessary, invisible for most of the action and appearing only as explosions of violence and insanity that sporadically intrude into the relatively intelligible world of the protagonists, as when the mayor's wife asks Sofia to be her maid and precipitates the beating, jailing, and domestic servitude of Sofia and the rape of Squeak or when the English engineers casually eradicate the Olinka village in the process of turning the jungle into a rubber plantation.

The point of view of pastoral is conventionally simple, artless and naïve—values rendered, of course, by means that are complex, subtle, and sophisticated—and can become the locus of a sustained attack on the mores of the mainstream society. Walker's protagonist Celie (whose name by various etymologies means "holy," "healing," and "heavenly"), is in these respects an exemplary pastoral protagonist, for her defining quality, and thus the defining quality of the narrative, is innocence. If this innocence subjects her to violation at the outset of the story, it also figures as a capacity for wonder and thus for experience. Celie learns, and as she learns her pastoral community develops, in a movement that implicitly restores a submerged Edenic ideal of harmony between individual human beings and between humanity and the natural order.

It is this development that makes *The Color Purple* a narrative—tragicomedy as well as pastoral—and provides striking affinities with the late Shakespearean romances. Kermode has defined romance as "a mode of exhibiting the action of magical and moral laws in a version of human life so selective as to obscure, for the special purpose of concentrating attention on these laws, the fact that in reality their force is intermittent and only fitfully glimpsed." Certainly the moral laws of Walker's novel, subtitled in the original hard-cover edition *A Moral Tale*, have magical power, producing consequences that are not in naturalistic terms remotely credible. Nettie, Samuel, and the children miraculously return from the sea after their ship is reported missing, to provide a conclusion that brings together all the far-flung characters in a celebration that is part family reunion, part assertion of a new social order that will supplant the old (the celebration takes place on the Fourth of July, a date on which, as Harpo explains to a representative of the younger generation, white people are busy "celebrating they independence from England" and consequently black people "can spend the day celebrating each other"). Shortly before this climactic juncture, Shug returns from her last heterosexual fling to find Celie and Albert reconciled and living in platonic harmony, a reversal prompted by Albert's recognition that "meanness kill." Shortly before *this* development Celie inherits a house, a store, and the information that her children are not the product of incest. And this last windfall comes after the success of Celie's company, Folkspants,

Ltd., an enterprise purveying androgyny to Depression-era black sharecroppers. The comic impetus of Walker's story is so powerful that it absorbs questions of probability and motivation. As Northrop Frye has noted of analogous Shakespearean plots, "What emerges at the end is not a logical consequence of the preceding action, as in tragedy, but something more like a metamorphosis."

In Shakespearean romance the metamorphosis is both social and metaphysical. It is social in that it involves a redemptive conclusion absorbing all the principal characters, whether or not they seem to deserve redemption. Moreover, as J. H. P. Pafford observes in writing of *The Winter's Tale*, the element of tragedy in romances derives from the suffering characters must undergo because of the misbehavior of a powerful male figure; this figure nevertheless "always shares to the full in the final blessings, and, however guilty and responsible for the suffering of others, he is ultimately absolved by facile excuse, if any is needed at all." In *The Color Purple* the most important agent of suffering is also a (relatively) powerful male figure, Celie's husband Mr. _____, whose unarticulated name, in the manner of epistolary fictions since Richardson's *Pamela*, suggests fearful effacement of an identity too dangerous to reveal and whose transformation is signaled by a renaming that at once diminishes and humanizes. In this case, the gratuitous absolution is also a conversion that affects descendants, for both Mr. _____ (who is transformed into a little man given to collecting shells and called merely Albert) and his son, Harpo, are absolved by becoming integrated into a female-defined value community, "finding themselves" at last in the traditionally female roles of seamstress and housekeeper.

The metamorphoses of romance are not limited to the social order, and they have an analogous metaphysical dimension in *The Color Purple*, where Celie's progress also serves to redefine the proper relation between human beings and the natural world they inhabit. Shug's disquisitions on religion and on the behavior required by a redefined God are consonant with the pastoral's characteristic fusion of reverence and hedonism and with a long tradition that uses pastoral convention to attack the excesses and misconceptions of established religious practice. "God love all them [sexual] feelings," Shug assures a scandalized Celie. "That's some of the best stuff God did," and she goes on to maintain, "God love admiration. . . . Not vain, just wanting to share a good thing." In the ensuing critique of prevailing religious beliefs, this undemanding God emerges as not only sexless—an "it" rather than a "he"—but also radically decentered: not one but many and in fact, according to Shug, "everything that is or ever was or ever will be. And when you can feel that, and be happy to feel that, you've found It." Like the value systems governing traditional romances, the nurturing pantheism this novel affirms as an ideal also figures implicitly as a preexisting state or Edenic norm that must be restored before human beings can attain social equilibrium. Celie only embraces it completely in the greeting of her last letter, which describes the celebratory reunion of all the principal characters: "Dear God. Dear stars, dear trees, dear sky, dear peoples. Dear Everything. Dear God."

Finally, Shakespearean romances provide precedent and rationale for an aspect of *The Color Purple* that readers have found particularly anomalous, the "Africa" passages, which in effect disrupt the American action for some forty pages, when a whole cache of withheld letters from Nettie is suddenly revealed. These letters detail the story of Nettie's adoption by a missionary family and her subsequent travels to New York, England, Senegal, Liberia, and finally the unnamed country of the Olinka. In the Olinka village she recapitulates Celie's discoveries, decrying the irrationality of the sex-gender system, becoming increasingly committed to the nonhuman, asexual God, and achieving a heterosexual version of Celie's stable, loving relationship. The function of the "Africa" section is clearly to provide analogies and contrasts to the dominant action. In this function, as in its seeming violation of realist conventions, it parallels scenes in the romances taking place in what Frye has called the "green world," a pastoral landscape that serves as a "symbol of natural society, the word natural referring to the original human society which is the proper home of man" and is "associated with things which in the context of the ordinary world seem unnatural, but which are in fact attributes of nature as a miraculous and irresistible reviving power." This "green world" is "particularly the world in which the heroine . . . dies and comes back to life," and as such it is the locus of Nettie's reincarnation as correspondent and conarrator.

The village of the Olinka, with its organically round huts, its roofleaf religion, its restorative myths of black hegemony, and its simple agrarian economy, is in some respects, and especially initially, an idyllic counter to the world that Celie must dismantle and remake. In its geographic distance from the world of the main action, in the length of time the daughter-heroine spends there (as missing and presumed dead), in its structural function of healing old wounds through a marriage and the founding of a family, and in its recapitulation of major themes of the containing drama, this generic "Africa" most resembles the Bohemia of *The Winter's Tale*—with one signal difference. Whereas Perdita in *The Winter's Tale* learns from the pastoral Bohemia, which in many respects remains an ideal, Nettie in *The Color Purple* ends up criticizing the Olinka society, which she first perceives as a natural and self-determining black community but soon finds sexist and fatally vulnerable to incursions by the encompassing white empire. By contrast, Celie's world becomes more woman-centered and more self-sufficient as it develops, finally containing and assimilating even elements of the white community in the person of Sofia's former charge, Miss Eleanor Jane, who leaves her own home to work for Sofia.

But this one difference in many ways completely inverts the emphasis of the romance, suggesting the extent to which Walker unsettles this structural paradigm in the process of applying it. As a marginal and marginalizing work, *The Color Purple* not only reveals the central preoccupations of the tradition within which it locates itself but succeeds in turning a number of these preoccupations inside out, at once exposing the ideology that informs them and insinuating the alternative meanings that, by insisting on its own centrality, the paradigm has suppressed.

II

One of the chief preoccupations of romance as a genre is the relation between men and women. *The Winter's Tale*, which, in this as in other respects, is the closest structural analogue to *The Color Purple*, deals with the unmotivated jealousy and cruelty of a man who is also a ruler, his loss of his wife and daughter for a period of sixteen years, and their restoration (both had been preserved in "green worlds") after he atones and comes to terms with his own misdeeds. The restoration is bittersweet: on the one hand, time has elapsed and many opportunities are gone for good; on the other hand, a young central couple restores the succession and suggests a more humane and rational future, both for this family and for the state that they govern.

Allowing for the fact that in *The Color Purple* the female roles of mother, daughter, wife, and lover are slippery to the point of being interchangeable, the plot of *The Winter's Tale* has clear affinities with the plot of *The Color Purple*—and a very different focus. Despite the attention given to the main female characters, the play is *about* the father and ruler, Leontes, about his crime, his punishment, and his eventual, though partial, restitution. By analogy *The Color Purple* ought to be about Mr. _____, about *his* crime, punishment and eventual restitution. And of course Mr. _____ goes through all these stages, emerging at the conclusion as an integral part of the new society embodied in the family that surrounds him. But *The Color Purple* is not his story. This point is especially important in view of the fact that Steven Spielberg seized on the underlying romance structure of Walker's novel when he made it into a film; he reinscribed Mr. _____ (whom he renamed simply Mister, so that the title of authority became this character's identity) at the center of the story, making his change of heart the turning point of the action and involving him in supplementary scenes that show him coming to reembrace his estranged family. Even more striking, Spielberg went on to reinscribe the law of the father exactly where Walker had effaced it, by providing Shug with a textually gratuitous "daddy," who is also a preacher and thus the representative of the Christian white father-God explicitly repudiated in the passage that gives the book its title. This father asserts his power by refusing to *speak* to Shug until she and all the inhabitants of the evolving new society who have gathered in the alternative structure of the juke joint are themselves assimilated to the Christian church and give *voice* to Christian hymns. Spielberg's restorative instinct here was unerring, for Walker uses the Afro-American motif of "finding a voice" primarily to decenter patriarchal authority, giving speech to hitherto muted women, who change meanings in the process of articulating and thus appropriating the dominant discourse. Spielberg replaced this entire narrative tendency with its reverse, not only restoring voice to the father but making paternal words uniquely efficacious: the film's Mister is shown visiting Washington, talking to bureaucrats, and in substance becoming the agent of the climactic reunion between Celie and Nettie.

In the novel, on the other hand, the emphasis is skewed away from this male discovery of identity. If Albert and Harpo "find themselves," it is within a context of redefinition that not only denies male privilege but ultimately denies that the designations "male" and "female" are meaningful bases for demarcating difference. In a fictional universe governed by the written "dialect" of Celie and initially conditioned by the paternal injunction *"You better not never tell nobody but God. It'd kill your mammy,"* speech among women turns out to be revivifying rather than death-dealing, especially inasmuch as such speech has the potential to bring about romance's characteristic reconstitution of society.

The reconstitution of society is largely a matter of redefinition, presented as the inevitable corollary of taking seriously the view from underneath, not only figuratively but also literally. For example, Celie's detached description of heterosexual intercourse, which prompts Shug to observe, "You make it sound like he going to the toilet on you," leads her into a revisionary discussion of female anatomy:

> You never enjoy it at all? she ast, puzzle. Not even with your children daddy?
> Never, I say.
> Why Miss Celie, she say, you still a virgin.
> What? I ast.
> Listen, she say, right down there in your pussy is a little

button that gits real hot when you do you know what with
somebody. It git hotter and hotter and then it melt. That the
good part. But other parts good too, she say. Lot of sucking go
on, here and there, she say. Lot of finger and tongue work.

     Button? Finger and *tongue*? My face hot enough to melt
itself.

Shug begins by replacing conventional terminology for the female genitals,
shifting emphasis from the lack or hole of patriarchal representation to a
"little button" that "git hotter and hotter and then it melt"—a mixed
metaphor from the point of view of the dominant discursive practice, which
of course has only recently begun to acknowledge the existence of buttons
that behave in this way. The consequence is immediately clear to Celie: if the
important organ is not a hole but a button, then stimulation can come from
such androgynous appendages as "finger and tongue," and intercourse is not
only insufficient but unnecessary for female sexual pleasure. Shug's
redefinition of the word "virgin" in this passage is equally threatening to
patriarchal control over women's bodies, in that it places priority not on
penetration, and thus on the social mechanism for guaranteeing ownership
of children, but on enjoyment, making the woman's own response the index
of her "experience."

    In the development of the story, Celie, along with the appositely named
Squeak, acquires a voice and becomes a producer of meanings, while Shug
and Sofia, articulate all along, increase their authority until it is evident that
female voices have the power to dismantle hierarchical oppositions that
ultimately oppress everyone and to create a new order in which timeworn
theories about male and female "natures" vanish because they are useless for
describing the qualities of people. Near the conclusion, the transformed Mr.
_____, now happily calling himself only Albert, tries to explain his
admiration for Shug: "To tell the truth, Shug act more manly than most men.
I mean she upright, honest. Speak her mind and the devil take the
hindmost." But Celie takes issue with these categories. "Harpo not like this,
I tell him. You not like this. What Shug got is womanly it seem like to me.
Specially since she and Sofia the ones that got it." Albert continues to worry
the problem—"Sofia and Shug not like men . . . but they not like women
either"—until Celie makes the relevant distinction: "You mean they not like
you or me." On the basis of such redrawn lines the entire immediate society
reconstitutes itself, in the manner of Shakespearean romance, around a
central couple. This couple is not only black, it is aging and lesbian. Yet
clearly Celie and Shug are intended to suggest the nucleus of a new and self-
sustaining society: the triply marginalized become center and source.

III

The issue of voice—and especially of voice as a way of appropriating discourse and remaking meanings—returns this discussion to the writer whom Walker has repeatedly claimed as her "foremother," Zora Neale Hurston, and to *Their Eyes Were Watching God*, in which the protagonist, Janie, discovers her voice and uses it to assert her own authority in a world full of speechmakers and tale-tellers. Janie's voice, first muted by the pathos of her Nanny's stories, emerges to threaten her first husband but then is subsumed to the "big voice" of Jody Starks until the moment of the insult that by the logic of the narrative kills him: "Humph! Talkin' bout *me* lookin' old! When you pull down yo' britches, you look lak de change uh life." Janie's relationship with Tea Cake reinforces the association of language and sexual potency—"He done taught me de maiden language all over," Janie tells her best friend Pheoby—and finally raises her to a level of equality that is to some extent both sexual and narrative, for in "the muck," the fertile Florida bottomland where Tea Cake takes her, "she could listen and laugh and even talk some herself if she wanted to. She got so she could tell big stories herself from listening to the rest."

"The muck" in this novel plays the role of a "green world" in Shakespearean romance: it is a magical, somehow "more natural" realm that shapes both the outside world and the conclusion toward which the narrative tends. Tea Cake describes it in unmistakably pastoral terms: "Folks don't do nothin' down dere but make money and fun and foolishness," and the narrator elaborates: "Pianos living three lifetimes in one. Blues made and used right on the spot. Dancing, fighting, singing, crying, laughing, winning and losing love every hour. Work all day for money, fight all night for love. The rich black earth clinging to bodies and biting the skin like ants." Precisely because "the muck" is a "green world," however, it represents a transitory stage in Janie's passage toward achieving her own identity, a passage that the romance paradigm further implies will lead to achieving the basis for a reconstituted society. The heterosexual idyll with Tea Cake is thus not the culmination of the plot but a transformative moment that leads to the culmination. In other word, the theme of finding a voice does not supplement the heterosexual romance plot of *Their Eyes Were Watching God* but supplants that plot, just as the story of Janie's *telling* her story frames and in framing displaces the ostensible main story of Janie's quest for heterosexual love.

The action of *Their Eyes Were Watching God* begins with a homecoming, but against the evidence the Eatonville residents eagerly collect—the "overhalls" that Janie wears and her manifestly mateless state—

this is a triumphal return. The whole of the ensuing narrative aims to establish that triumph, displayed especially in the significance of Janie's ability to tell her own story. The capacity to tell this story rests on two conditions. The first is that there be a story to tell, a plot, a completed action in Aristotle's terms. But because a completed action is one that has ended, the quest for heterosexual love must terminate in order to be appropriated by discourse, and the only terminus that will preserve the fulfillment of the quest while imposing closure on it is the apparently tragic one of Tea Cake's death. Rather paradoxically, then, the killing of Tea Cake becomes part of the larger *comic* impetus that establishes Janie's voice and gives him a fictional "life" that she can possess wholly: "Of course he wasn't dead. He could never be dead until she herself had finished feeling and thinking. The kiss of memory made pictures of love and light against the wall. Here was peace."

The appropriative move goes further. In appropriating Tea Cake in the form of her story, Janie brings the "horizons" so important in the development of her aspirations—she undertook her "journey to the horizons in search of *people*"—back to Eatonville, the black community that functions as the locus of black storytelling in this novel. "Ah done been tuh de horizon and back and now Ah kin sit heah in mah house and live by comparisons," she tells Phoeby, but the closing image of the narrative affirms that the horizon has with her: "She pulled in the horizon like a great fish-net. Pulled it from around the waist of the world and draped it over her shoulder. So much of life in its meshes! She called in her soul to come and see." And this looping, "netting" action also contains the novel, which begins at the end of Janie's story and comes back to it, drawing the whole "life" of the plot in its meshes.

The central action of *Their Eyes Were Watching God* is thus Janie's telling of her story, and the climax of this central action is the pulling in of the horizon, a dramatization of the fact of closure that establishes Janie as an accomplished storyteller. If one condition of this action is a completed story that can be told, a second condition is an audience capable of hearing it. Janie's privileged listener is her best friend, Pheoby, whose credentials as audience are her empathy and equality with the narrator, to the point of being at least potentially interchangeable with her. "You can tell 'em what Ah say if you wants to," Janie assures her. "Dat's just the same as me 'cause mah tongue is in mah friend's mouf." The image implies that the relation of female narrator to female audience is nonhegemonic and reversible. But like so many of the images associated with storytelling in this book it is also highly sexual, suggesting further that the narratorial couple composed of Janie and Pheoby has displaced the heterosexual couple as the desired union that motivates and finally terminates the action. The commencement of

Janie's "conscious life" dates from a revelation in which the spectacle of bees fertilizing the blossoms of a pear tree led to the conclusion "So this was a marriage!" but Janie's subsequent three marriages somewhat miraculously produce no children. The real fertilization seems to occur when Janie combines with Pheoby to give birth to her story after she has returned to Eatonville, the town of tale-tellers. This story addresses the values governing her community, its misplaced emphasis on possession, status, class, and sexual hierarchy, all legacies of its founder Jody Starks. In narrating, Janie moves to renovate the society that she has rejoined, transforming it at last into a female speech community embracing the playful, nonhierarchical values that constitute the lesson she draws from her experience—an Edenville.

Walker clearly picks up on these implications in her own revision of *Their Eyes Were Watching God*. In *The Color Purple* a homosexual romance plot replaces the heterosexual one, with the appetizing Tea Cake ("So you sweet as all dat?" Janie inquires when she learns his name) transformed into Celie's lover and mentor Sugar Avery. Moreover, the drama of Celie's epistolary self-creation revolves around the discovery of a female audience that finally fulfills the ideal of co-respondence. Celie initially writes to God as an alternative to speech. The process of finding her speaking voice is a process of finding her audience, first in Sofia, then in Shug, but she is not able to deliver the Old Testament–style curse that in turn delivers her from bondage until she is assured of the existence of Nettie, her ideal audience, who also tells a story leading to identical conclusions about the nature of spiritual and social reality—as if her sister's tongue were in her mouth.

IV

Thus in *Their Eyes Were Watching God*, Hurston's ostensible frame tale decenters what it appears to comprehend, shifting the story of heterosexual love to the margin even as it contains and completes that story. It behaves, that is, like the frame or margin that Jacques Derrida has discussed under the rubric of the *parergon*. Conventionally extrinsic, supplementary, or inessential to that which it borders, a parergon is simultaneously intrinsic and essential, inasmuch as the priority of the center depends entirely on the oppositional relation of center to margin. Yet to call attention to this margin is to destroy its marginality, for the parergon is what it is by virtue of "disappearing, sinking in, obliterating itself, dissolving just as it expends its greatest energy." To call attention to the margin is to render it no longer marginal and consequently to collapse the center in a general unsettling of oppositional hierarchies.

This turning of attention to what is not conventionally in the center—
most obviously to conventionally marginal characters—is of course a
characteristic activity of conventionally marginal writers: black women, for
example. And of course to give voice to marginality—to let the margins
speak—is to mix a metaphor intolerably, for a speaking margin cannot be a
margin at all and in fact threatens to marginalize what has hitherto been
perceived as the center. Or, rather, such a phenomenon tends to destabilize
precisely the hierarchical oppositions that give margin and center clearly
demarcated meanings.

Such hierarchical oppositions are the basis of traditional genres. In
the paradigm of the Shakespearean romance they guarantee the distinction
between major and minor characters, between dominant and peripheral
lines of action, and between classes, sexes, and generations—all of which
may become confused during the development of the plot but must be
sorted out so as to fall into place in a conclusion that at once reconciles
apparently conflicting elements and confirms their inherent differences:
the ritual marriage. This conclusion makes its model of unity the
patriarchal family and its model of continuity the order of succession in
which power passes from father to son. Distinctions of class, gender, and
generation coincide with distinctions between major and minor, dominant
and peripheral, on the levels of character and plot. These distinctions are
unalterable, a premise that becomes the basis for both the tragic and the
comic aspects of pastoral tragicomedy.

But these distinctions are destabilized in *Their Eyes Were Watching
God* and *The Color Purple*, novels that Rachel Blau DuPlessis has identified
as employing a "narrative strategy of the multiple individual," in which the
female hero "encompasses opposites and can represent both sociological
debate and a psychic interplay between boundaries and boundlessness" and
eventually "fuses with a complex and contradictory group; her power is
articulated in and continued through a community that is formed in direct
answer to the claims of love and romance." Not only is the traditional
heterosexual couple supplanted as emphasis of the action, but it is replaced
by interchangeable versions of the same-sex couple: mother and daughter,
sisters, lovers, narrator and audience. The roles of the characters have
become slippery and permeable.

Perhaps most significant, the mother-daughter relation is
continuously transformed. Dianne Sadoff observes the extent to which
both novels suppress or overtly repudiate traditional mothering—Janie
hates her Nanny and produces a story with Pheoby rather than children in
any of her three marriages; Celie loses her children, and their foster-
mother subsequently dies—and suggests that such suppressions or

repudiations "question anxiety-free matrilineage." The issue is particularly important in light of the role of literary foremother that Walker has assigned to Hurston, and Sadoff uses what she perceives as an unacknowledged theme of failed mothering within the two novels to bolster readings that discern "ruptures" within *Their Eyes* and "scars of concealment" within *The Color Purple*, with its imbedded claims of unproblematic descent from the mother tale.

But the preceding discussion of the two novels might suggest, rather, that the issue is less one of the failure of mothering than of a redefinition, in which mothering is presented as a wholly relational activity. In *The Color Purple* children create mothers by circulating among women who in other contexts are daughters, sisters, friends, wives, and lovers. Celie's children pass first to Corrine, then to Nettie. Squeak takes on Sofia's children when Sofia goes to jail, and Sofia later mothers Squeak's daughter Suzie Q and—with exasperated acknowlegment that even unwilling nuture can engender filial affection—the white girl Eleanor Jane. And Celie's love affair with Shug begins from an erotic exchange that is poignantly figured as a mutual reparenting: "Then I feels something real soft and wet on my breast, feel like one of my little lost babies mouth. Way after while, I act like a little lost baby too."

In *Their Eyes Were Watching God*, mothering is intimately allied with production of a powerful narrative that enjoins a world view and a series of prescriptions about how to live. Nanny's story of Janie's lineage, which begins from what appears to be a piece of maternal wisdom, "De nigger woman is de mule uh de world so fur as Ah can see," concludes with the demand that Janie marry the man who, in Hurston's wonderfully apt conflation of social class and phallic power, owns "de onliest organ in town." While Janie ultimately repudiates this version of her story as unlivable, her repudiation is explicitly dissociated from an agonistic Oedipal model in which the child kills the parental figure in order to revise this parent's master narrative. If the narrative logic by which an ensuing action is figured as a consequent action indicates that Janie is responsible for the death of two husbands, the same logic makes Nanny's death the consequence of her *own* story, for Nanny's acknowledgment that she is dying, "Put me down easy, Janie, Ah'm a cracked plate," occurs at the end of the narrative in which she coerces Janie into marrying Logan Killicks. In replacing Nanny's story about sexual oppression with an alternative story about sexual love that paradoxically enables her to live independently and alone—"by comparisons"—Janie in effect takes on the maternal function, in company of course with her listener, Pheoby. She becomes author of her own story, both source and subject of maternal wisdom, in effect giving birth to herself.

Clearly in Walker's and Hurston's novels mothers are no guarantors of succession or legitimacy, and mothering is a slippery and even reversible relationship. Furthermore, Walker has suggested that the same sort of observation holds for literary motherhood among black women writers. Indeed, in her essay "In Search of Our Mothers' Gardens" she elides the distinction between biological and literary motherhood in the same way that in *The Color Purple* she elides the distinction between mothering and other, conventionally contrary female functions. Mothers are artists, artistic precursors are mothers, and in either case the mother's creation may be inseparable from the daughter's: perhaps Phillis Wheatley's mother "herself was a poet—though only her daughter's name is signed to the poems we know." This collaborative model of maternal influence suggests a subversively extended family romance, in which the mother as cocreator is simultaneously parent of the writer and lover or spouse. Most disruptive for the absolute status of all these role definitions, she may even become the daughter of her own daughter. DuPlessis has suggested that in fulfilling or completing her biological mother's work the twentieth-century woman writer is inclined to dramatize her mother's situation, recreating her mother as a character and revising her destiny by reinscribing it in the fiction. Alice Walker, who gave birth to her stepmother when she created Celie, also uses *The Color Purple* to revise her relation to the woman she has elsewhere called her foremother. Gates points out that the photograph of Hurston parenthetically described in Walker's essay "Zora Neale Hurston: A Cautionary Tale and a Partisan View"—"(I have a photograph of her in pants, boots, and broadbrim that was given to me by her brother, Everette. She has her foot up on the running board of a car—presumably hers, and bright red—and looks racy)"—is in essence the photograph of Shug Avery that fascinates Celie in *The Color Purple*: "I see her there in furs. Her face rouge. Her hair like somethin tail. She grinning with her foot on somebody motocar." In recreating her relationship to Hurston as a reciprocal and interactive one, Walker dramatizes Hurston's literary role as the undoer of inessential and divisive hierarchies. In casting Hurston as Shug, she revises theories of influence as they apply to black women.

What is finally at stake in readings of the two novels is the centrality of the paradigms and values informing what mainstream Western society chooses to call literature. To invoke these paradigms and values as if they exhausted the possibilities, and to castigate Walker and Hurston for failure to realize them, is to judge according to assumptions rather like those of the white community that Sofia ridicules in *The Color Purple*. It is like maintaining that slavery failed because blacks didn't have sense enough to handle it. In this chapter I have suggested, on the contrary, that by treating the marginal as central and thereby unsettling the hierarchical relations that structure "mainstream" genres, Walker and Hurston manage to handle very well the conventions that threaten to enslave them in a system of representation not of their own making.

DIANE GABRIELSEN SCHOLL

With Ears to Hear and Eyes to See: *Alice Walker's Parable* The Color Purple

To call *The Color Purple* a radical novel is not to make a surprising charge, considering the alarming number of critics who have protested the novel's raw language, its frank depiction of sexual expression, particularly lesbianism, and its bitter castigation of male and female sex roles. Its somewhat avant-garde epistolary narration also might earn the novel my designation of "radical," since the major portion of the letters are penned by a semi-literate black woman.

However, my claim for the radically *Christian* nature of the novel might meet with surprised opposition, given the vague spiritualist cast of the author's own theology and the pantheism expressed by Shug Avery in the novel's apparent theological center: "I believe God is everything. . . . Everything that is or ever was or ever will be. And when you can feel that, and be happy to feel that, you've found It." Indeed, Celie's letters to God give way in *The Color Purple* to her communication with her lost sister, a trade with which she seems quite happy, and her increasing self-reliance leaves her little need or inclination to continue her relationship with the Christian God of her earlier and more vulnerable days.

While the generalized awareness of God's presence in "a blade of corn" and in "the color purple" is not definitively Christian, the novel's Christianity instead rests in its qualities of extended parable, its movement through a

From *Christianity and Literature* 40, no. 3 (Spring 1991). © 1991 Conference on Christianity and Literature.

realistically improbable sequence of narrative reversals toward a conclusion that defies realistic expectations. In fact, the world of the novel is figuratively turned upside down in the course of Celie's changing fortunes; and such radical alterations, the stuff and substance of the Gospels' paradoxical stories, inform the story of Celie with an energy that is distinctly biblical.

Readers consistently have argued that such improbable turns and reversals of fortune render the novel both unrealistic and unconvincing. Thus, Trudier Harris challenges the fundamental character changes Celie undergoes throughout the novel's unpredictable course and, in particular, takes on Alice Walker's choice of resolution for the novel: "While the reader is inclined to feel good that Celie does survive, and to appreciate the good qualities she has, she or he is still equally skeptical about accepting the logic of a novel that posits so many changes as a credible progression for a character." Such radical changes ask "more of the reader than can be reasonably expected."

Harris picks a central bone of contention with Walker, charging that in the novel "the issues are worked out at the price of realism." In fact, almost immediately following its publication *The Color Purple* was attacked for its lack of verisimilitude. "Black people don't talk like that," charged a leading black women's magazine that turned down the opportunity to print excerpts from the novel. Walker's essay "Coming in from the Cold" rejects this allegation, maintaining that she used the voice and language of her step-grandmother for Celie. But Walker indicates here a concern that goes well beyond the faithful recording of dialect:

> Celie's speech pattern and Celie's words reveal not only an intelligence that transforms illiterate speech into something that is, at times, very beautiful, as well as effective in conveying her sense of the world, but also what has been done to her by a racist and sexist system, and her intelligent blossoming as a human being despite her oppression demonstrates why her oppressors persist even today in trying to keep her down. For if and when Celie rises to her rightful, earned place in society across the planet, the world will be a different place, I can tell you.

Walker suggests the figurative possibilities for Celie's character and for the novel as a whole, and she leads us toward a recognition of *The Color Purple*'s necessary resolution, a major transformation of Celie's place in the world and, more significantly, a transformation of the world itself. The means to this interesting but problematic resolution is parable, which defies realism's effort to convey the "ordinary" and plausible course of events in its depiction of a topsy-turvy world where the unlikely and unpredictable are indeed most likely to happen.

The novel is most obviously the story of Celie's changing fortunes, and its central pattern displays a kinship to Victorian novels as Celie gradually overcomes the oppressive conditions of her despised situation, achieving in the end the prosperity and family security she has longed for. A black Jane Eyre? Celie seems to be one, though in moving toward its concluding reunion scene *The Color Purple* takes its readers through an even more dizzying series of ironic reversals than does the nineteenth-century novel. Celie, sexually abused by her father and married against her will to the infamous Mr., learns to love the provocative blues singer Shug Avery and then herself, acquires self-esteem and financial independence as a maker of pants, becoming increasingly more expressive in their fabric and design, and learns to her surprise and satisfaction that her real father, lynched before she could remember him, has left her a house and a dry goods store. Near the end of the novel she lacks nothing but her sister Nettie, whose letters from the mission field in Africa were long denied her by the malicious Mr. but are regained through the ministrations of wily Shug. When the steamship on which Nettie and her family have been returning to America is torpedoed during World War II, Celie's well of fortune seems to have dried up. But Nettie and her new husband Samuel, together with Celie's grown children whom she has not seen since her supposed "daddy" spirited them away in their infancy, are restored to Celie at the novel's close to her complete happiness.

Too good to be true? The story's outward attempt at successful resolution is belied by the energetic tension throughout, for Celie's story is marked by narrative reversals, ironic in their defiance of expectations and often comical in their improbable and unpredictable nature. Repelled by Mr.'s insensitive sexual advances, she likens men to frogs and finds herself powerfully attracted to his mistress instead: "First time I got the full sight of Shug Avery long black body with it black plum nipples, look like her mouth, I thought I had turned into a man." Shug makes no effort to hide her contempt for adoring Celie at first, but gradually she is won over by Celie's enduring kindness and becomes her lover and strongest ally, leaving Mr. baffled and much put out. This reversal of alliances is thoroughly in character for the novel. Celie loses her children, the unwelcome results of her "daddy's" incestuous violence, only to learn that they are alive and have been adopted by the missionaries Samuel and Corinne. Similarly, after Nettie is lost to Celie, she reappears when her withheld letters are found in Mr.'s trunk by ally Shug, letters chronicling her years spent in missionary service in the very household where the children Adam and Olivia are being reared. Nettie's letters further reveal that she and Celie share another father, the industrious shopkeeper who was lynched for his success, thereby removing from the children the taint of incestuous origins and from Celie the burden of an abusive "daddy."

Such ironic reversals are the stuff of which *The Color Purple* is made. Lovesick Harpo moons after Sofia but finds he is no match for her physical strength and prepossessing size. He likes washing dishes, while she likes to chop wood. Embarrassed by his failure to control his wife as his father dominates the submissive Celie, he embarks on a marathon eating binge designed to make him Sophia's match but winds up tearful and sick, consoled in Celie's arms. When he and Sofia part, he takes up with Squeak, a diminutive shadow of her predecessor, who begins as Sofia's feisty combatant but who at the end of the story has become her loyal friend, entrusting Sofia with the care of her child while she pursues her singing career. Harpo and Sofia provide for their children and for Squeak's (she by this time has resumed her rightful name of Mary Agnes) in a large and spontaneous extended family, a considerable reversal of their first expectations of married life.

Sofia's personal fortunes shift considerably during the course of the novel, too. Jailed for attacking the mayor and his wife, behavior they find most unbecoming in a black woman, she is mercilessly beaten and sentenced to solitary confinement. Due to the improbable intervention of Harpo's mistress Squeak, she is freed to work as a maid for the mayor's wife, the job she originally refused with contempt in the scene which resulted in her jailing. Having gone to some effort to teach the mayor's wife to drive a car, Sofia is at last rewarded with Miz Millie's offer to drive her home to see her children for Christmas. But even before they set out the trip seems doomed, according to Sofia's account which Celie records in her letter:

> Well, say Sofia, I was so use to sitting up there next to her teaching her how to drive, that I just naturally clammed into the front seat.
>
> She stood outside on her side the car clearing her throat.
>
> Finally she say, Sofia, with a little laugh, This *is* the South.
>
> Yes ma'am, I say.
>
> She clear her throat, laugh some more. Look where you sitting, she say.
>
> I'm sitting where I always sit, I say.
>
> That's the problem, she say. Have you ever seen a white person and a colored sitting side by side in a car, when one of 'em wasn't showing the other how to drive it or clean it?

> I got out the car, opened the back door and clammed in.
> She sat down up front. Off us traveled down the road, Miz
> Millie hair blowing all out the window.

Relegated to passenger status in the back seat, Sofia has a short-lived
Christmas. Miz Millie proves unequal to the task of backing up and clearing
Jack and Odessa's yard, where Sofia's children have been staying in their
mother's absence. Her frantic gear-stripping leaves the car unable to make
the journey home, and Jack must drive both the mayor's wife and Sofia back
in his pickup.

The crux of the story is the ironic role-shifting between Sofia and the
mayor's wife. Sofia, outwardly the recipient of the mayor's charity, is
obviously the most capable member of his household, secretly admired and
feared by the family. Her competence is proven when she must assume the
upper hand as driving instructor to Miz Millie, who nonetheless insists on
changing roles back to the familiar pattern when she installs Sofia in the back
seat. Ironically, the roles are reversed again by her failure to turn around in
Jack and Odessa's yard, which leaves Sofia the obedient and helpful servant
to the outward eye, as she sacrifices her afternoon with her children, but
which makes her the silent victor as she chalks up still another instance of
white incompetence and mismanagement. "White folks is a miracle of
affliction."

It is the conspicuous nature of these ironic reversals throughout *The
Color Purple* that gives the novel its qualities of parable. Such narrative turns,
contrary to expectation and to precedent, suggest of course the arbitrary
nature of assigned roles for men and women and for black and white people,
as the characters burst the bonds of acceptable behavior. But such reversals
have a deeper, unsettling effect as well: they push us beyond the comfortable
assumptions of our culture-bound lives and serve to upset our certainties
about the larger reality in which we live. Sofia winds up in the driver's seat,
figuratively speaking, both in this episode and much later when the mayor's
problem-besieged family continues to seek her advice. Celie's husband leaves
behind his abusive behavior to take up women's work, emerging improbably
as her confidante and not her tormentor.

Such narrative turns cause us to remember the parables, in which it is
not the priest or the Levite who offer aid to the traveler set upon by robbers
but the unlikely Samaritan who binds up his wounds and pays for his lodging;
the prodigal son gets a warm welcome when he returns, overshadowing his
dutiful brother. John Crossan in *The Dark Interval: Towards a Theology of Story*
addresses the contradiction at the heart of parables, which "are meant to
change, not to reassure us." He characterizes parable as the opposite of myth,

which has as its aim restoration of order and reconciliation. "Parable brings not peace but the sword, and parable casts fire upon the earth which receives it." Is this not what *The Color Purple*, weaving craftily from one narrative reversal to another, does to us? Crossan maintains both a destructive and a creative role for parable:

> The surface function of parable is to create contradiction within a given situation of complacent security but, even more unnervingly, to challenge the fundamental principle of reconciliation by making us aware of the fact that *we made up* the reconciliation. Reconciliation is no more fundamental a principle than irreconciliation. You have built a lovely home, myth assures us; but, whispers parable, you are right above the earthquake fault.

So Celie's narrative characteristically pulls the rug out from under us, sweeping away our certainties with an unsettling procession of contradictions.

But Celie's letters to God which reveal the radically changing nature of events in her life are only part of *The Color Purple*. Nettie's letters to Celie comprise another part, and although Nettie fails to acquire a voice the way Celie does, never emerging as a spellbinding narrator, there is method to her narrative inclusions. She writes from the other side of the world about a cultural experience that is in some respects the reverse of that in which Celie lives: most human beings are black, and white people are the minority. The Africans with whom Nettie lives tell a different version of the creation story from Genesis, one which emphasizes white people as an aberration, an interruption or reversal of the usual case, and which puts the blame on black people for casting out their unacceptable white children, Adam and Eve. In this embedded parable from the other side of the world, the theme of betrayal and guilt within the human family is underscored, an ironic commentary on the treatment Celie, Sofia, and other black characters have received at the hands of white people throughout their lives.

Nettie's letters provide other embedded parables within the novel, among them the story enacted for the missionaries as part of the welcoming ceremony that marks their arrival in the African village. A wealthy chief plants cassava fields, yams, cotton, and millet to sell to white traders. He grows increasingly greedy and soon takes over the land on which the roofleaf grows to cultivate more crops for sale. When a storm destroys the roofs of the village during the rainy season, villagers fall ill and die. Only after several years have enough roofleaves grown back to adequately protect the villagers, who continue to suffer adverse fortune due to their self-serving and now banished chief. Here again are the themes of betrayal, resulting destitution, and culpability, described as the intrinsic story of the African village and not the story imposed by the white oppressors alone. It is a story that suggests Mr.'s brutal treatment of Celie on the other side of the world and also her "daddy's" betrayal of her trust, and it serves to put such actions in a new light, causing readers to look beyond the oppression of blacks by the white establishment as the prevailing condition for brutality and betrayal.

Such embedded parables set in a counter-continent serve their place within the overall parable. *The Color Purple* ends with a scene of reconciliation, a reunion that begins when Celie makes her peace with a contrite Mr., who has taken up sewing and housekeeping and collects seashells. More significantly for Celie, he is willing to talk about their past and attempts to understand and apologize for his excessive domination. They resume their relationship on a radically altered basis—as members of an extended family that embraces Shug, Harpo and Sofia and their combined brood, and finally Nettie, Samuel, Olivia, Adam, and African Tashi as well. The resolution of the novel offers us an apocalyptic vision of the "peaceable kingdom" established by human beings in search of love and justice.

But in order to establish the "peaceable kingdom" it has been necessary to turn the world figuratively upside down, to reverse roles and to subvert the structure of a society dominated by white people with the occasional complicity of black victims of oppression, such as Mr. and Celie's "daddy" Alphonso. While it might seem that all contradictions are resolved in the concluding reunion scene, in fact the existence of an exploitative and racist society, in which oppressors and victims both reveal their propensity for self-seeking and domination, sets the reconciliation firmly on an "earthquake fault." Tashi and Adam have undergone the African rite of scarification, a figurative fall from the innocence of childhood, and they know that visibly marked as they are they face an uncertain future in the American South. The problems of the world outside the reunited "family" suggest the "made-up" nature of the resolution. *The Color Purple*, then, confronts us with an ending that is not an ending, the ultimate paradox in a series of narrative paradoxes.

Much critical attention has been given to the novel's derivation from black folklore which, as Keith E. Byerman maintains, provides contemporary African-American writers "access to their racial history, not only as a content of struggles for freedom, literacy, and dignity, but also as a form of dialectical experience, practice, and belief." For Byerman, "folklore serves in this literature as the antithesis of closed, oppressive systems"; it "can be made to contradict the representations of the past and of reality offered by apologists for oppression." Contemporary African-American writers tend to produce "open-ended stories which do not force a resolution on conflicts which are, both in literary and historical terms, inherently unresolvable."

Byerman judges Walker's novel to be lacking when it is measured by these standards:

> Walker seeks to resolve the dialectic by making all males female (or at least androgynous), all destroyers creators, and all difference sameness. In this process, she must move outside the very conflicts that generated the sewing, the blues singing, and the voice of Celie herself. Such an effort makes sense for one who wishes to articulate a political position; resolution creates sacred, utopian space which justifies the ideology on which it is based. But this creation is in fact another system that requires the same denial of history and difference as the order it has supplanted. To live "happily ever after," as the folk characters do in *The Color Purple*, is ironically, to live outside the folk world.

Byerman views Walker's choice of an "allegorical" form as an effort to "transcend history," and he charges that in so doing Walker "has neutralized the historical conditions of the very folk life she values."

Such an evaluation of the novel's resolution, however, seems to overlook the obvious figurative implication of the ending. Certainly *The Color Purple* fails to close with convincing realism, and indeed such a conclusion would be totally out of keeping with the highly improbably developments in the novel. Walker chooses instead to resolve the novel in a vision of peace and plenty, a vision that would be deluding as a realistic possibility (given the reader's awareness of the oppressive conditions that continue to threaten the characters) but serves to point us toward the end of history. The novel's ending is then both a false bottom and a figurative depiction of ultimate redemption.

Furthermore, the ahistorical feature of Walker's resolution which Byerman regards as its deficiency is consistent with the requirements of its nature as parable. It is in the nature of biblical parable to transcend the precise historical moment without avoiding the historical implications of story and its multiple ways of being heard and understood. The biblical parables emerge from their historical context to strike the listener or reader in other contexts, and in this sense the stories are always new, never to be resolved fully but instead open and subject to shifting significance. Jesus attests to the "openness" of parable in Matthew 13:52 when he teaches his disciples: "Therefore every scribe who has been trained for the kingdom of heaven is like a householder who brings out of his treasure what is new and what is old."

Walker's sense of story, deriving from black folklore its heightened awareness of paradox and of a subversive dialectic, draws from the Bible's storytelling also, and particularly from the radical stories of the Gospels, punctuated by ironic reversals and rife with a subversive principle of contradiction and mystery as they are. Folklore shares some of the qualities of parable both in narrative structure and in the pervasive element of secrecy, the sense of hidden mystery accessible only to the initiated.

Henry Louis Gates, Jr., describes the indebtedness of African-American authors, including writers of early slave narratives and contemporary figures such as Walker, to the African traditional figure of the "signifying monkey" who interprets the Word of God and serves to baffle, mystify, and contradict in stories from African folklore. According to Gates, "signifying" in African-American culture retains a relationship to its origin in folklore, since it implies speaking with an element of "doubleness," often with an ironic or satirical intent and meaning. While such "signifying" might indeed be a feature of the dialogue reported by Celie in *The Color Purple*, the most obvious way in which the novel maintains the character of a mysterious or "hidden" text is in Celie's original effort to write letters to God, letters that reveal but simultaneously conceal from the world the abuse inflicted on her by her "daddy." The letters therefore have a contradiction at their core and convey a kind of "doubleness," "signifying" themselves.

Certainly Jesus' role is characteristically that of "signifier," demonstrated in Matthew when the disciples ask him to explain his habit of speaking in parables. "To you it has been given to know the secrets of the kingdom of heaven, but to them it has not been given" (13:11) he answers them. "For to him who has will more be given, and he will have abundance; but from him who has not, even what he has will be taken away." "This is why," he explains, "I speak to them in parables, because seeing they do not see, and hearing they do not hear, nor do they understand." Frank Kermode characterizes the world depicted by Jesus in the book of Matthew as "a world of paradox," in which

> Jesus' followers are of more value than sparrows, yet God, who is with the sparrows when they fall (10:30), will nevertheless not prevent men from falling; for, according to the most bleakly majestic paradox of all, "He that findeth his life shall lose it: and he that loseth his life for my sake shall find it" (10:39). Under this new authority the world is turned upside down; it becomes unacceptable to "the wise and prudent" and acceptable only to the simple or silly, to "babes" (11:25). Indeed, to accept it requires ignorance of all that the new

authority does not vouchsafe (11:27); yet by another disorienting paradox this apparently impossible charge becomes an easy yoke and a light burden (11:28–30).

The "riddling" nature of Jesus' teachings conspires with the unpredictability of the parables to create a "world of paradox" essentially similar to Celie's world of seeming radical disorder, an improbable world of shifting meanings in which practically no one at the end occupies the same place in which he or she began.

Crossan calls parable "the dark night of story," but he confers upon it the power that enables the reader's transcendence. Parables, he maintains, "shatter the deep structure of our accepted world and thereby render clear and evident to us the relativity of story itself. They remove our defenses and make us vulnerable to God. It is only in such experiences that God can touch us, and only in such moments does the kingdom of God arrive." In *The Color Purple* the concluding reunion is then like the story's false bottom, giving way after the preparatory narrative reversals to the novel's true transcendent ground as it points beyond history without evading the historical circumstances of racial violence and oppression.

Walker's writing indicates the author's commitment to a new social order. "I believe in change: change personal, and change in society," she says in an interview. "I have experienced a revolution (unfinished, without question, but one whose new order is everywhere on view) in the South. And I grew up—until I refused to go—in the Methodist Church, which taught me that Paul *will* sometimes change on the way to Damascus, and that Moses—that beloved old man—went through so many changes he made God mad."

Yet she has resisted a narrow didacticism in *The Color Purple*, an overstated and obvious endorsement of social change, and certainly some of her critics who maintain that she subjugates the art of storytelling to her ideology in this novel have overlooked the tension, the dialectic, the intentional paradox both of her narrative turns and of her improbable resolution. Her biblical heritage is one shaping influence on her art in this powerful novel, and it is this same heritage that prepared her to read the fiction of another Georgia author, Flannery O'Connor. In Walker's essay "Beyond the Peacock," a tribute to O'Connor, she characterizes the author she admires:

> She believed all the mysteries of her faith. And yet, she was incapable of writing dogmatic or formulaic stories. No religious tracts, nothing haloed softly in celestial light, not even any happy endings. It has puzzled some of her readers and

annoyed the Catholic Church that in her stories not only does good not triumph, it is not usually present. Seldom are there choices, and God never intervenes to help anyone win. To O'Connor, in fact, Jesus was God, and he won only by losing.

O'Connor, like Walker, understood the essential role of parable as an agent of change, of transfiguring redemption. The reader need only think of the ironic reversals in a story such as "Parker's Back" or the shifting fortunes in "The Displaced Person."

It is the capacity of parable to unsettle our complacency, to prevent our ossification, to open up new possibilities that usher in the kingdom of God. Walker's methodical destruction of all our social certainties is her means to the revelation, her provocative challenge issued in the spirit and the narrative technique of the Gospels. In extending this challenge she effects a transcendence of history by appearing to resolve the conflicts at the heart of *The Color Purple*, but only so that her parable can unsettle us more profoundly, striking at the roots of our historical circumstance as we, like the householder in Matthew 13, uncover in the treasure "what is new and what is old."

TUZYLINE JITA ALLAN

The Color Purple: *A Study of Walker's Womanist Gospel*

> Change means growth, and growth can be painful. But we sharpen self-definition by exposing the self in work and struggle together with those whom we define as different from ourselves. . . . For Black and white, old and young, lesbian and heterosexual women alike, this can mean new paths to our survival.
>
> Audre Lorde, *Sister Outsider*

Womanism has brought Alice Walker and her characters safely to the land of psychic freedom after a perilous journey fraught with fear, self-hate, and guilt. The transforming agent (and transporting agency) is "womanish" gall, the courage to be daring in the face of a conspiracy of conformity and, if not silence, acquiescence. A traditionalist in the sense of one who believes in the authenticating capacity of orality, Walker locates womanism in the speech culture of black women. Being or "acting womanish," Walker writes, is "the folk expression" black female adults used to describe young girls who were overly curious, "audacious," and eager to enter the world of grown-ups. Womanishness is similar to, yet different from, its nonfolk correlative, precociousness. While both suggest prematurity or early ripening, the former takes on the added elements of willfulness and excessive curiosity,

From *Womanist and Feminist Aesthetics: A Comparative Review* by Tuzyline Jita Allan. © 1995 Tuzyline Jita Allan.

119

which are not necessarily a part of precocity. "Womanish," I think, links better with the West African pidgin expression "big woman" (pronounced "big ooman"), used also by adults (male and female, though it is female-derived) to refer to the sassy demeanor of young females. Since both expressions also provoke the contradictory response of disagreement over the young person's refusal to be circumscribed and tacit approval and admiration for the rebellious spirit, Walker's term, given the history of African retentions in African American folk culture, may very well have its origin in the West African version.

To distinguish further the black feminist writer from her white counterpart, Walker adds to the folk quality of reckless boldness, which she defines as "wanting to know more and in greater depth than is considered 'good' for one," the attributes of woman-centeredness (an appreciation or love of other women "sexually and/or non-sexually"), and a unified vision of the world. Couched in this definition of womanism is Walker's criticism of white liberal feminism, especially what she regards as its qualified resistance to the status quo and self-seeking amelioration in the face of massive global oppression. For Walker, the battle against patriarchal society and its multiple sins of sexism, racism, classism and homophobia (among others) needs the womanist spirit of defiance and irreverence, on the one hand, and the desire for social integration, on the other. Woolf's dialectics of resistance and compliance in *Mrs. Dalloway* and Drabble's deterministic model in *The Middle Ground* seem to justify Walker's unease with white feminism, yet a closer look at Walker's own feminist consciousness reveals a slow, torturous progress toward her emancipating womanist ethos. Walker's confident rebellion in *The Color Purple* is the culmination of a long struggle against despair, as well as racial and sexual fragmentation. The path to womanist victory in Walker's fiction is strewn with physically and psychically battered women, victimized as much by self-hate as by an oppressive racist and sexist social system.

In a 1973 interview Walker defined the subject of her creative imagination: "I am committed to exploring the oppressions, the insanities, the loyalties, and the triumphs of black women . . . the most fascinating creations in the world." More precisely, the focus of Walker's attention is the Southern black woman and until *The Color Purple* her personal "oppressions" and "insanities" far out-numbered her "triumphs." The female characters in both Walker's first novel, *The Third Life of Grange Copeland*, and first collection of short stories, *In Love & Trouble*, are too close to their creator's near-suicide experience (involving an unwanted pregnancy in her final college year in 1965) to escape the mood of "completely numbing despair" that crisis engendered. In *The Third Life of Grange Copeland* both male and female characters are caught beneath a brutally oppressive social machinery, but it is the women who are crushed by the double weight of racism and sexism. Grange Copeland tries to regain the manhood he lost to Shipley, the white man who "owned" him, by beating his wife, Margaret. Himself reduced to an object by Shipley, Grange in turn strips Margaret of her humanity, rendering her indistinguishable from "their dog." Beaten and silenced, Margaret suffers alone, a silent sacrifice to brute masculinity. Not even in the murder of her unwanted child and her own suicide does Margaret show defiance. On the contrary, these acts, as Trudier Harris points out, "are a bow of defeat, a resignation," bearing the marks of one who, like a dog, "had spent the last moments on her knees."

In a second cycle of sadomasochistic violence, Brownfield and Mem repeat and expand the life-denying behavior of the earlier generation. Brownfield, aptly described by Bettye Parker-Smith as "a worm, a wretched, contemptible maggot," displaces his powerlessness within the dominant social structure onto women whom he treats with unrelieved venom. Having sexually used and abused Josie (his father's mistress) and her daughter, Lorene, Brownfield reaches for the prize female, Mem, the superior woman with education and middle-class promise. Brownfield's gradual but certain destruction of Mem dramatizes the plight of black women vis-á-vis black men in a society that devalues blackness but privileges maleness. Mem and her fellow victims in *The Third Life* succumb to the guilt the black cultural economy produces to punish those women who fail to yield to male authority. Feeling partly responsible for white society's emasculation of black men, these women offer themselves in atonement, their self-sacrifice demanding from them total submission to male desire. This religion of submission, the driving force in the lives of Walker's early female characters, earns Mem the title of "saint," the dubious honor accorded her by Grange, her husband's father, for her incredible feat of self-erasure. Mem's pathological passivity shocks the sensibilities. Advantaged by education and class, she chooses nonetheless to put herself in the service of an illiterate reprobate who gets his kicks from cutting her down to manageable size. Brownfield strips Mem of her language (forcing her to drop her "damn proper" idiom for "talk like the rest of us poor niggers"), her claim to her own body (by continuously beating and impregnating her), and, finally, her being (by murdering her). Like Margaret, Mem is no better than "an old no-count dog," deprived of the will to fight back by an urge to make Brownfield "feel a little bit like a man." The overwhelming sense of female victimization that permeates *The Third Life of Grange Copeland* is most likely one of the reasons why Walker called it "a grave book." Despite her inclusion of Ruth, the third-generation female who projects the self-confidence of a later day,

Walker does not escape the cultural guilt economy that trades black female identity for black male gratification.

The theme of thwarted black female identity continues in the short stories of *In Love & Trouble*. Here, too, the twin scourges of sexism and racism beat women to their knees where they remain, hopeless supplicants before a mercilessly brutal social structure. "Her Sweet Jerome" offers a haunting example of female self-destruction. Mrs. Jerome Franklin Washington III, referred to throughout the story as "she" (except for the one instance in which she calls herself by the coveted marital name), embodies the principle of self-negation. Lacking a name of her own, she has no recourse to an identity separate from her role as wife, a position she won only after a Herculean show of effort and which she is determined to keep at any cost. Not surprisingly, news that "her cute little man is sticking his finger into somebody else's pie" sends her reeling from her precarious perch into madness and death. By the time her frenzied search for her husband's lover ends in the shocking discovery of a pile of books rather than another woman, Mrs. Jerome Franklin Washington III has not only lost her reason but has transmogrified into a beast: "Her firm bulk became flabby. Her eyes were bloodshot and wild. She smelled bad from mouth and underarms and elsewhere . . . she has taken to grinding her teeth and tearing at her hair as she walked along." In the end, as she burns her determined and contingent self out of existence, the effect is not pathos but relief.

Marriage as entrapment is also the theme in "Roselily," a story of deep psychological turmoil framed by a seemingly benign social transaction. Roselily is getting married and upon the culture-bound text of wedding vows she inscribes her own text, one that indicts at once her culture for its offer of marriage as women's salvation and herself for believing in the efficacy of that idea. In her interior monologue we find Roselily's real story, the tale of a life crippled by loneliness, poverty, back-breaking labor, and the desperate search for escape. Rescue for this mother of four comes in the form of marriage to a man whose manner and religion spell domination. The married space, filled with images of her veiled face and promises of more babies, will be, as Roselily rightly intuits, just as confining as her beleaguered past. It will not allow her "to live for once" and yet it is her only chance at "respect" for herself and her children. As with Mem, there are intimations of a rebellious spirit in Roselily, manifested, for instance, in the desire "to strike [the preacher] out of the way, out of her light, with the back of her hand." But the blow is directed instead at herself in the final scene where, in a significant shift to an omniscient narrative perspective, we are shown Roselily, cowed and "feel[ing] ignorant, *wrong*, backward" as she walks behind her husband into a second round of bondage.

The female character in "Really Doesn't Crime Pay?" acts as spoil for two men: her husband, who married her only because her brown skin is the closest thing to the real but unattainable object of his desire, a white woman; and her lover, a phoney artist and plagiarist. The narrator (it is not clear if the name "Myrna," which appears in parenthesis below the title, is hers) is one of those silent and unsung black female artists Walker would later celebrate in the womanist prose of "In Search of Our Mothers' Gardens," but for now the character is a willing accomplice to the rape of her mind and body. For Ruel (her husband), she is a sex object to be made perpetually desirable with preening, perfumes, and lotions. Her "sweetened . . . body" is his play thing. Mordecai Rich, too, uses her body but it is her creative mind that serves him better. A writer without words of his own, he steals her story, publishes it in his name, and leaves town. Madness is the logical consequence of this symbolic silencing, and as the narrator attempts to saw off her husband's head in his sleep, it is clear that protest and resistance must replace passivity if the black woman is to survive. Her husband's murder averted, the narrator, therefore, finds another death-dealing act of protest: the birthcontrol pills she swallows "religiously" each day will certainly kill Ruel's chances for the children he so desperately wants. And in the end when she is "quite, quite tired of the sweet sweet smell of [her] body," she "will leave him . . . forever without once looking back."

Such signs of budding resistance in *In Love & Trouble* are few but their very presence amidst the intractable oppressive forces that govern the lives of these women suggests that their author is contemplating a re-evaluation. Walker's "personal historical view of Black women," notes Mary Helen Washington, "sees the experiences of Black women as a series of movements from a woman totally victimized by society and by men to a growing, developing woman whose consciousness allows her to have control over her life." Clearly, the goal of female self-understanding is not a crucial component of Walker's aesthetics in either *The Third Life of Grange Copeland* or *In Love & Trouble*; instead, these works mark, in Walker's trajectory of black womanhood, the mule-of-the-world stage in the development of black female consciousness. Lowest in the hierarchy of white and male social privilege, Walker's early women are, to use Washington's apt word, "suspended," caught between sexism and racism. This angle of Walker's artistic vision sheds light on her decision to expunge from the final version of *The Third Life of Grange Copeland* a first draft which "began with Ruth as a Civil Rights lawyer in Georgia going to rescue her father, Brownfield Copeland, from a drunken accident, and to have a confrontation with him." Such a beginning would have opened the window on an entirely different view of womanhood, the kind that will reach full flowering in *The Color*

Purple but is only slowly emerging on the pages of *The Third Life of Grange Copeland* and *In Love & Trouble*.

The new strain of black femaleness we get a peek at appears not only in Ruth (who, in her historically "correct" place as a third-generation woman, begins to claim the lost voice of her predecessors) but also in the weather-beaten women of *In Love & Trouble*. Like the powerful example of female subterfuge via denial of fertility in "Really, Doesn't Crime Pay?" the title character in "The Revenge of Hannah Kemhuff" exacts a heavy price from her white oppressor. When Sara Marie Sadler denies Hannah the chance to feed her starving self and children during the hunger-filled Depression simply because she looked neat in her hand-me-down clothes, Hannah loses everything she values: her children, her pride and hope, and her life. But with the last ounce of energy left in her withered body, she turns Tante Rosie's root-working magic on Sarah to make sure that her enemy is deprived of the right to exist, too. Hannah's revenge is a mild but potent act of self-affirmation; like the young woman who disobeys her father's command to give up her white lover in "The Child Who Favored Daughter," a refusal for which she pays with her life, or like the mother who rejects her daughter's new-found ideology of solipsism in "Everyday Use," Hannah is a harbinger of the reconstituted image of black womanhood found in Walker's later fiction.

Walker has criticized white American writers for "end[ing] their books and their characters' lives as if there were no better existence for which to struggle." Unlike black writers who strive toward "some kind of larger freedom," white writers, she says, tend to thick[en]" their writings with the "gloom of defeat." Of course, she is quick to point to the generalized character of her observation, noting that the comparison "perhaps does not really hold up at all." Walker's rethinking on this matter may have something to do not only with the weakness of her comparison but also with the suspicion that her own fiction, especially in its early stages, is as painful as, say, Faulkner's or O'Connor's. Her movement toward the womanist optimism of *The Color Purple* can be seen as simultaneously an acknowledgment and a rejection of the lure of defeat that permeates *The Third Life of Grange Copeland* and *In Love & Trouble*.

While Walker considers concrete experience invaluable to the creative process (many of her characters, including Celie, have real-life analogues and some of her stories are renditions of her mother's tales—part of her effort to legitimize the black female experience), she also believes, with Camus, that "though all is not well under the sun, history is not everything." But the re-creation of history *is*, for it allows "connections [to be] made . . . where none existed before, the straining to encompass in one's glance at the varied world the common thread, the unifying theme through immense diversity, a fearlessness of growth, of search, of looking, that enlarges the private and the public world." And so after capturing the poignant but narrow vista of recollected scenes from her native South in *The Third Life of Grange Copeland* and *In Love & Trouble*, Walker positions her creative lens for what she believes to be the hallmark of art, "the larger perspective." *The Color Purple* is the site of this diffuse creative activity but first the path must be cleared through *Meridian*.

Midway between despair and hope, *Meridian* is a novel that meets life at the cross-roads and agonizes over the road to be taken. Meridian Hill, the main character, is a curious amalgam of the traditional female of Walker's early fiction and the liberated woman of her later work. How to become the latter, that is, a self-constituting being, is the essence of her story. Meridian must claw her way through layers of culturally induced guilt to reach a convincing plateau of selfhood, a feat that paralyzes both her will and body and barely lifts her above empty despair. First is the guilt she must carry because her mother is not "a woman who should have had children." An ambitious and self-motivating woman, Meridian's mother in her early adulthood had embraced motherhood in order to find out the tantalizing secret behind the "mysterious inner life" of "the mothers of her pupils," women who seemed to have found contentment in the drudgery of their lives. What she discovered after six children was that her imaginings about these women had lured her siren-like into motherhood, a cultural institution that insists on female self-negation. It was not "euphoria" that gave these mothers the contented look, as Meridian's mother had previously surmised, but, rather a mind-binding pain carefully concealed from the world's judgment. Like them, having lost all claim to selfhood, "she was not even allowed to be resentful." The effect was the feeling of "being buried alive, walled away from her own life, brick by brick"; perishing in the process were her creativity and all traces of affection for all children, especially her own. Thus, "for stealing her mother's serenity, for shattering her mother's emerging self . . . Meridian felt guilty from the very first."

Meridian's second wave of guilt stems from the first: to prevent her son from robbing her of her own life, Meridian gives him away. Convinced that her act has saved two lives—hers and her son's, both of which she had wanted to terminate—Meridian is nonetheless wracked by "an almost primeval guilt" sanctioned by that stern, unyielding cult known as "Black Motherhood," whose tradition of self-sacrifice her mother had personified and Meridian now betrays by abandoning her son. The communal voice of condemnation, one that Shug Avery in *The Color Purple* would later simply ignore, follows her to Saxon College where she "curs[ed] her existence . . . that could not live up to the standard of motherhood that had gone before." But as thoughts of suicide give way to active participation in the struggle for racial equality,

Meridian begins to see a larger picture, one in which her act of betrayal, as well as the monument of black motherhood, pales beside the terrible reality of racial hatred.

The larger perspective provided by Saxon College and the civil rights movement also brings with it some self-understanding for Meridian. Her fear of sex, for instance, which had manifested itself earlier in her relationship with Eddie, her son's father, resurfaces in her brief romance with Truman as tangible evidence that she does not fill the stereotype of woman as object of male sexual gratification. Meridian had resisted Eddie, a man she did not love, with legs that looked "like somebody starched them shut." Truman seems to stand a better chance because with him she "felt she had discovered a missing sense" that she can gratify through "hot, quick, mindless" love-making with him. But sex with Truman turns out to be as mechanical as it was with Eddie; her mind oversees the process with vigilance and deliberation. Once again, the sex act leaves her unfulfilled and pregnant. This time, however, her speedy termination of both the pregnancy and the relationship with Truman point to an emerging sense of self as subject. When Truman returns to her with the directive, "*Have* my beautiful black babies," Meridian hears the male voice of authority that in an earlier time had blocked the growth of Margaret and Mem Copeland, and she reacts with swift vengeance:

> And she drew back her green book bag and began to hit him. She hit him three times before she even knew what was happening. Then she hit him again across the ear and a spiral from a tablet cut his cheek. Blood dripped onto his shirt. When she noticed the blood she turned and left him to the curiosity of the other students crowding there.

With this blood-letting ritual, Meridian posits herself as subject rather than object, but this act of hegemonic reversal proves costly. Retribution comes in the form of alienation and psychic disorientation. Her tenuous relation with the black community (she finds the God of the black church, for instance, incomprehensible), coupled with her lack of positive female role models (except for her father's grandmother, Feather Mae, whose religion of "physical ecstasy" she hopes to inculcate), assists her slide into voluntary solitariness. But even from here, Meridian intends to engage the world on her own terms. One-by-one she sheds the features of male-structured identity—status, material comfort, romantic love, respect for the law—for a self-definition located in challenge and self-sacrifice.

As Meridian throws her starved and emaciated body in front of an army tank in an effort to prevent school children from viewing the body of

Marilene O'Shay, murdered by her jealous husband, or as she comforts Lynne Rabinowitz, the woman Truman married and has abandoned to return to the love he thinks he and Meridian shared, it is obvious that the logic of her self-identity defies conventional thinking on womanhood. As Anne Marion terminates her friendship with Meridian, she captures the sense of bafflement and misunderstanding that Meridian's problematic new self provokes: "Meridian, I can not afford to love you. Like the idea of suffering itself, you are obsolete." This remark is only half-true. That side of Meridian that insists on self-punishment is obviously obsolete, for it is a throwback to a time when women like Margaret or Mem Copeland cast themselves as willing victims. But there is another side to Meridian: that which has engendered an alternative economy of selfhood, namely the will to act on her own behalf. As if unable to withstand the weight of this momentous act of defiance, Meridian's (female) body literally disintegrates after it is taken over by a mysterious disease referred to only as "her illness." But it is a bold spirit that chafes beneath the husk that remains to her, a spirit strengthened by a new self-concept: "For she understood, finally, that the respect she owed her life was to continue, against whatever obstacles, to live it, and not to give up any particle of it, without a fight to the death, preferably *not* her own." Here, indeed, is the blueprint for the brave new world to be ushered in *The Color Purple*.

You Can't Keep a Good Woman Down, Walker's second collection of short stories, serves as a test site for the theme of female liberation. But a disproportionate emphasis on such trendy aspects of the women's movement as pornography, abortion, and rape gives these stories a thick polemical flavor, relieved neither by the thematic richness of *In Love & Trouble* nor the subtle complexity of *Meridian*. With such titles as "How Did I Get Away with Killing One of the Biggest Lawyers in the State? It Was Easy," "Porn," "The Abortion," and "You Can't Keep a Good Woman Down," Walker not only captures the prevailing mood of the times but also seems intent that the psychological distance between the free spirits in this collection and their fettered predecessors from *In Love & Trouble* will not go unnoticed. In "The Abortion" the protagonist's attitude toward the self/other dichotomy, previously a burden for Walker's female characters, speaks to the topical character (as well as the undecorated literalness) of these stories. Lying in a recovery room after aborting her child, Imani intones: "Well . . . it was you or me, Kiddo, and I chose me." Self-abnegation is a thing of the past for this group of women and they make no bones about it.

If female autonomy as represented in *You Can't Keep a Good Woman Down* has an aesthetically grating effect, in *The Color Purple* it receives its finest artistic expression, mainly because it is conjoined with another cherished idea of Walker's, namely, life as a harmonious whole. In the essay

"Saving the Life That Is Your Own" Walker writes: "It has been said that someone asked Toni Morrison why she writes the kind of books she writes, and that she replied: 'Because they are the kind of books I want to read.' This remains my favorite reply to that kind of question." *The Color Purple*, then, like Morrison's *Sula*, is a book Walker had to write. Indeed it is a book toward which she had been philosophically orienting herself throughout her writing career.

Two habits of thought led Walker irreversibly to *The Color Purple*: an insatiable curiosity that borders on rebelliousness, and an unshakable belief in the interrelatedness of the multifarious strands of existence. Walker's essays provide valuable insight into these shaping forces. Regarding her penchant for the curious, she writes: "Curiosity is my natural state and has led me headlong into every worthwhile experience (never mind the others) I have ever had." Apart from engendering a desire for exploration (resulting in trips to Africa, Cuba, China, Europe, Zora Neale Hurston's grave site, and the homes of Flannery O'Connor and William Faulkner), Walker's curious mind is also drawn to what Barbara Christian calls "the forbidden." Taboo has always held a fascination for Walker because it means another challenge that she must meet. In college, for instance, confronted with the law prohibiting racial mixing, social and genetic, Walker recalls in *Living by the Word* that she responded in characteristic fashion: "I actively combatted it by having numerous friendships with white women and children, and by dating white men. I later married, had a child by, and divorced a white man."

Walker's curiosity is an integral element in her quest for truth. Dissatisfied with the limited vision of existing systems of knowledge, she feels the need for a new truth, one that will come about "only . . . when all the sides of the story are put together, and all their different meanings make one new one." This re-made story will affirm the oneness or "wholeness" of life, the connectedness of all living forms. With the intensity of a Romantic, Walker has managed to turn the idea of the unity of nature into a personal religion. It permeates her poetry and prose. Commenting on the relations between Blacks and Jews, for example, she writes: "Every affront to human dignity necessarily affects me as a human being on the planet, because I know every single thing on earth is connected." Walker's neo-pantheistic message of the "world [as] God" and "full humanity . . . [as] a state of oneness with all things" reaches evangelistic heights in the essay "The Universe Responds," in which she sums up an account of a stray dog with this evocation:

> I think I am telling you that the animals of the planet are in desperate peril, and that they are fully aware of this. No less than human beings are doing in all parts of the world, they are

seeking sanctuary. But I am also telling you that we are connected to them at least as intimately as we are connected to trees. Without plant life human beings could not breathe. Plants produce oxygen. Without free animal life I believe we will lose the spiritual equivalent of oxygen. "Magic," intuitions, sheer astonishment at the forms the Universe devises in which to express life—itself—will no longer be able to breathe in us.

The human link in this ecological chain of being is of particular concern to Walker. It is humans, in her view, who pose a threat to the chain because of their proclivity for fragmentation: "Everything around me is split up, deliberately split up. History split up, literature split up, and people are split up too. It makes people do ignorant things." Walker sees an irony in this separatist tendency, based on her contention that genetically pure individuals or racial groups are a rarity. She cites her own mixed ancestry—African, Cherokee, Indian, and white—as an example of the inherently heterogeneous characteristic of human beings, and decries America's reluctance to come to terms with its consanguinity as the root cause of its spiritual dis-ease:

> One of the reasons our country seems so purposeless (except where money is concerned) is that Americans, even (and perhaps especially) genetically, have been kept from acknowledging and being who they really are. There are fewer "white" people in America, for instance, and even fewer "black" ones. This reality is a metaphor for countless other areas of delusion. In our diversity we have been one people— just as the peoples of the world are one people—even when the most vicious laws of separation have forced us to believe we are not.

Womanist ideology, therefore, born out of Walker's insistence on new ways of perceiving self and other, is not revisionist, but revolutionary. Its goal is change and its target the "splits" of race, sex, and class that divide humanity. *The Color Purple*, which enacts this revolutionary vision, is the kind of book that, according to Christine Froula, Woolf in 1931 had predicted would emerge from the female unconscious, but only after fifty years. Although Walker assigns *The Color Purple* to the genre of historical novel, the text works more to subvert rather than exemplify that male-identified category. In a clever literary move, Walker utilizes the traditional historical model only to explode it. Rape, racial and sexual oppression, and colonialism position themselves in the novel as cultural imperatives to give the impression of business as usual. However, slowly but persistently these structures are undermined and by the end of the novel their raison d'etre has been totally invalidated and supplanted by the foundations of a moral imperative. As Froula accurately points out, *The Color Purple* "undoes the patriarchal cultural order and builds upon new ground."

One of the pillars of the patriarchal stronghold brought down in the novel is the idea of woman as marginal. In the beginning of the novel, Celie, the fourteen-year-old protagonist, is locked within a cultural text that defines her as an object. Raped, beaten, silenced, and sold into marital slavery by the man she thinks is her father, Celie begins to doubt her humanity, and as her debasement continues in the hands of Mr. _____, she actually entertains thoughts of self-erasure: "He beat me like he beat the children . . . I make myself wood. I say to myself, Celie, you a tree. That's how come I know trees fear man." Rendered nonhuman by patriarchal law, Celie is deprived even of the self-protective mechanism of anger, a right every human being exercises in the event of an assault to her/his personhood. Listening to Sofia's personal narrative of the justifiable use of anger, Celie responds:

> I can't even remember the last time I felt mad . . . I used to get mad at my mammy cause she put a lot of work on me. Then I see how sick she is. Couldn't stay mad at her. Couldn't be mad at my daddy cause he my daddy. Bible say, Honor father and mother no matter what. Then after while every time I got mad, or start to feel mad, I got sick. Felt like throwing up . . . Then I start to feel nothing at all.

Celie's inscription as object is at once metaphoric and literal.

Embedded within this cultural text, however, is a subtext that reveals Celie as patently human and female. Far from being "dumb," as her Pa has labeled her, Celie is intelligent, perceptive and creative. For instance, even though she is too young to understand the full implications of her rape by Pa, she knows enough to steer her sister, Nettie, away from a similar fate. Further, during an accidental encounter with Olivia, the infant daughter whom Pa gave away, Celie's innate intelligence allows her to immediately recognize her own child. In addition, Celie possesses a creative core that manifests itself not only in quilt-making but also in a poetic imagination. Shug's flamboyance, for example, inspires Celie to write that "she look so stylish it like the trees all around the house draw themself up for a better look." And later, trying to capture the wicked side of Shug's personality, Celie notes, "But evil all over her today. She smile, like a razor opening." Harpo's despondency over his inability to tame Sofia is conveyed with the same richness of metaphor: "Harpo sit on the steps acting like he don't care. . . . He look out toward the creek every once in a while and whistle a little tune. But it nothing compared to the way he usually whistle. His little whistle sound like it lost way down in a jar, and the jar in the bottom of the creek." Celie's gift for words is evident throughout the text. Her letters bear the imprint of a keen, perceptive mind, one that is capable of interpreting (not just documenting) reality.

Also contrary to the predominating cultural text, Celie is sexually alive. As a victim of extended rape—first by Pa and then by Albert, who "go[es] to the toilet on [her]"—she is expected to be drained of any sexual desire of her own. Indeed, her premature menopause, probably induced by the trauma of sexual abuse, is read as a symbol of her de-sexing. In the minds of Pa and Mr. _____, Celie is neither a man nor, devoid of her periods, a woman. Therefore, for Pa she is a beast of burden that is auctioned off to the first bidder, and for Mr. _____, who purchases her, she is a sperm repository. But far from being sexually inert, Celie is ripe with desire to be spent not on a man ("I don't even look at mens," she confesses) but on Shug Avery ("The most beautiful woman I ever saw"). Shug's picture excites her and she almost loses control while bathing Shug's sick but tantalizing body: "First time I got the full sight of Shug Avery long black body with it black plum nipples, look like her mouth, I thought I had turned into a man." But unlike a man who at such a moment would most likely think of rape, the supreme act of female devaluation, Celie raises physical desire to the level of the spiritual: "I wash her body, it feel like I'm praying. My hands tremble and my breath short." The fact is that though in the patriarchal sexual economy Pa can describe Celie as no longer "fresh," according to Shug, she is "still a virgin," and making love to Shug is tantamount to her first sexual act. That Celie's sexuality, like her humanity, can remain intact under a prolonged male siege is evidence that contradicts and invalidates her dominant image as pathological victim.

Celie's transgressive act of desire puts into proper prospective Clarissa's furtive lesbianism in *Mrs. Dalloway*. The similarities in the sexual geographies of these women are so striking as to reward the effort to distinguish between their attempts to establish a radical sexuality. Like Celie, Clarissa incarnates a homoerotic force threatened to be contained by marriage and motherhood, both of which act as encroachments that wreak havoc on their bodies; Clarissa is left pale and weak by influenza and Celie enters early menopause. Ironically, the heterosexist configuration is broken with the birthing process, reconfirming the virginity of both women. Clarissa "could not dispel a virginity preserved through childbirth which clung to her like a sheet" and Celie is said to be "still a virgin" after two children with Pa and sexual experiences with Mr. _____ during which she renders herself invisible. Sexually revived, Celie convincingly resists patriarchal reappropriation, as she settles in a libidinal economy in which coupling is for pleasure. On the contrary, Clarissa's expression and subsequent denial of her passion for Sally Seton, begins the process by which she sees her (sexual) self through the distorting lense of convention. As "the perfect hostess," Clarissa is locked into a vicious matrix of libidinal renunciation and maintenance of a sexless class order, a sado-masochistic act symbolized by her sheathed (and sheeted, postnatal) virginity. Accorded the same sexual advantage, Celie and Clarissa make different choices that betray their (and their creators') differing relations to the patriarchal order.

In the textual configuration of sexual politics, Sofia and Shug abandon Meridian's subterfuge and Celie's subtlety for the tactics of confrontation. Armed with a self-definition that defies male-determined social categorization, Sofia and Shug claim the center as the space to enact their humanity, vigorously resisting any attempt to be pulled into the margins. Having cut her way through layers of male intransigence, Sofia, for instance, believes she has earned her place in the center: "All my life I had to fight. I had to fight my daddy. I had to fight my brothers. I had to fight my cousins and my uncles. A girl child ain't safe in a family of men." And in the extended "family of men," Harpo, Sofia's husband, intends to keep her under male tyranny. But his attempt, inspired by his father's example, is met with swift retaliation: "Next time us see Harpo his face a mess of bruises. His lip cut. One of his eyes shut like a fist. He walk stiff and say his teef ache." Clearly, the taming of Sofia is not as easy as Harpo had been led to think.

Shug Avery is equally unmalleable; in her case no one has dared pin her down to a preconceived idea of her identity because in word and deed she is determined to remain unshackled. She embodies the truth contained in her advice to Celie: "You have to git man off your eyeball, before you can see anything a'tall." Shug does not compartmentalize reality. Rather, she sees it as a continuum that in its capaciousness allows her to love (sexually) man and woman, victim and victimizer (Celie and Albert); to relegate the care of her children to someone else without feeling guilty (unlike Meridian or Woolf's Clarissa); and to conceive of God as "everything . . . that is ever was or ever will be." Shug, like Morrison's Sula, "has been endowed with dimensions of other possibility" and therefore "whatever she is, is a matter of her own choices." This is the state of selfhood that Meridian aspired toward but could not attain because the scapegoat mentality that derives from female secondariness (the type Kate Armstrong exhibited in her obsessive desire to please) undermined her potential.

Unburdened by guilt or any of the cultural strictures designed to constrain women, Shug is the quintessential free spirit. She sees nothing wrong, for instance, in liking Anna Julia and at the same time hurting her by stealing her husband (Albert). And if she can share Albert with Celie, why should she not share Celie with Albert? Although falling in love with nineteen-year-old Germaine, a "child . . . a third of my age," scares Shug as much as it jolts Celie, it is another experience that has been dropped on Shug's path and she will not walk away from it. Multiple, even chaotic, experience is her domain. She sums up her liberationist philosophy in her response to Albert's declaration that society will condemn Celie if she abandons her housekeeping chores and runs off to Memphis: "Why any woman give a shit what people think is it mystery to me." Other not-so-bold women rally around this battle cry: Celie finally breaks out of her cocoon with self-prophesying words: "I'm pore, I'm black, I may be ugly and can't cook . . . But I'm here," and Mary Agnes expresses herself in song and with Grady, Shug's husband. It is clear from these acts of self-affirmation that Walker is moving us from one reality into another.

In Walker's womanist universe the collapse of male-erected boundaries that separate woman from her self is a necessary first step toward coalition-building. Women must themselves be whole before they can be part of a wholeness. Speech or the end of silence is the key marker of female selfhood. As bell hooks puts it, "Silence is the condition of one who has been dominated, made an object; talk is the mark of freeing, of making one subject." With their voice no longer dammed up, women's creativity, which before appeared in trickles, explodes, and in the place of "sister's choice," the quilt Celie was unsure she and Sofia could perfect, we have a human quilt in which segmented realities of sex, race, and culture are woven into one, unbroken pattern. Celie, for example, exercises the power of voice by speaking the truth to Albert, who had silenced her and hid Nettie's letters away from her. "Until you do right by me," she tells him, "everything you touch will crumble." And as Celie's and Albert's fates take different turns—Celie flourishing both creatively and financially in Folkspants, Unlimited, her Memphis-based business, while Albert wallows in filth and lassitude—it is clear that Celie's "curse" has a moral authority that must be reckoned with. Albert's gradual understanding of the new dispensation of peaceful coexistence releases him from "meanness" that "kill[s]" into a human community of love where he learns that life is something to be enriched, not diminished. He revives his sewing talent, which has been buried under years of masculine posturing, becomes an avid shell collector, participates in the communal feeding of yam to Henrietta, who needs it to combat a rare blood disease, and learns to listen. Albert sums up his transformation in a conversation with Celie: "I'm satisfied this the first time I ever lived on Earth as a natural man. It feel like a new experience." "Natural" man, in Walker's cosmology, has shed his gender-based superiority complex and is ready to coexist with "natural" woman, who no longer sees herself as inferior.

If Celie's voice is instrumental in the resolution of sexual difference, Sofia's plays a key role in bridging the racial gap. Against life-threatening odds, Sofia claims her right to speech as she defends her humanity against a remark from the mayor's wife and her body from assault by the mayor. These two bigots share a racial ideology designed to keep Sofia in eternal serfdom as surely as Albert's sexist mentality held Celie in vassalage. Sofia is savagely beaten, imprisoned, and confined to servitude in the mayor's household, the very fate she had tried to resist. As her instinct for revenge simmers down and she slowly repairs her voice, Sofia feels it is time to set the racial record straight. The occasion for speaking the truth presents itself through Eleanor Jane, the mayor's daughter, who admits to her husband that "Sofia raise me, practically." When Eleanor Jane demands of Sofia a confession of love for her son, Reynolds Stanley Earl, she is in fact asking for Sofia to dismiss the feelings of hurt and humiliation that have built up over a period of eleven-and-a-half years of servitude and, instead, to embrace her oppressors as though they were her benefactors. This reality is not lost on Sofia and she responds appropriately: "No ma'am . . . I do not love Reynolds Stanley Earl." Pressed further, she adds, "I don't feel nothing about him at all. I don't love him, I don't hate him." When Eleanor Jane accuses her of being "unnatural" and unlike "the other colored women [who] love children," Sofia hammers back with an even more painful truth: "I love children . . . But all the colored that say they love yours is lying" because they can no more love their oppressor, which is what young Reynolds will become when he grows up, than they can "the cotton gin," the symbol of their oppression.

This exchange between the races, like its sexual counterpart between Celie and Albert, is a necessary preamble to Walker's new constitution, which seeks a peaceful cohabitation of human beings. It clears the air for the settling of differences, because the point Sofia hopes to get across to Eleanor Jane is that although she has been ground down by her oppressors, she has shown a great deal of humanity by the mere fact that she harbors no hate for them. Asking her for love, therefore, is a thinly disguised act of subjugation because it denies Sofia the right to anger as surely as she had earlier been denied the right to speech. Eleanor Jane must have gotten the message, because by the end of the novel she, like Albert, has broken away from self-concern to participate in the urgent matter of feeding Henrietta the life-saving yam diet. And for the unconverted who ask, "Whoever heard of a white woman working for niggers?" after they hear that she is helping Sofia run Celie's shop, Eleanor Jane has a question of her own: "Who ever heard of somebody like Sofia working for trash." Having heard the whole of Sofia's story from her mother, Eleanor Jane is now in a position to understand that differences need not cancel out mutual respect,

The theme of racial and sexual reconstruction is played out on a large canvas in *The Color Purple*. Nettie's retelling of the African story contains some equally harsh truths, but like the ones told to Albert and Eleanor Jane, hers, too, clear the way for reconciliation. On the racial front, European mythologizing of Africa and its people as backward and mired in poverty is revised to reveal Europe as the cause of the problem it blames the victims for. Not only did Europe rob Africa of priceless art and artifacts that fill up many a museum in the West, but Europe is also responsible for the destruction of African cities and the enslavement of "millions and millions of Africans." The economic rape of Africa continues as European companies push Africans out of the land, destroying their way of life in the process, to make room for rubber and cacao trees, the goods of the marketplace. From this angle, therefore, the philanthropy of such westerners as Doris Baines, who sent two young African girls to England to study medicine and agriculture and "built a hospital, a grammar school [and a] college" in her home town, seems inconsequential. In Walker's womanist perspective, however, Doris Baines sketches a picture of hope for the races as she heads for England with her "grandchild" Harold, the son of one of the young women she had helped to educate, by her side. It seems as if Doris has had time to reconsider her earlier colonialist belief that "an African daisy and an English daisy are both flowers but totally different kinds."

Just as Europe's racial myths are challenged in the novel, so are Africa's sexist attitudes held up to public view. The oppressive African mentality, according to Walker, is rooted in self-centeredness, and sexist Africans are as guilty of this crime as are racist (American) whites. "I think Africans are very much like white people back home," Nettie writes, "in that they think they are the center of the universe and that everything that is done is done for them." Through Nettie, Walker, true to her womanist courage, chastises African men for their subjugation of women. So deeply has the belief in male dominance—with female subordination as its corollary—been ingrained in men and women that a mother can say about her girl-child: "A girl is nothing to herself; only to her husband can she become something," which is, of course, "the mother of his children." Thus education is reserved for boys who, when they become men, will care for their wives. The idea of a dependent woman is fixed in the Olinka psyche. "There is always someone to look after Olinka Woman," Tashi's father declares, that "someone" being, of course, a man. This sexually oppressive climate replicates the one that nearly stunted Celie's and Nettie's growth under Pa, as Nettie rightly observes: "There is a way that the men speak to women that reminds me too much of Pa. They listen just long enough to issue instructions. They don't even look at women when women are speaking." Those women, such as Tashi's aunt, who fight against this cultural effort to reduce them to ciphers, are sold into slavery, an act that completely effaces their individuality.

Like the system that imprisoned Celie, this canvas of overwhelming masculinity does not escape womanism's brush of change. Young Tashi, reincarnating her aunt's fighting spirit, begins to reveal signs of interiority which are misread in this phallic economy as her slowly "becoming someone else." Tashi, in fact, molds a personality uniquely her own, and the true test of her liberation comes with her rejection of Adam's marriage proposal because of her fear that in America Adam would want to turn her into someone else—a skimpily dressed, light-skinned (most likely, bleached) woman without a scarred face. Tashi thus sets the terms of marital agreement: she will not trade in her individuality—"the scarification marks on her cheeks" or her black skin, for example—for love. That Adam's reassurance of Tashi goes beyond the promise of eternal fidelity to the scarring of his own face is an indication that relations between women and men have reached a new threshold. Both offshoots of rigidly gendered societies, Tashi and Adam symbolize an emergent sexual consciousness that allows for difference without penalty or privilege.

"Womanist is to feminist as purple is to lavender," Walker writes in *In Search of Our Mothers' Gardens*. Appearing at the end of a list of womanist determinants, this metaphor is intended as a visual illustration of the ideological gap between womanism and feminism. The shade of difference is a matter of depth or intensity. While both modes of thought originate from the same wellspring of resistance to patriarchal domination, womanism intensifies the struggle by fighting from several fronts because it believes that patriarchy, like the Gorgon, is many-headed. More than simply being aware of the "multiple jeopardies of race and class, not the singular one of sexual inequality," the womanist writer is artistically committed to a radical restructuring of society that will allow for the dissolution of boundaries of race, sex and class. What Froula calls "Walker's recreated universe" in *The Color Purple* is a womanist paradigm that offers a rigorous critique of white feminist practices. Complicity in patriarchal thought, the Achilles' heel of the woman writer, is particularly acute in Woolf and Drabble, for example, and the diluted resistance it engenders in their fiction is a blind spot in the white feminist aesthetic that womanism intends to illuminate.

However, while this critique of mainstream feminism rests on legitimate grounds, the *carpe diem* urgency of womanism's dismantle-and-rebuild message seems to overlook Walker's own arduous progress toward her liberatory aesthetic. In other words, Walker's fiction reveals that her feet were held to patriarchal fire long enough for her to be able to appreciate the degree to which the female psyche has been scarred by marginality. The creative imagination of both black and white women has been held captive by the masculine complex (as studies such as Hazel Carby's *Reconstructing Womanhood* and Sandra Gilbert and Susan Gubar's *The Madwoman in the Attic* affirm) and escape routes have often been short-circuited by such other social exigencies as race and class. There is no doubt that Walker has reached a clearing in *The Color Purple*, a space where female subjectivity redefines itself as autonomous and at the same time "as self in relationship." Her creative lens has long pointed in this direction but, as I have demonstrated hers has been an odyssey fraught with doubt, despair, and hope. The picture of Meridian, finally self affirming but totally alienated, that ends that novel stands in sharp contradistinction to the portrait of celebration which rounds off *The Color Purple*.

However, the effort expended toward the achievement of womanism's holistic worldview by no means minimizes its success. The womanist perspective is an important contribution to the feminist project. As Linda Alcoff puts it, "You cannot mobilize a movement that is only and always against: you must have a positive alternative, a vision of a better future that can motivate people to sacrifice their time and energy toward its realization." That the womanist goal holds such a vision is indisputable. What is problematic is the essentialist implication of womanism's self-definition. A womanist as "black feminist" or "feminist of color" not only excludes white feminists whose creative vision approximates the womanist ideal (Agnes Smedley, for example) or those who might choose to incorporate aspects of womanism in their writing, especially in the wake of the recent push for inclusiveness in feminist theory. It also assumes that by virtue of being black or nonwhite, a feminist is necessarily womanist. The example of Buchi Emecheta, which is the subject of the next chapter, seems to complicate Walker's effort to racially limit the womanist ethic.

LINDA SELZER

Race and Domesticity in The Color Purple

An important juncture in Alice Walker's *The Color Purple* is reached when Celie first recovers the missing letters from her long-lost sister Nettie. This discovery not only signals the introduction of a new narrator to this epistolary novel but also begins the transformation of Celie from writer to reader. Indeed, the passage in which Celie struggles to puzzle out the markings on her first envelope from Nettie provides a concrete illustration of both Celie's particular horizon of interpretation and Walker's chosen approach to the epistolary form:

> Saturday morning Shug put Nettie letter in my lap. Little fat queen of England stamps on it, plus stamps that got peanuts, coconuts, rubber trees and say Africa. I don't know where England at. Don't know where Africa at either. So I still don't know where Nettie at.

Revealing Celie's ignorance of even the most rudimentary outlines of the larger world, this passage clearly defines the "domestic" site she occupies as the novel's main narrator. In particular, the difficulty Celie has interpreting this envelope underscores her tendency to understand events in terms of

From *African American Review* 29, no. 1 (Spring 1995). © 1995 Indiana State University.

personal consequences rather than political categories. What matters about not knowing "where Africa at"—according to Celie—is not knowing "where Nettie at." By clarifying Celie's characteristic angle of vision, this passage highlights the intensely personal perspective that Walker brings to her tale of sexual oppression—a perspective that accounts in large part for the emotional power of the text.

But Walker's privileging of the domestic perspective of her narrators has also been judged to have other effects on the text. Indeed, critics from various aesthetic and political camps have commented on what they perceive as a tension between public and private discourse in the novel. Thus, in analyzing Celie's representation of national identity, Lauren Berlant identifies a separation of "aesthetic" and "political" discourses in the novel and concludes that Celie's narrative ultimately emphasizes "individual essence in false opposition to institutional history." Revealing a very different political agenda in his attacks on the novel's womanist stance, George Stade also points to a tension between personal and public elements in the text when he criticizes the novel's "narcissism" and its "championing of domesticity over the public world of masculine power plays." Finally, in praising Walker's handling of sexual oppression, Elliott Butler-Evans argues that Celie's personal letters serve precisely as a "textual strategy by which the larger African-American history, focused on racial conflict and struggle, can be marginalized by its absence from the narration."

By counterposing personal and public discourse in the novel, these critics could be said to have problematized the narrative's domestic perspective by suggesting that Walker's chosen treatment of the constricted viewpoint of an uneducated country woman—a woman who admits that she doesn't even know "where Africa at"—may also constrict the novel's ability to analyze issues of "race" and class. Thus Butler-Evans finds that Celie's "private life preempts the exploration of the public lives of blacks," while Berlant argues that Celie's family-oriented point of view and modes of expression can displace race and class analyses to the point that the "nonbiological abstraction of class relations virtually disappears." And in a strongly worded rejection of the novel as "revolutionary literature," bell hooks charges that the focus upon Celie's sexual oppression ultimately deemphasizes the "collective plight of black people" and "invalidates . . . the racial agenda" of the slave narrative tradition that it draws upon. In short, to many readers of *The Color Purple*, the text's ability to expose sexual oppression seems to come *at the expense of* its ability to analyze issues of race and class.

But it seems to me that an examination of the representation of race in the novel leads to another conclusion: Walker's mastery of the epistolary form is revealed precisely by her ability to maintain the integrity of Celie's and Nettie's domestic perspectives even as she simultaneously undertakes an extended critique of race relations, and especially of racial integration. In particular, Walker's domestic novel engages issues of race and class through two important narrative strategies: the development of an embedded narrative line that offers a post-colonial perspective on the action, and the use of "family relations"—or kinship—as a carefully elaborated textual trope for race relations. These strategies enable Walker to foreground the personal histories of her narrators while placing those histories firmly within a wider context of race and class.

Both the novel's so-called "restriction of focus to Celie's consciousness" and one way in which Walker's narratology complicates that perspective are illustrated by the passage quoted above. Celie's difficulty interpreting the envelope sent by Nettie at first only seems to support the claim that her domestic perspective "erases" race and class concerns from the narrative. But if this short passage delineates Celie's particular angle of vision, it also introduces textual features that invite readers to resituate her narration within a larger discourse of race and class. For where Celie sees only a "fat little queen of England," readers who recognize Queen Victoria immediately historicize the passage. And if the juxtaposition of the two stamps on the envelope—England's showcasing royalty, Africa's complete with rubber trees—suggests to Celie nothing but her own ignorance, to other readers the two images serve as a clear reminder of imperialism. Thus Africa, mentioned by name for the first time in this passage, enters the novel already situated within the context of colonialism. Importantly, Walker remains true to Celie's character even as she recontextualizes the young woman's perspective, because the features of the envelope Celie focuses upon are entirely natural ones for her to notice, even though they are politically charged in ways that other features would not be (for example, Celie might have been struck by more purely personal—and more conventional—details, such as the familiar shape of her sister's handwriting). Embedded throughout *The Color Purple*, narrative features with clear political and historical associations like these complicate the novel's point of view by inviting a post-colonial perspective on the action and by creating a layered narrative line that is used for different technical effects and thematic purposes. That Celie herself is not always aware of the full political implications of her narration (although she becomes increasingly so as the novel progresses) no more erases the critique of race and class from the text than Huck's naïveté in *Huckleberry Finn* constricts that work's social criticism to the boy's opinions. This individual letter from Nettie thus provides readers with a textual analogue for the novel's larger epistolary form, illustrating one way in which the novel's domestic perspective is clearly "stamped" with signs of race and class.

But it is not only through such narrative indirection and recontextualization that the novel engages issues of race and class. Walker's domestic narrative undertakes a sustained analysis of race through the careful development of family relationships—or kinship—as an extended textual trope for race relations. Any attempt to oppose political and personal discourses in the novel collapses when one recognizes that the narrative adopts the discourse of family relations both to establish a "domestic ideal" for racial integration and to problematize that ideal through the analysis of specific integrated family groupings in Africa and America.

I. "She says an African daisy and an English daisy are both flowers, but totally different kinds"

Important throughout the narrative, the kinship trope for race relations is articulated most explicitly late in the novel when a mature Celie and a reformed Albert enjoy some communal sewing and conversation. Celie herself raises the issue of racial conflict by drawing on the Olinka "Adam" story that has been handed down to her through Nettie's letters. Beginning with the explanation that ". . . white people is black peoples children," the Olinka narrative provides an analysis of race relations expressed explicitly in terms of kinship.

According to the Olinka creation narrative, Adam was not the first man but the first white man born to an Olinka woman to be cast out for his nakedness—or for being "colorless." The result of this rejection was the fallen world of racial conflict, since the outcast children were, in Celie's words, "so mad to git throwed out and told they was naked they made up they minds to crush us wherever they find us, same as they would a snake." Offered specifically as an alternative to the Judeo-Christian account of Adam, this parable also offers readers an alternative account of Original Sin—defined not in terms of appropriating knowledge or resisting authority but precisely in terms of breaking kinship bonds: "What they did, these Olinka peoples, was throw out they own children, just cause they was a little different." Significantly, by retelling the Olinka narrative, Celie is able to express naturally some rather sophisticated ideas concerning the social construction of racial inferiority, since the myth defines that inferiority as a construct of power relations that will change over time. For the Olinka believe that someday the whites will "kill off so much of the earth and the colored that everybody gon hate them just like they hate us today. Then they will become the new serpent."

The Olinka creation narrative also raises a question central to the novel's larger design: Is progress in race relations possible? Some Olinka, notes Celie, answer this question by predicting that the cycle of discrimination will repeat itself endlessly, that ". . . life will just go on and on like this forever," with first one race in the position of the oppressor and then the other. But others believe that progress in racial harmony is possible—that Original Sin may be ameliorated—through a new valorization of kinship bonds: ". . . the only way to stop making somebody the serpent is for everybody to accept everybody else as a child of God, or one mother's children, no matter what they look like or how they act." These latter Olinka, then, express a *domestic ideal* for race relations, one that counters the sin of discrimination—based on an ideology of essential difference—with an ethic of acceptance that is grounded upon a recognition of relation, or kinship.

But the universalist ethos of the domestic ideal for race relations is put to the test by the larger narrative's development of historically situated, integrated kinship groupings in both Africa and America. Of particular importance are two family groupings: the white missionary Doris Baines and her black African grandchild in Africa, and Sophia and her white charge Miss Eleanor Jane in America. In both cases the specific integrated domestic groupings serve to expose and to critique the larger pattern of racial integration found in their respective countries.

Nettie meets Doris and her adopted grandson on a trip from Africa to seek help for the recently displaced Olinka in England, a trip Nettie calls "incredible" precisely because of the presence of an integrated family on board ship: It was "impossible to ignore the presence of an aging white woman accompanied by a small black child. The ship was in a tither. Each day she and the child walked about the deck alone, groups of white people falling into silence as they passed." Compared to the overtly racist actions of the other whites who ostracize Doris and her grandson, the English missionary's relationship with the boy at first seems in keeping with the ethic of treating all people as "one mother's children." Indeed, Doris describes her years as the boy's "grand*mama*" as "the happiest" years of her life. Furthermore, Doris's relationship with the African villagers also seems preferable to that of other white missionaries because, rather than wanting to convert "the heathen," she sees "nothing wrong with them" in the first place.

But the relationship between the white woman and her African grandson is actually far from ideal, and Nettie's letters subtly question the quality of their "kinship." If the boy seems "fond of his grandmother"—and, Nettie adds, "used to her"—he is also strangely reticent in her presence and reacts to Doris's conversation with "soberly observant speechlessness." In contrast, the boy opens up around Adam and Olivia, suggesting that he may feel more at home with the transplanted black Americans than with his white grandmother. Indeed, the boy's subdued behavior around his grandmother raises questions about the possibility of kinship across racial lines, while his ease with the black Americans suggests that feelings of kinship occur almost spontaneously within racial groups.

The nature of Doris's honorary "kinship" with the Akwee villagers is questioned more seriously still, beginning with her reasons for taking up missionary work in the first place. As a young woman Doris decided to become a missionary not out of a desire to help others but in order to escape the rarefied atmosphere of upper-class England and the probability of her eventual marriage to one of her many "milkfed" suitors, "each one more boring than the last." Although Doris describes her decision to go to Africa as an attempt to escape the stultifying roles available to women in English society, it is important to note that Nettie does not take Doris's hardships very seriously and draws upon fairy-tale rhetoric to parody the woman's upper-class tribulations: "She was born to great wealth in England. Her father was Lord Somebody or Other. They were forever giving or attending boring parties that were not fun." From Nettie's perspective as a black woman familiar with the trials of the displaced Olinka, Doris's aristocratic troubles seem small indeed, and Nettie further trivializes the white woman's decision to become a missionary by emphasizing that the idea struck Doris one evening when she "was getting ready for yet another tedious date."

The self-interest that prompts Doris to become a missionary also characterizes the relationship she establishes with the Akwee upon her arrival in Africa. There she uses her wealth to set up an ostensibly reciprocal arrangement that in fact reflects her imperial power to buy whatever she wants: "Within a year everything as far as me and the heathen were concerned ran like clockwork. I told them right off that their souls were no concern of mine, that I wanted to write books and not be disturbed. For this pleasure I was prepared to pay. Rather handsomely." Described as a mechanism that runs "like clockwork," Doris's relationship to the Akwee clearly falls short of the maternal ideal for race relations expressed in the Olinka myths. In fact, Doris's relationship to the villagers is decidedly *pa*ternal from the outset, since her formal kinship with the Akwee begins when she is presented with "a couple of wives" in recognition for her contributions to the village. The fact that she continues to refer to the Olinka as "the heathen" in her discussions with Nettie implies that, in spite of her fondness for her grandson, Doris never overcomes a belief in the essential "difference" of the Africans attributed to her by the Missionary Society in England: "She thinks they are an entirely different species from what she calls Europeans. . . . She says an African daisy and an English daisy are both flowers, but totally different kinds." By promoting a theory of polygenesis opposed to the Olinkan account of racial origins, Doris calls into question her own ability to treat the Akwee as kin. The true nature of her "reciprocal" relationship with the Akwee is revealed when she unselfconsciously tells Nettie that she believes she can save her villagers from the same displacement the Olinka suffered: "I am a very wealthy woman," says Doris, "and I *own* the village of Akwee."

Stripped of both the religious motivation of the other missionaries and the overt racism of the other whites, Doris Baines through her relationship with the Akwee lays bare the hierarchy of self-interest and paternalism that sets the pattern for race relations in larger Africa. Indeed, from the moment that young Nettie first arrives in Africa she is surprised to find whites there "in droves," and her letters are filled with details suggestive of the hegemony of race and class. Nettie's description of Monrovia is a case in point. There she sees "bunches" of whites and a presidential palace that "looks like the American white house." There Nettie also discovers that whites sit on the country's cabinet, that black cabinet members' wives dress like white women, and that the black president himself refers to his people as "natives"—as Nettie remarks, "It was the first time I'd heard a black man use that word." Originally established by ex-slaves who returned to Africa but who kept "close ties to the country that bought them," Monrovia clearly reveals a Western influence in more than its style of architecture, and its cocoa plantations provide the colonial model of integration that defines the white presence elsewhere in Africa—from the port town "run by a white man" who rents out "some of the stalls . . . to Africans" all the way up to the governor's mansion where "the white man in charge" makes the decision to build the road that ultimately destroys the Olinka village. Indeed, the later displacement of the Olinka villagers by the English roadbuilders—the main action in the African sections of *The Color Purple*—simply recapitulates the colonial process of integration already embedded in Nettie's narrative of her travels through the less remote areas of Africa.

From her eventual vantage point within the Olinka's domestic sphere, Nettie becomes a first-hand witness to this process of colonization—a process in which she and the other black missionaries unwittingly participate. For although Nettie's reasons for going to Africa differ from Doris Baines's in that they, like those of the other black missionaries, include a concern for the "people from whom [she] sprang," she is trained by a missionary society that is "run by white people" who "didn't say a thing about caring about Africa, but only about duty." Indeed, missionary work is tied to national interest from the time Nettie arrives in England to prepare for the trip to Africa:

> . . . the English have been sending missionaries to Africa and
> India and China and God knows where all, for over a hundred
> years. And the things they have brought back! We spent a

morning in one of their museums and it was packed with jewels, furniture, fur, carpets, swords, clothing, even *tombs* from all the countries they have been. From Africa they have *thousands* of vases, jars, masks, bowls, baskets, statues—and they are all so beautiful it is hard to imagine that the people who made them don't still exist. And yet the English assure us they do not.

Charting the course of empire through a catalogue of the material culture appropriated by missionaries from "all the counties they have been" (and, chillingly, from peoples who no longer exist), this passage brilliantly underscores Walker's ability to maintain the integrity of the narrative's personal perspective—here that of a young girl's wonder at her first glimpse into the riches of her African heritage—even as she simultaneously invites readers to resituate that perspective in a wider context of race and class. In fact, throughout the African sections of the novel, Walker's embedded narrative enables readers to sympathize with the hopes and disappointments of the black missionaries while it simultaneously exposes the limitations of their point of view.

This narrative complexity becomes especially important in the passages concerning Samuel and Corrine's Victorian aunts, Theodosia and Althea, whom the narrative asks readers both to sympathize with and to judge harshly. On the one hand, as representatives of a group of black women missionaries who achieved much against great odds, the narrative asks readers to see these women and their accomplishments as "astonishing":

> . . . no sooner had a young woman got through Spelman Seminary than she began to put her hand to whatever work she could do for her people, anywhere in the world. It was truly astonishing. These very polite and proper young women, some of them never having set foot outside their own small country towns, except to come to the Seminary, thought nothing of packing up for India, Africa, the Orient. Or for Philadelphia or New York.

On the other hand, the narrative levies its harshest criticism of missionary work not against the white missionary Doris Baines but against Aunt Theodosia—and particularly against the foolish pride she takes in a medal given to her by King Leopold for "service as an exemplary missionary in the King's colony." The criticism is levied by a young "DuBoyce," who attends one of Aunt Theodosia's "at homes" and exposes her medal as the emblem of the Victorian woman's "unwitting complicity with this despot who worked to death and brutalized and eventually exterminated thousands and thousands of African peoples." Like the other political allusions embedded in Walker's narrative, the appearance of Du Bois in Aunt Theodosia's domestic sphere recontextualizes Nettie's narrative, and his comments serve as an authoritative final judgment upon the entire missionary effort in Africa.

By structuring Nettie's letters around missionary work, then, Walker achieves much. First, that work provides Nettie and the other black missionaries with a practical and credible pathway into the African domestic sphere. Second, the institutional, historical, and ideological connections between philanthropy and colonialism enable Walker to use that domestic sphere and the example of Doris Baines's integrated family to expose the missionary pattern of integration in larger Africa. Finally, the embedded narrative line enables Walker to remain true to her characters even as she anatomizes the hierarchy of race and class that is first pictured in miniature on Nettie's envelope.

II. "He said he wouldn't do it to me if he was my uncle"

If the integrated family of Doris Baines and her adopted African grandson exposes the missionary pattern of integration in Africa as one based on a false kinship that in fact *denies* the legitimacy of kinship bonds across racial lines, the relationship between Miss Sophia and her white charge, Miss Eleanor Jane, serves an analogous function for the American South. Sophia, of course, joins the mayor's household as a maid under conditions more overtly racist than Doris Baines's adoption of her Akwee family: Because she answers "hell no" to Miss Millie's request that she come to work for her as a maid, Sophia is brutally beaten by the mayor and six policeman and is then imprisoned. Forced to do the jail's laundry and driven to the brink of madness, Sophia finally becomes Miss Millie's maid in order to escape prison. Sophia's violent confrontation with the white officers obviously foregrounds issues of race and class, as even critics who find these issues marginalized elsewhere in *The Color Purple* have noted. But it is not only through Sophia's dramatic *public* battles with white men that her story dramatizes issues of race and class. Her domestic relationship with Miss Eleanor Jane and the other members of the mayor's family offers a more finely nuanced and extended critique of racial integration, albeit one that has often been overlooked.

Like Doris Baines and her black grandson, Sophia and Miss Eleanor Jane appear to have some genuine family feelings for one another. Since Sophia "practically . . . raise[s]" Miss Eleanor Jane and is the one sympathetic person in her house, it is not surprising that the young girl "dote[s] on

Sophia" and is "always stick[ing] up for her," or that, when Sophia leaves the mayor's household (after fifteen years of service), Miss Eleanor Jane continues to seek out her approval and her help with the "mess back at the house." Sophia's feelings for Miss Eleanor are of course more ambivalent. When she first joins the mayor's household, Sophia is completely indifferent to her charge, "wonder[ing] why she was ever born." After rejoining her own family, Sophia resents Miss Eleanor Jane's continuing intrusions into her family life and suggests that the only reason she helps the white girl is because she's "on parole. . . . Got to act nice." But later Sophia admits that she does feel "something" for Miss Eleanor Jane "because of all the people in your daddy's house, you showed me some human kindness."

Whatever affection exists between the two women, however, has been shaped by the perverted "kinship" relation within which it grew—a relationship the narrative uses to expose plantation definitions of kinship in general and to explode the myth of the black mammy in particular. Separated from her own family and forced to join the mayor's household against her will, living in a room under the house and assigned the housekeeping and childraising duties, Sophia carries out role in the mayor's household which clearly recalls that of the stereotypical mammy on the Southern plantation. However, as someone who prefers to build a roof on the house while her husband tends the children, Sophia seems particularly unsuited for that role. And that is precisely the narrative's point: Sophia *is* entirely unsuited for the role of mammy, but whites—including and perhaps especially Miss Eleanor Jane—continually *expect* her to behave according to their cultural representations of the black mother. It is, in fact, these expectations that get Sophia into trouble in the first place, for when Miss Millie happens upon Sophia's family and sees her children so "clean," she assumes that Sophia would make a perfect maid and that Sophia would like to come and work in her household. Similarly, Miss Eleanor Jane assumes that Sophia must return her family feelings in kind, without considering Sophia's true position in her household. The young white woman's stereotypical projections become clear when she can't understand why Sophia doesn't "just love" her new son, since, in her words, "all other colored women I know love children."

An historical appropriation of domestic discourse for political ends, descriptions of the black mammy were used by apologists for slavery to argue that the plantation system benefited the people whom it enslaved by incorporating supposedly inferior blacks into productive white families. And Sophia explicitly ties her employers to such plantation definitions of racial difference: "They have the nerve to try to make us think slavery fell through because of us. . . . Like us didn't have sense enough to handle it. All the time breaking hoe handles and letting the mules loose in the wheat." But through

Sophia's experience in the mayor's household, the narrative demonstrates that it is Miss Millie, the mayor's wife, who is actually incompetent—who must be taught to drive by Sophia, for example, and who even then can't manage a short trip by herself. Thus, when she suddenly decides to drive Sophia home for a visit, Miss Millie stalls the car and ruins the transmission, the mistress unable to master driving in reverse. Too afraid of black men to allow one of Sophia's relatives to drive her back home alone, Miss Millie reveals her childlike dependence upon Sophia, who must cut short her first visit with her children in five years to ride home with the distraught white woman. Sophia's position as domestic within the mayor's household thus enables Walker to subvert the discourse of plantation kinship by suggesting that it actually supports a group of people who are themselves incompetent or, in Sophia words, "backward, . . . clumsy, and unlucky."

Predicated on this plantation model of integration, relations between whites and blacks throughout the American South reveal a false kinship not unlike that of Doris Baines and the Akwee. But in this instance the false kinship is doubly perverse because it conceals an elaborate network of actual kinship connections. Thus Miss Eleanor Jane's husband feels free to humor Sophia by referring to the importance of black mammies in the community— ". . . everybody around here raise by colored. That's how come we turn out so well"—while other white men refuse to recognize the children they father with black women. As Celie says of Mr. _____'s son Bub, he "look so much like the Sheriff, he and Mr. _____ almost on family terms"; that is, "just so long as Mr. _____ know he colored." Like the apologists for slavery, then, the Southern whites in *The Color Purple* keep alive a counterfeit definition of family while denying the real ties that bind them to African Americans.

In fact, the underlying system of kinship that exists in the American South has more to do with white uncles than black mammies, as is clear from the scene in which Sophia's family and friends consider various stratagems for winning her release from prison. By asking, "Who the warden's black kinfolks?," Mr. _____ reveals that kinship relations between whites and blacks are so extensive in the community that it may be assumed that *someone* will be related by blood to the warden. That someone, of course, is Squeak. Hopeful that she will be able to gain Sophia's release from the warden on the basis of their kinship, the others dress Squeak up "like she a white woman" with instructions to make the warden "see the Hodges in you." In spite of the fact that the warden does recognize Squeak as kin "the minute [she] walk[s] through the door"—or perhaps *because* he recognizes her—the warden rapes Squeak, denying their kinship in the very act of perverting it. As Squeak herself recounts, "He say if he was my uncle he wouldn't do it to me." Both an intensely personal and highly political act, Squeak's rape exposes the denial of kinship at the heart of race relations in the South and underscores the individual and institutional power of whites to control the terms of kinship—and whatever power those definitions convey—for their own interests.

It is specifically as an act of resistance to this power that Sophia comes to reject Miss Eleanor Jane's baby and thereby to challenge the Olinka kinship ideal for race relations. From the time her son is born, Miss Eleanor Jane continually tests out Sophia's maternal feelings for him, "shoving Reynolds Stanley Earl in her face" almost "every time Sofia turn[s] around." When an exasperated Sophia finally admits that she doesn't love the baby, Miss Eleanor Jane accuses her of being "unnatural" and implies that Sophia should accept her son because he is "just a little baby!"—an innocent who, presumably, should not be blamed for the racist sins of his fathers. From Sophia's vantage point as a persecuted black woman, however, Reynolds Stanley is not "just a sweet, smart, cute, *innocent* little baby boy." He is in fact the grandson and namesake of the man who beat her brutally in the street, a man whom he also resembles physically. A "white something without much hair" with "big stuck open eyes," Reynolds Stanley also takes after his father, who is excused from the military to run the family cotton gin while Sophia's own boys are trained for service overseas. To Sophia, Reynolds Stanley is both the living embodiment of and literal heir to the system that oppresses her: "He can't even walk and already he in my house messing it up. Did I ast him to come? Do I care whether he sweet or not? Will it make any difference in the way he grow up to treat me what I think?" Reminding Miss Eleanor Jane of the real social conditions that separate her from Reynolds Stanley in spite of his "innocence," Sophia articulates a strong position counter to the Olinka kinship ethic of treating everyone like one mother's children: ". . . all the colored folks talking bout loving everybody just ain't looked hard at what they thought they said."

In subverting the plantation model of kinship in general and the role of mammy that it assigns to black women in particular, then, Sophia's position as an unwilling domestic in the mayor's household underscores the importance of the personal point of view to the novel's political critique of race relations. Indeed, the personal point of view of *The Color Purple* is central to its political message: It is precisely the African American woman's *subjectivity* that gives the lie to cultural attempts to reduce her—like Sophia—to the role of the contented worker in a privileged white society.

III. "White people off celebrating their independence. . . .
Us can spend the day celebrating each other"

The Color Purple closes with a celebration of kinship, its concluding action composed of a series of family reunions: Sophia patches things up with

Harpo; Shug visits her estranged children (for the first time in thirty years); and the novel's two narrators, Celie and Nettie, are joyfully and tearfully reunited. Even Albert and Celie are reconciled, his change of heart signaled by his earning the right to have his first name written. Coming after Celie has achieved both economic independence and emotional security, the reunions at the end of *The Color Purple* testify to the importance of kinship to the happiness of every individual. Appropriately, then, when the two sisters fall into one another's arms at last, each identifies her kin: Nettie introduces her husband and the children, and Celie's first act is to "point up at [her] peoples . . . Shug and Albert." But in addition to suggesting that the individual realizes her full potential only *within* the supporting bonds of a strong kinship group (no matter how unconventionally that group might be defined), the conclusion to *The Color Purple* also addresses the vexing question posed by the Olinka Adam narrative: Is progress in race relations possible? By bringing to closure two earlier narrative threads—one dealing with Sophia and Miss Eleanor Jane, and the other with Sophia's relationship to work—the novel suggests that progress in race relations is possible. But the narrative's ending also contains arresting images of racial segregation in both Africa and America that complicate the idea of progress and ultimately move the narrative toward a final definition of kinship based on race

After their falling out over Reynolds Stanley, Sophia and Miss Eleanor Jane are reunited when the mayor's daughter finally learns from her family *why* Sophia came to work for them in the first place. Miss Eleanor Jane subsequently comes to work in Sophia's home, helping with the housework and taking care of Sophia's daughter Henrietta. Clearly an improvement in the domestic relationship between the two women, this new arrangement expresses Miss Eleanor Jane's new understanding of their domestic history together: To her family's question "Whoever heard of a white woman working for niggers?" Miss Eleanor Jane answers, "Whoever heard of somebody like Sophia working for trash?" For her part, Sophia's acceptance of Miss Eleanor Jane in her own home also signals progress, although when Celie asks pointedly if little Reynolds Stanley comes along with his mother, Sophia sidesteps the issue of her own feelings for the child by answering, "Henrietta say she don't mind him." Sophia's comment maintains the legitimacy of her own hard-earned attitudes toward the child, even as it reserves the possibility that different attitudes may be possible in future generations.

Sophia's employment in Celie's dry goods store also seems to signal an improvement in race relations, not only because it represents Sophia's final escape from her position as mammy but also because shops are used throughout *The Color Purple* to represent the status of economic and social integration between blacks and whites. Thus early in the novel Corrine, a

Spelman graduate, is insulted when a white clerk calls her "Girl" and intimidates her into buying some thread she doesn't want. Later the novel contrasts the histories of Celie's real Pa and Step-pa as store owners, histories that comment on the ability of African Americans to achieve economic integration into the American mainstream. Celie's real father, in the tradition of the American success story, works hard, buys his own store, and hires two of his bothers to work it for him. Ironically, his model of industry and enterprise fails, since the store's very success leads "white merchants . . . [to] complain that this store was taking all the black business away from them" Refusing to tolerate free competition from a black-owned and black-operated business, whites eventually burn the store and lynch Celie's Pa and his two brothers. The tragic history of Celie's real Pa thus compels readers to reinterpret Celie's family history in terms of the historical lack of access of African Americans to the "American Dream."

Believing that Celie's real Pa "didn't know how to git along," Alphonso, her step-pa, expresses a different path to economic integration:

> Take me, he say, I know how they is. The key to all of 'em is money. The trouble with our people is as soon as they got out of slavery they didn't want to give the white man nothing else. But the fact is, you got to give 'em something. Either your money, your land, your woman or your ass. So what I did was just right off offer to give 'em money. Before I planted a seed, I made sure this one and that one knowed one seed out of three was planted for *him*. Before I ground a grain of wheat, the same thing. And when I opened up your daddy's old store in town, I bought me my own white boy to run it. And what make it so good, he say, I bought him with whitefolks' money.

Alphonso's decision to pay off whites and buy a white boy to work in the dry goods store establishes him in the tradition of the trickster who plays the system for his own benefit; however, the model of integration he represents is finally seen as accommodationist. Alphonso, in fact, is identified with white power from the beginning of the novel, where he is seen going off with a group of white men armed with guns. After he has made his fortune, Alphonso recalls the compromised African president described in Nettie's letter—like him Alphonso lives in a house that now looks like a "white person's house," and like him he establishes paternalistic relationships with other blacks. Thus when Shug asks Alphonso's new wife, a "child" not "more than fifteen," why her parents allowed her to marry him, the girl replies: "They work for him. . . . Live on his land." Alphonso's marriage thus makes explicit the degree to which his identification with white paternalism shapes his domestic relationships with other blacks.

In the context of these earlier histories, Sophia's coming to work in Celie's dry goods store has wider significance than just her finding suitable work outside the home. Indeed, for the first time in its history the store has an integrated workforce, since Celie keeps the "white man" who works there even as she hires Sophia to "wait on" blacks and "treat 'em nice." In direct contrast to the white clerk who intimidated Corrine earlier, Sophia refuses to coerce customers and turns out to be especially good at "selling stuff" because "she don't care if you buy or not." Importantly, Sophia also resists the white clerk's attempts to define their relationship in the terms of plantation kinship: When he presumes to call her "auntie," she mocks him by asking "which colored man his mama sister marry." While race relations in Celie's integrated store are obviously not ideal, Sophia's employment there is nonetheless both a personal and a communal triumph: Sophia finds employment that suits her as an individual, and the black community is treated with new respect in the marketplace.

Significantly, these small steps toward progress in race relations come not from some realization of the Olinka ideal or any recognition of identity *between* the races but from an evolving separatism and parallel growth in racial identity *within* the African and African American communities. The possibility of treating everyone like "one mother's children" is achieved within but not between racial groups by the end of *The Color Purple*. Instead, the conclusion leaves readers with images of an emerging Pan-Africanism in Africa and a nascent black nationalism in the American South.

In Africa separatism is represented by the *mbeles*, warriors who "live deep in the jungle, refusing to work for whites or be ruled by them." Composed of men and women "from dozens of African tribes," the *mbeles* are particularly significant because they comprise a remnant group defined not by traditional village bloodlines but by their common experience of racial oppression and their shared commitment to active resistance, which takes the form of "missions of sabotage against the white plantations." In the *mbeles*, *The Color Purple* accurately depicts the historical origin of many African "tribes" or nations in the reorganization of older societies decimated by colonization. Their plans for the white man's "destruction—or at least for his removal from *their continent*"—also reflect a nascent pan-Africanism among the disenfranchised. Including among their number "one colored man . . . from Alabama," the *mbeles* represent a form of kinship that is defined by racial rather than national identity.

In America, a parallel growth in black identity is suggested by Celie's final letter in *The Color Purple*. Indeed, the spirit of celebratory kinship with which the novel closes is achieved by Celie's group specifically in isolation from whites, as Harpo explains: "White people busy celebrating they independence from England July 4th . . . so most black folks don't have to work. Us can spend the day celebrating each other." By juxtaposing "white people" and "black folks," Harpo distinguishes his kinship group from the kinship of whites, defined by privilege and national identity. Importantly, the "folks" that Harpo refers to now include Celie's African daughter-in-law, Tashi. Also significantly, that group does *not* include Miss Eleanor Jane, no matter how strained her relationship with her own family or how successful her reunion with Sophia. Tashi's easy integration into the black community effaces her earlier fears that coming to America would rob her of all kinship ties, leaving her with "no country, no people, no mother and no husband and brother." Instead, Tashi's quick acceptance by the Southern women, who make a fuss over her and "stuff her" with food, suggests once again that feelings of black identity make it easy for people to treat others as "one mother's children."

But if the conclusion to *The Color Purple* suggests that feelings of racial identity can transcend national boundaries, the novel provides no such reassurances that the boundaries between races can be successfully negotiated. That sober conclusion is confirmed by the outcome of two other attempts at integration. The first is that of Shug's son, a missionary on an Indian reservation in the American West. The American Indians refuse to accept her son, Shug explains, because "everybody not a Indian they got no use for." The failure of Shug's son to become integrated into the American Indian community contrasts with Mary Agnes's successful integration with the mixed peoples of Cuba, but her experience there also emphasizes the importance of racial identity to kinship definitions. Indeed, it is because she is a person of color that Mary Agnes is recognized as kin: Even though some of the Cuban people are as light as Mary Agnes while others are "real dark," Shug explains, they are "all in the same family though. Try to pass for white, somebody mention your grandma." Thus in Cuba—as well as in Africa and North America—feelings of racial identity among marginalized peoples become the basis for definitions of kinship by novel's end.

Finally, it is not surprising that, in elaborating her domestic trope for race relations, Walker is able to foreground the personal experience of her narrators while simultaneously offering an extended critique of racial integration. As Walker's integrated families remind us, the black family has seldom existed as a private, middle-class space protected from the interference of the state; therefore, the African American household is particularly inscribed with social meanings available for narration. Rather than opposing public and private spheres, Walker's narrative underscores their interpenetration. If her narrative does reveal an opposition, it is not between public and private discourse but between the universalist ethos of the Olinka ideal for race relations and the historical experience of African Americans as reflected in the narrative's analysis of specific integrated family groupings. For if the Olinka ideal questions the true nature of kinship in the novel's integrated families, these families also serve to criticize the Olinka myth for tracing the origins of racial discrimination back to some imaginary sin of black people, rather than to real, historical discrimination by whites.

It may be, however, that the growing sense of racial separatism at the conclusion to the *The Color Purple* is not necessarily at odds with the Olinka ideal for race relations. Past discrimination itself may dictate that improved relations between the races must begin with the destruction of false relations—the discovery of kinship among the disenfranchised the necessary first step, perhaps, toward recognizing all others as part of the same family. Like the Olinka Adam myth, the conclusion in Walker's novel raises the question of the future of race relations, but also like that myth, the novel offers no certain predictions. One thing is certain, however. Critics who believe that *The Color Purple* sacrifices its ability to critique the public world of blacks in favor of dramatizing the personal experience of its narrators not only run the risk of reducing the narrative's technical complexity, but also of overlooking the work's sustained critique of racial integration levied from *within* the domestic sphere. Through its embedded narrative line and carefully elaborated kinship trope for race relations, *The Color Purple* offers a critique of race that explores the possibility of treating all people as "one mother's children"—while remaining unremittingly sensitive to the distance that often separates even the best of human ideals from real historical conditions.

DEBORAH E. McDOWELL

Generational Connections and Black Women Novelists—
Iola Leroy *and* The Color Purple

As Iola finished, there was a ring of triumph in her voice, as if she were reviewing a path she had trodden with bleeding feet, and seen it change to lines of living light. Her soul seemed to be flashing through the rare loveliness of her face and etherealizing its beauty. Everyone was spellbound. Dr. Latimer was entranced, and, turning to Hon. Dugdale, said, in a low voice and with deep-drawn breath, 'She is angelic!' . . . 'She is strangely beautiful! . . . The tones of her voice are like benedictions of peace; her words a call to higher service and nobler life.'

As soon as dinner over, Shug push back her chair and light a cigarette. Now is come the time to tell yall, she say.

Tell us what? Harpo ast.

Us leaving, she say.

Yeah? say Harpo, looking round for the coffee. And then looking over at Grady.

Us leaving, Shug say again. Mr. _____ look struck, like he always look when Shug say she going anywhere. He reach down and rub his stomach, look off side her head like nothing been said. . . .

From *"The Changing Same": Black Women's Literature, Criticism, and Theory* by Deborah E. McDowell. (Essay originally titled "'The Changing Same': Generational Connections and Black Women Novelists—*Iola Leroy* and *The Color Purple*.") © 1995 Deborah E. McDowell.

Celie is coming with us, say Shug.

Over my dead body, Mr. _____ say.

You satisfied that what you want, Shug say, cool as clabber.

Mr. _____ start up from his seat, look at Shug, plop back down again. He look over at me. I thought you was finally happy, he say. What wrong now?

You a lowdown dog is what's wrong, I say. It's time to leave you and enter the creation. And your dead body just the welcome mat I need.

The character being *spoken about* in the first passage is Iola Leroy, the title character of Frances E. W. Harper's 1892 novel, thought, until recently, to be the founding text of a black women's tradition in the novel. A group of men are giving their approval of an impromptu speech that Iola has just delivered on the ennobling effects of suffering and the necessity for Christian service. They lay stress, simultaneously, on her physical beauty and saintliness.

In the second passage, from Alice Walker's 1982 novel, *The Color Purple*, Celie, the novel's central character is *speaking*, along with her spiritual guide and lover, the itinerant blues singer Shug Avery. Celie's, unlike Iola's, is an audience of hostile, disapproving men; nevertheless, with force and resoluteness, Celie announces her plans to move on in search of personal fulfillment and spiritual growth.

I cite these two passages as examples of two strikingly different images of black female character in black women's fiction—one "exceptional" and outer-directed, the other "ordinary" and inner-directed; two different approaches to characterization, one external, the other internal; and finally, two different narrative voices, one strained, stilted, genteel, and inhibited, the other spontaneous, immediate, fresh, and authoritative.

Although the passages are different, the novels from which they are excerpted share important basic patterns. Both novels recount the problems of familial separation and reunion, of lost and found identities. More significantly, however, these novels represent the two most salient paradigms in the black female literary tradition in the novel. Although manipulated differently, depending on the author, these paradigms derive from a common center in black women's novels. Both revisionist in impulse, they are revealed, most graphically, in the depiction of black female characters. Borrowing from Susan Lanser's *The Narrative Act*, I call these paradigms, simply, public and private narrative fiction. I see them posed respectively and most dramatically in France E. W. Harper's *Iola Leroy* and Alice Walker's *The Color Purple*.

Of necessity, I use these terms, not literally, but metaphorically, for as Lanser notes correctly, "obviously all fictional narration is 'public' in the sense that it was written to be published and read by an audience. What I am distinguishing here are fictional narrative acts designed for an apparently public readership [or one "outside" the text] and those narratives designed for reception only by other characters and textual figures."

In the following discussion, I would like to adapt and modify Lanser's distinction between public and private point of view to posit a provisional distinction between public and private narrative fiction. I wish to distinguish here between those novels by black women that seem to imply a public readership (or one outside the black cultural community) and those that imply a private readership or one within that cultural matrix. Given the complexity and ambiguity inherent in questions about audience, one can only speculate about the audience for whom a specific text seems intended. To be certain, authors cannot determine conclusively who their actual readers are. Nevertheless, all writers begin by fictionalizing or imagining an audience. As Peter Rabinowitz notes, authors "cannot make artistic decisions without prior assumptions (conscious or unconscious) [stated or implied], about their audience's beliefs, knowledge, and familiarity with conventions," literary and/or social. Each text, then, selects, encodes, and images its targeted audience—what Wolfgang Iser calls its "implied reader"—through the style, language, and strategies it employs. (That does not preclude, of course, its being read by those outside the targeted reading group.)

I have chosen character as a way of examining these paradigms even though the current wave of literary/theoretical sophistication calls into question "naive common-sense categories of 'character,' 'protagonist,' or 'hero,'" and rejects the "prevalent conception of character in the novel" which assumes that "the most successful and 'living' characters are richly delineated autonomous wholes." For, despite such positions, imaging the black woman as a "whole" character or "self" has been a consistent preoccupation of black female novelists throughout much of their literary history. That these writers frequently use the *bildungsroman*—a genre that focuses primarily on the gradual growth and development of a "self" from childhood to adulthood—attests strongly to this preoccupation. It seems appropriate, therefore, to allow critical concerns of black women's novels to emerge organically from those texts, rather than to allow current critical fashion to dictate what those concerns should be.

In considering character in black women's fiction as a structure that reflects dominant paradigms in their tradition, other critical questions arise. Although the scope of this essay does not permit me to explore them in full and equal detail, the following interlocking questions are implied in my consideration of characterization. In that one of the most challenging aspects of characterization for any writer is the authentic representation of speech, what is the relationship between race/gender and literary voice? In turn, what is the relationship between author and audience, for that relationship largely determines and explains, not only narrative voice, but also a range of artistic strategies and structures. What do the configurations and variations of character in black women's fiction reveal about patterns of literary influence among black women writers, about their literary history?

But examining how black women writers approach characterization is not a purely aesthetic question, for in raising questions about this literary structure, one simultaneously confronts political and cultural questions that must be embedded in their historical context, not articulated solely in terms of our own. For black women novelists of the nineteenth century, character as aesthetic structure was tightly coupled to character as a complex of moral attributes, most clustered around sexuality.

Largely because of the negative construction of their sexual identity, black women novelists treated sexuality with caution and reticence. This pattern is clearly linked to the network of social and literary myths perpetuated throughout history about black women's libidinousness. It is well known that during slavery the white slave master helped to construct an image of black female sexuality that shifted responsibility for his own sexual passions onto his female slaves. They, not he, had wanton, insatiable desires that he was powerless to resist. The image did not end with emancipation. So persistent was it that black club women devoted part of their first national conference in July 1895 to addressing it, thereby working to fulfill their motto, "Lifting as We Climb."

Though myths about black women's lasciviousness were not new to the era, a letter from one J. W. Jacks, a white male editor of a Missouri newspaper, made them a matter of urgent concern to black club women. Forwarded to Josephine S. Pierre Ruffin, editor of *The Woman's Era*, the letter attacked black women's virtue, supplying "evidence" from other black women. According to Jacks, when a certain Negro woman was asked to identify a newcomer to the community, she responded, "the negroes will have nothing to do with 'dat nigger,' she won't let any man, except her husband, sleep with her, and we don't 'sociate with her."

Mrs. Ruffin circulated the letter widely to prominent black women and to heads of other women's clubs around the country, calling for a conference to discuss this and other matters of direct concern to black middle-class women. Given this historical context, it is not surprising that black women novelists of the nineteenth and early twentieth centuries dealt quietly with issues of black sexuality.

Of course, reticence about sexuality in literature during these periods was certainly not peculiar to black women writers; however, black women's unique psychosexual history in turn-of-the-century United States casts a different and important light on a more general cultural convention. Black women writers responded to the myth of black women's sexual licentiousness by insisting fiercely on their chastity. In attempting to overcome their heritage of rape and concubinage—a fight the club women waged—they stripped the characters they created of *all* sexual desire. In such works as Emma Dunham Kelley's *Megda* (1891), Frances E. W. Harper's *Iola Leroy* (1892), and Pauline Hopkins's *Contending Forces* (1900), black heroines struggle to defend and preserve the priceless gem of virginity. Conscious of the fact that a reconstruction of black female sexuality was required, these writers assumed a revisionist mission in their work, one based on a belief that they could substitute reality for stereotype. That substitution would assist a larger and related mission: to elevate the image of the entire black race. In so doing, they naively believed, they could eliminate caste injustices.

This impulse is, at once, the greatest strength and the greatest weakness of these early texts, for it results, without exception, in the creation of static, disembodied, larger-than-life characters. These early black heroines are sexually pure, invariably exemplary, characterized by their self-sacrifice and by their tireless labor for the collective good. Ironically, despite the early writers' efforts to revise homogenized literary images, they succeeded merely, and inevitably, in offering alternative homogenization; they traded myth for countermyth, an exchange consistent with their public mission. The countermyth dominates *Iola Leroy* and is evident most strikingly in Iola's conscious choice to glorify the virtues of motherhood and domesticity, the mainstays of the mid-nineteenth-century cult of true womanhood.

Although this ideology of domesticity conflicted sharply with the majority of black women's lives, Harper, like the majority of black writers of her era—both men and women—ironically accommodated her "new" model image of black womanhood to its contours. As Barbara Christian observes, "Since positive female qualities were all attributed to the white lady," black writers of the nineteenth century "based their counterimage on her ideal qualities, more than on [those] of any real black women." The image of the Lady combined and conflated physical appearance with character traits. Immortalized particularly in the Southern antebellum novel, the image required "physical beauty [that is, fair skin] . . . fragility, refinement and helplessness." "The closest black women could come to such an ideal, at least physically," Christian continues, "would . . . have to be the mulatta, quadroon, or octoroon."

Iola fulfills this physical requirement. "My! but she's putty," says the slave through whose eyes we first see her. "Beautiful long hair comes way down her back; putty blue eyes, and jis ez white ez anybody is dis place." This ideal dominates novels by black women in the nineteenth century, due, as Alice Walker argues reasonably, to a predominantly white readership "who could identify human feeling, humanness, only if it came in a white or near-white body." She concludes, "'Fairness' was and is the standard of Euro-American femininity."

By giving Iola a role to play in the larger struggle for race uplift, Harper modified the image of the Southern lady, but it is important to note that Iola's role in the struggle is enacted within the boundaries of the traditional expectations of women as mothers and nurturers, expectations that form the cornerstone of the cult of true womanhood. According to Iola, "a great amount of sin and misery springs from the weakness and inefficiency of women." In "The Education of Mothers," one of the two public speeches she gives in the novel (public speaking being largely reserved for men in the text), she appeals for "a union of women with the warmest hearts and clearest brains to help in the moral education of the race." Not only does the content of such speeches contribute to Iola's exemplary image, the style and language do also.

Ordinary or black folk speech has been historically devalued by the standard (white) English-speaking community, a devaluation that, as John Wideman maintains, "implies a linguistic hierarchy, the dominance of one version of reality over others." That devaluation and all that it implies is especially pervasive in Harper's era, in which, notes Arlene Elder, "Blacks were ridiculed in white plantation and Reconstruction humor for the rough rhythms, slurred words, malapropisms, and quaint images in their language. In order to escape this degrading image, [early] black novelists sped to the other extreme of creating cultured mulattoes" who used the elegant, elaborate, and artificial language found in much of the popular fiction of their day. At every point that Iola speaks in the novel, it is in the form of a carefully reasoned oration in defense either of her virtue or of some moral or social ideal. Even in conversations at home with family and friends, Iola expounds, as in the following example:

> To be the leader of a race to higher planes of thought and action, to teach men clearer views of life and duty, and to inspire their souls with loftier aims, is a far greater privilege than it is to open the gates of material prosperity and fill every home with sensuous enjoyment.

In significant contrast to Iola's formal oratory is the folk speech of the novel's secondary characters, captured particularly well in the opening chapter titled "Mystery of Market Speech and Prayer Meeting." The chapter describes the slaves' masterful invention of a coded language to convey information to each other, unsuspectedly, about battles won and lost during the Civil War. Their rich and imaginative language is self-consciously mediated in this chapter and throughout the novel by the stilted and pedantic voices of the narrator and the novel's major character. Nowhere is this pattern more strikingly illustrated in the novel than in the passage that describes the reunion between Iola's uncle, Robert, and his mother, from whom he was separated as a child. "Well, I'se got one chile, an' I means to keep on prayin' till I find my daughter," says Robert's mother. "I'm so happy! I feel's like a new woman!" In contrast, Robert responds: "My dear mother . . . now that I have found you, I mean to hold you fast just as long as I live. . . . I want you to see joy according to all the days wherein you have seen sorrow."

In *Iola Leroy*, the propaganda motive, the hallmark of public discourse, largely explains these extreme differences of speech styles between the principal characters—all educated mulattoes—and the minor characters—all illiterate and visibly black servants and workers. The implications of such differentiations are clear: the speech of these secondary characters (which Iola finds "quaint," "interesting," and "amusing") must be mediated and legitimated by the more accepted language of the major characters.

In the course of *Iola Leroy*, as Iola fulfills her role as exemplary black woman, she comes to resemble a human being less and less and a saint more and more. We learn very little about her thoughts, her inner life. Nothing about her is individualized, nor does this seem to be Harper's chief concern, for she is creating an exemplary type who is always part of some larger framework. That larger framework is moral and social in *Iola Leroy*, and every aspect of the text, especially character, must be carefully selected to serve its purpose. All of the novel's characters are trapped in an ideological schema that predetermines their identities. Every detail of Iola's life, down to the most personal experiences of family life, is stripped of its intimate implications and invested with social and mythical implications. It is significant that of all the Old Testament types, she identifies with Moses and Nehemiah, for "they were willing to put aside their own advantages for their race and country."

Iola's role as social and moral exemplar is paralleled by the novel's role as exemplum. Like its title character, *Iola Leroy* is on trial before the world. It aims for a favorable verdict by choosing its models carefully. Harper's most recognizable model is Harriet Beecher Stowe's *Uncle Tom's Cabin*, the most popular novel of the mid-nineteenth century in America. Space does not permit me to detail the striking similarities of plot, theme, style, and characterization between the two novels. Although Harper makes slight modifications, echoes of the most salient episodes of *Uncle Tom's Cabin* are present throughout *Iola Leroy*.

Harper's choice of *Uncle Tom's Cabin* as model is a logical and appropriate one, given the polemical and public role that she expected her novel to play, a role that Stowe's novel had played to unrivaled success with an audience comprised mainly of Northern white Christians. Harper addresses and appeals to this audience directly in the afternote of the novel:

> From threads of fact and fiction I have woven a story whose mission will not be in vain if it awakens in the hearts of our countrymen a stronger sense of justice and a more Christlike humanity in behalf of those whom the fortunes of war threw, homeless, ignorant and poor, upon the threshold of a new era.

Those Northern whites might be more inclined to lend their assistance to this homeless and displaced lot if the images of black life that Harper and her black contemporaries valued and affirmed accorded with that audience's horizon of social and literary expectations. In this respect, *Iola Leroy* is in company with a number of novels by black writers of its era, all dedicated to a public mission, all foundering on the shoals of two contradictory attempts: "to conform to the accepted social [and] literary . . . standards of their day and their almost antithetical need to portray their own people with honesty and imagination."

The need to portray their people with honesty and imagination has been paramount for contemporary black women novelists. For many—Alice Walker, Toni Morrison, Gayl Jones, and Sherley Anne Williams, among others—that need has compelled them to transform the black female literary ideal inherited from their nineteenth-century predecessors. Although these recent writers have preserved the revisionist mission that inspired that ideal, they have liberated their own characters from the burden of being exemplary standard bearers in an enterprise to uplift the race. The result is not only greater complexity and possibility for their heroines, but also greater complexity and artistic possibility for themselves as writers. The writings of Alice Walker are suggestive examples of this paradigm shift.

In "Beyond the Peacock," an essay in her collection *In Search of Our Mother's Gardens*, Walker writes, "each writer writes the missing parts to the other writer's story. And the whole story is what I'm after." To Walker, a major, if not *the* major, missing part is the story of what she calls the "black black" heroine, described in the essay "If the Present Looks Like the Past." Unlike *Iola Leroy* and the other nineteenth-century black women characters that Walker surveys in the essay, the black black heroine can neither pass for white nor be protected by class privilege. While Walker isn't the only black female novelist to problematize the Iola Leroy type, she has made a particularly suggestive and controversial attempt in the Celie letters of *The Color Purple*. These letters can be read as Walker's effort to write the missing parts of *Iola Leroy* and other black women's texts in its tradition. In other words, Celie is a revision of a revision of black female character, an unvarnished representation.

Whereas *Iola Leroy* as character is largely indistinguishable from the Southern Lady and is devoted to the mission of middle-class racial "uplift," Celie is a poor, visibly black, barely literate drudge devoted simply to avoiding and surviving the brutalities inflicted on her by every man with whom she comes into contact. Unlike Iola, no ornate and elevated speeches come trippingly to Celie's tongue. She speaks in black folk English, and, unlike Harper, Alice Walker provides none of the self-conscious assurances to the reader—apostrophes, contractions, corrections from more "well-spoken" characters—that she knows the "standard."

But perhaps Celie's most striking distinction from Iola is her sexual experience. Iola survives attempted rape; Celie does not. Celie is unable to fend off attacks on her virtue by predatory men as her very first letter makes starkly clear: "You gonna do what your mammy wouldn't. First he put his thing up gainst my hip and sort of wiggle it around. Then he grab hold my titties. Then he push his thing inside my pussy." Although Celie's introduction to sexuality is rape, as her narrative unfolds, she, unlike Iola, discovers how vital healthy sexual experiences are to the development of her self-esteem and her creative powers. Significantly, the only form of sexuality that aids that process is expressed with a woman, one of the few lesbian relationships explored in black women's literature.

Iola and Celie reflect their authors' divergent approaches to characterization as well. Whereas Harper approaches Iola's character largely from the outside through her physical characteristics and through what others say about her, Walker reveals Celie's character completely from the inside. Everything we learn about Celie is filtered through her own consciousness and rendered in her own voice.

In *Iola Leroy*, self is sacrificed to the collective mission and the result is a static symbol rather than a dynamic character. In *The Color Purple*, the collective mission, as imaged by Harper, is sacrificed to the self, and the result is the creation of a character in process, one more complex and thoroughly realized than Iola Leroy.

Iola's energy is invariably directed outside of herself, and the narrative's action is correspondingly social and public in emphasis. Celie's energy, on the other hand, is primarily directed inward, and the narrative action of *The Color Purple* is correspondingly psychological, personal, and intimate in emphasis.

Like *Iola Leroy*, *The Color Purple* fits primarily into the private paradigm, suggested by its choice of the epistolary mode—by definition, personal and private—and the finite focus of the Celie letters. One of their most striking features is the conspicuous absence of any reference to the "outside" world. Except for an occasional reference to Macon, Memphis, and one to World War I, the world is shut out. Instead, like epistolary novels generically, *The Color Purple* emphasizes the psychological development of character.

Celie begins her story at age 14, in the form of letters to God, the only one who can hear her, she thinks. Feeling isolated and ashamed, she tells Him of her life of brutality and exploitation at the hands of men. Writing is all-important to Celie; her last resounding word to her sister, Nettie, before they separate is, "Write."

While Celie's letters are an attempt to communicate with someone outside herself, they also reveal a process of self-examination and self-discovery in much the same way the letter functioned for the protagonists in Richardson's *Clarissa* and *Pamela*. In other words, Celie's growth is chartable through her letters to God, which are essentially letters of self-exploration, enabling her to become connected to her thoughts and feelings. That connection eventually liberates her from a belief in a God outside herself, whom she has always imaged as "big and old and tall and graybearded and white," and acquaints her with the God inside herself.

The spiritual dimension of Celie's discovery of the God-in-self has striking implications for her experience as a writer—for a writer she is, first and foremost. A self-reflexive novel, *The Color Purple* explicitly allegorizes much about the process and problematics of writing. It dramatizes the relationship between writer and audience and its effect on narrative authority and autonomy, to forceful voice. *The Color Purple* makes clear that the black woman writer has written primarily without an audience capable of accepting and appreciating that the full, raw, unmediated range of the black woman's story could be appropriate subject matter for art.

The Celie letters addressed to God indicate her status as a writer without an audience, without a hearing, a predicament she recognizes only after discovering that her husband has intercepted and hidden in a trunk letters her sister Nettie has written to her from Africa over a thirty-year period.

As Celie recovers from the shock, she announces to Shug that she has ceased to write to God, now realizing that "the God I had been praying and writing to is a man, and just like all the other mens I know. Trifling, forgitful, and lowdown." When Shug cautions Celie to be quiet, lest God hear her, Celie responds defiantly, "Let 'im hear me, I say. If he ever listened to poor colored women the world would be a different place."

Celie's decision to cease writing to God and to begin writing to her sister, Nettie, marks a critical point in both her psychological development and in her development as a writer. Significantly, before Celie discovers that God is not listening, her letters to him record passive resignation, silence, and blind faith in his benevolence. She can suffer abuses in this life, she confides to Sofia, because "[it] soon be over. . . . Heaven last all ways." In these letters, she identifies with Squeak who speaks in a "little teenouncy voice." She "stutters," "mutters," her "throat closes," and "nothing come[s] out but a little burp." Celie admits that she "can't fix [her] mouth to say how [she] feel[s]." Appropriately, these letters record a distinct split between what she thinks and what she feels and says. For example, when Nettie leaves for Africa, she expresses sadness at leaving Celie to be buried by the burden of caring for Mr. _____ and his children. Celie writes, "It's worse than that, I think. If I was buried, I wouldn't have to work. But I just say, Never mine, never mine, long as I can spell G-o-d I got somebody along." Similarly, when Celie thinks she sees her daughter, Olivia, at the drygoods store in town, she strikes up a conversation with the woman who has custody of the child. The woman makes a joke about the child's name, and Celie writes: "I git it and laugh. It feel like to split my face." The image of the split functions here, as in so many novels by women, as a sign of the character's tenuous sense of self, of identity, if you will. The image objectifies the split between Celie's outer and inner selves that will ultimately be made whole as the novel develops.

It is further significant that none of the letters addressed to God is signed. In their anonymity, their namelessness, the letters further underscore Celie's lack of individuality. When she begins to write to Nettie, however, her inner and outer selves become connected. Her thoughts are fused with her feelings, her actions, her words, and the letters assume a quality of force and authority, at times, of prophecy, as seen in Celie's conversation with Mr. _____ before she leaves for Memphis:

> Until you do right by me, everything you touch will crumble.
>   He laugh. Who you think you is? he say. You can't curse nobody. Look at you. You black, you pore, you ugly, you a woman. Goddam, he say, you nothing at all.

> Until you do right by me, I say, everything you even
> dream about will fail.

Celie concludes: "I'm pore, I'm black, I may be ugly and can't cook. . . . But I'm here." Thus these letters addressed to Nettie are alternately signed, "Your sister, Celie" and "Amen," an expression of ratification, of approval, of assertion, of validation. The suggestion is clear: Celie is now ratifying, asserting, and validating her own words, her own worth, and the authority of her own experience. Celie's validation of her linguistic experience is central to that process.

Celie's story underscores sharply, as Iola's does not, the argument of many students of language that "ordinary" discourse can be continuous with "poetic," or "literary" discourse, and that any assumed distinctions between the two are unsupported by linguistic research. For considerations of African American literature that argument is especially critical, for if both forms of discourse can be continuous with each other, the need for an external and legitimating filter is eliminated.

In wanting to teach her to "talk correctly," Jerene and Darlene, Celie's helpers in her Folkspants, Unlimited, enterprise, imply the popular belief that ordinary black speech must be "corrected" in order to have literate status, but Celie comes to understand that "only a fool would want you to talk in a way that feel peculiar to your mind."

The narrative links Celie's refusal to talk in a manner peculiar to her mind with a change in audience. That refusal—the mark of psychic wholeness as well as of narrative authority and autonomy—is licensed and buttressed by the sympathetic audience she imagines. Significantly, Celie directs her letters away from God, a "public" and alien audience outside herself and toward her sister, Nettie, a private, familial, familiar, and receptive audience. The qualitative differences between the letters to God and those to Nettie imply a causal connection between a receptive audience (imaged as one with "kinship" ties to the writer) and the emergence of a forceful, authoritative, and self-validating narrative voice.

The question that immediately arises, however, is, given this connection, what explains the comparative lack of force and authority in Nettie's letters? How do they serve the narrative? Early reviewers of *The Color Purple* rightly saw Nettie's letters as lackluster and unengaging compared to Celie's. While Nettie's letters advance the narrative line, they disrupt the immediacy and momentum of Celie's. That notwithstanding, Nettie's letters do function to unify the narrative by repeating its central images and concerns. Most significantly, they continue and expand its commentary on the act of writing and the role that context and circumstances play in the creative process.

But the Nettie letters have perhaps the most striking and intriguing suggestions for Alice Walker as a writer, for her discovery of her own voice. For Walker, as for so many women writers, the process of that discovery begins with thinking back through and reclaiming her female ancestors. While much has been made (with Walker's encouragement) of Walker's obvious debt to Zora Neale Hurston, there has been virtually no acknowledgment that she owes an equal, though different, debt to black women writers before Hurston. In "Saving the Life That Is Your Own: The Importance of Models in the Artist's Life," Walker admits that her need to know the oral stories *told* by her female ancestors, stories that Hurston transcribed in her folklore and writing, was equal to her need to know the stories *written* by nineteenth-century black women. Even if they had to be transformed or rejected altogether, the experiences that these earlier writers recorded were crucial to Walker's development as a writer.

In an interview with Gloria Steinem, Walker remarks that "writing *The Color Purple* was writing in my first language" in its "natural, flowing way." In the novel, that language is Celie's, not Nettie's, indicating that Walker identifies her own writing voice with Celie's. However, that identification does not require that she reject Nettie's. Both the oral and the literate are parts of her literary ancestry and she conjoins them in the Celie and Nettie letters, respectively, reinforcing one of the novel's central themes: female bonding. Together their letters form a study of converging contrasts that are homologous with the relationship between Frances E. W. Harper and Alice Walker.

As their letters reveal, the correspondences between the sisters' experiences are striking, even strained and over-determined. Much of what Nettie writes to Celie describing the situation in Africa—the breakdown of male/female relationships, the power of male domination, and the bonding between women—is replicated in Celie's experiences in the rural South. Nettie writes to Celie of the paved roads in Africa; Celie, to her, of those in Georgia. Nettie describes her round and windowless African hut; Celie, Shug's difficulty including windows in her plans for a round house in Memphis.

While the sisters' experiences converge at these critical points, they diverge at others, perhaps most importantly in the voice, content, and style of their epistles. While Celie's letters are written in black folk English and record her personal trials and near defeat, Nettie's, written in more formal language, record the trials and decimation of a people and their culture. Nettie's personal relationships with Samuel, Corinne, and their children seem dwarfed and insignificant compared to the destruction of the Olinka culture. In other words, while the majority of Celie's letters can be said to represent the private paradigm of the African American female tradition in the novel, the majority of Nettie's letters can be said to represent the public paradigm. I say "majority" because Nettie's letters to Celie are, significantly, in two distinct linguistic registers. Her first letters to Celie focus on personal matters and are largely indistinguishable from Celie's letters:

> Dear Celie, the first letter say,
> You've got to fight and get away from Albert. He ain't no good.
> When I left you all's house, walking, he followed me on his horse. When we was well out of sight of the house, he caught up with me and started trying to talk. You know how he do. . . .

The next letter reads: "I keep thinking it's too soon to look for a letter from you. And I know how busy you is with all Mr. _____ children. . . ." Shortly after these letters, Nettie writes to Celie of the events leading to her decision to go to Africa as a missionary, explaining her agreement to help build a school in exchange for furthering her education. That letter reads:

> . . . When Corinne and Samuel asked me if I would come with them and help them build a school . . . I said yes. But only if they would teach me everything they knew to make me useful as a missionary. . . . They agreed to this condition, and my real education began at that time.

From this point on, Nettie's letters shift from the personal to the social, the political, the historical. They assume the quality of lecture and oration, losing the intimacy more appropriate in correspondence to a sister. Nettie's has become an educated imagination, shaped by the context within which she moves as well as by her function as a missionary in a colonizing enterprise.

Although Celie and Nettie are separated by an ocean, by their lifestyles—one ordinary, the other exceptional—and by the style of their epistles—oral and literate—these separate realities become integrated in the novel and held in sustained equilibrium. Each sister is allowed to exist as an independent entity; each, through her letters, is allowed to speak in her own voice without apology, mediation, or derision.

While one might expect it, there is no apology, mediation, or derision on Walker's part for her predecessor, Frances E. W. Harper, the impulses of whose work she incorporates in the voice and experiences of Nettie. Reminiscent of Iola, Nettie guards her virginity. Her self-conscious and ambiguous description of her developing passion for Samuel brings to mind Iola's reticence about sexuality. In one letter Nettie recounts to Celie her "forward behavior" with Samuel. As she and Samuel embraced, Nettie writes, "concern and passion soon ran away with us," and "I was transported by ecstasy in Samuel's arms."

But the more important resemblance between Nettie and Iola is their sacrifice of personal needs and wishes for a larger social purpose. Nettie is swept up in a social movement and energized by its unofficial motto: "OUR COMMUNITY COVERS THE WORLD." She is, in her words, working for the "uplift of black people everywhere." The concept of racial uplift, of corporate mission, so central to *Iola Leroy*, is explicit in Nettie's letters and acts as counterpoint to Celie's more private and personal concerns. Further, together these letters objectify the pattern of intertextual relations among black women writers, a pattern which departs from what Harold Bloom describes in *The Anxiety of Influence* and *A Map of Misreading*. Bloom's linear theory of the oedipal war between literary fathers and sons does not hold among black women writers, many of whom reverently acknowledge their debts to their literary foremothers. Unlike Bloom, I see literary influence, to borrow from Julia Kristeva, in the intertextual sense, each text in dialogue with all previous texts, transforming and retaining narrative patterns and strategies in endless possibility.

This pattern of literary influence from Harper to Walker departs in significant ways from that among black men. Henry Gates's description of intertextuality in his discussion of Richard Wright, Ralph Ellison, and Ishmael Reed, for example, characterizes the formal relations between them as largely adversarial and parodic. While there is certainly much to parody in Harper's *Iola Leroy*—most notably, the uplift concept and the excesses of formality that generally attended it—Walker refrains from doing so, and perhaps, therein, lies a fundamental distinction between African American male and female literary relations. We might argue that Walker has transformed and updated the concept of "uplift," associated almost exclusively with Harper and her generation, for a kind of uplift functions metaphorically in *The Color Purple*. The novel elevates the folk forms of rural and southern blacks to the status of art. In a similar fashion, it takes the tradition of letters and diaries, commonly considered a "female" tradition (and therefore inferior), from the category of "non-art" and elevates it to art.

But while Walker retains uplift as metaphor in *The Color Purple*, she rejects the burden it imposes on the writer, a burden that black writers have shouldered to their detriment throughout their literary history in service to a corporate mission. Certainly a major consequence of that mission for the writers of Harper's generation was a homogenized literary era that inhibited the writers' discovery of their unique voices.

The Color Purple is rich with images of voice, of singing, that complement and comment upon the novel's controlling metaphor of writing as seen in Celie's description of an exchange between Shug and Mary Agnes, a.k.a. Squeak:

> Shug say to Squeak, I mean, Mary Agnes, You ought to sing in public Mary Agnes say, Naw. She think cause she don't sing big and broad like Shug nobody want to hear her. But Shug say she wrong.
>
> What about all them funny voices you hear singing in church? Shug say.
>
> What about all them sounds that sound good but they not the sound you thought folks could make? What bout that?

Mary Agnes does go on to become a blues singer in her own right, singing in her own unimitative voice. Moreover, the narrative clearly implies that she can sing in public only when she discovers her own name (Mary Agnes, not Squeak) and her own "private," unique voice.

The Color Purple underscores the regrettable fact that black writers have not been permitted the freedom to discover and then to speak in their unique voices largely because they have been compelled to use their art for mainly propagandistic (public) purposes. Ntozake Shange makes that point in her collection of poems *nappy edges:* "We, as a people, or as a literary cult, or a literary culture / have not demanded singularity from our writers, we could all sound the same, come from the same region, be the same gender, born the same year." She adds, "we assume a musical solo is a personal statement / we think the poet is speakin for the world, there's something wrong there, a writer's first commitment is to the piece itself, then comes the political commitment."

The work of Frances E. W. Harper implies no such choice. Her age demanded the reverse. The morality of black women was being rampantly impugned; black people were suffering rank injustices, when they were not being lynched in teeming numbers. Without question, the writer lifted the pen in an act of political intervention.

Walker sacrifices the impulse to uplift the race, if that means sanitizing it, although hers, no less than Harper's, is a project whose aim is cultural transformation. She envisions a new world—at times utopian in dimension—in which power relations between men and women, between the colonizers and the colonized, are reconfigured to eliminate domination and promote cooperation. Further, in the structural arrangement of the letters—Celie's first, then Nettie's, then alternation of the two—she shows that self-development and corporate mission are not mutually exclusive but can be consonant with each other.

The Color Purple reflects Walker's awareness that the literary manifestations of racial uplift (or any social movement for that matter) are explained, in part, by the relationship between writer and audience. Unlike Harper, Walker could choose to ignore the fact that her audience was predominantly white, a choice strongly influenced, as was Harper's, by the social realities and literary circumstances of her place and time.

We might pinpoint specifically the emergence of black nationalism in the 1960s and 70s and the rise of the women's movement that followed closely on its heels. During this period, the writers and critics who formed the cultural arm of the larger political movement became convinced, as Houston Baker notes, that "their real audience, like the nation to come, was black." Accordingly, they directed "their energies to the creation of a new nation and their voices to an audience radically different from any [they] had ever conceived of," a black audience which would include, as never before, ordinary blacks from ghetto communities. They fashioned a critical methodology, termed the "black aesthetic," a "system of isolating and evaluating the artistic works of black people which reflect the special character and imperatives of black experience."

Like the black aestheticians, those women in the vanguard of the women's movement's second wave called for women's release from unreal and oppressive loyalties. Feminist criticism became one literary manifestation of that political stance. Similar in spirit and methodology to the largely male-dominated black aesthetic movement, feminist critics likewise repudiated and subverted what they considered alien, male-created literary standards, and began to describe and analyze a female aesthetic that reflected women's unique culture.

It is necessary to note that, ironically, in their earliest formulations, the objectives and practices of both the black aesthetic and feminist criticism often came dangerously close to insisting on a different and no less rigid set of aesthetic orthodoxies. Despite their own prescriptive leanings, however, these two modes of critical inquiry must be credited with opening up unprecedented possibilities for black and women writers. In isolating and affirming the particulars of black and female experience, they inspired and authorized writers from those cultures to sing in their different voices and to imagine an audience that could hear the song.

The narrative strongly implies that that audience is comprised mainly of Walker's "sisters," other black women. Its structure and plot—two black sisters writing to each other—lend this reading some support. It is not that Walker can or even desires to exclude readers outside this group; it is simply that she addresses her letters to them.

I am all too aware that this suggestion raises at least two glaring empirical paradoxes: the novel has been enormously successful with a very diverse readership, a large part of which is white, while often criticized by those to whom it seems addressed. However, the premise is recommended and supported by a major thread in the novel's plot: the act of reading letters that are written and intended for other eyes.

Just as the novel's letters lend themselves to Walker's reflexive depiction of the act of writing, they simultaneously lend themselves to her reflexive depiction of the act of reading. They offer a compelling model of the relationship Walker implies between herself and her readers, her own correspondents, her audience of "kissin' friends" who enter by the "intimate gate," to borrow from Zora Neale Hurston. In choosing them as her auditors and their experiences as her story, she has made the private public, and, in the process, created a new literary space for a black and a female idiom against and within a traditionally Eurocentric and androcentric literary history.

1984

It is a commonplace of current critical discourse to acknowledge that ideas of literary history or "tradition" are most appropriately read as narratives, the details of which are often selected in the interest of etching unitary and coherent story lines. By turns, these stories ignore discontinuities, explain them away, or assimilate them into existing narratives, all the while prompting readers to accept certain textual priorities and reading protocols. For these reasons, many look with suspicion, if not scorn, on ideas of tradition, even finding the very term tradition, a "critical fable intended to encode and circumscribe an inner and licit circle of empowered texts." Within dominant narratives of African American literary history, the circle of empowered texts have tended to include few by women and fewer still by those from the nineteenth century. Many fault the dominant plot of racial protest and the reading codes and priorities it established—both derived mainly from texts by men—with obscuring, until recently, the texts of a "black women's tradition."

Positing such a category as a clear and uncomplicated entity rests on no less powerful a fable, complete with its own textual consecrations and reading codes. But more importantly, constructing that category as a separate and "alternative" entity leaves intact and unexamined the reigning critical paradigm against which women writers are inevitably judged. What I call the racial recognizability quotient, or the "blackness" factor, constitutes the critical center of gravity of that paradigm, which circles ceaselessly around variations on two interlocking questions: What is the relationship between race and color? What is the relationship between color and emancipatory narrative strategies? The priority that nineteenth-century black women writers placed on "whiteness," which Molly Hite reads rightly as "the most overused element of characterization," has thrown into question the credentials of nineteenth-century novels by black women as "black" texts, a dispute resting on the widely accepted equation: race = color. Anticipating the passing novels that dominated the 1920s and '30s, many of these nineteenth-century works can seem to be nudging readers in a different, if you like, a modernist, direction by implying vexing questions about race: How do we recognize *"blackness" and assign it a value in the social order in the absence of the visible mark of color?*

In preparing the introduction to Four Girls at Cottage City, *the questions I posed indicated that I could only recognize "blackness" as it had already been constructed throughout Afro-American literary history: What is "black" about this book? How does it alter existing assumptions about nineteenth-century literature by* black *women? What formal and thematic features, what narrative strategies give these books a black woman's signature? Because this list of questions derived from the existing critical framework that assumes tautologically that blackness is always and self-evidently about itself, they ricocheted back on me. A different set of questions must be posed here, questions alert to the nuances of textual detail and narrative moment that distinguish this text and others like it from those with which it is invidiously compared.*

According to conventional critical grids and the hierarchies of "race consciousness" they inscribe, the writings of Emma Dunham Kelley are read as "race neutral" and thus apolitical foils to the more political and "race conscious" works of Ida B. Wells-Barnett, Frances E. W. Harper, and Anna Julia Cooper on one side and, say, Charles Chesnutt, on the other. Such zero-sum dichotomies are even more relentlessly pursued by critics unconditioned and opposed to the religious vocabularies that animate Kelley's work, which sits squarely in the discourse of spiritual writings and the tradition of religious movement: These provide the most logical contexts for reading her work, which is less an aberration in one stream of post-Reconstruction African American writing than might at first appear.

Mrs. A. E. Johnson's Clarence and Corinne *is a text that compares favorably to* Four Girls at Cottage City. *In her introduction to the Schomburg edition of* Clarence and Corinne, *Hortense Spillers urges readers who "smuggle in race" to be mindful of how the "narrative's subtitle insinuates its own supplementary meanings.* God's Way *renders the* other *theme of the work." That the novel was published by the American Baptist Publication Society establishes up front its evangelical designs, against which contemporary reading audiences are conditioned. The* what *and* how *of Johnson's writings, Spillers continues, are altogether less significant than the fact that she wrote: "the very act of writing itself is far more important than any particular outcome." She concludes that "even though* Clarence and Corinne *does not answer any of the expectations of a post-modernist reading protocol, it is a type of story that we must learn to read again for precisely that reason." Spiller's defense of Johnson generalizes easily to Emma Dunham Kelley and amounts to a recertification of her work. But however much we strain to read writers like Kelley and Johnson "in their own write," to quote Henry Louis Gates, they are inevitably subordinated in a linear logic of progress, by what Susan Sontag terms the relentless "rhythm of advent and supersession," which controls our understanding of literary history in many of its details.*

In juxtaposing Frances E. W. Harper's Iola Leroy *and Alice Walker's* The Color Purple, *I attempted to transcend that logic, implied in the popular notion that fiction by black women gets "better and better" with each generation, especially in its delineation of black female character. But a supersessional logic emerged nonetheless in the essay's reading strategies, which show a tendency to privilege twentieth-century over nineteenth-century texts, even while calling for non-hierarchical ways of considering them together. That tendency is reflected in my decision to evaluate* Iola Leroy *as character and text in terms of Celie and* The Color Purple, *the latter representing in my mind some kind of high-water mark in writing fiction with political intent. The essay associates emancipatory narrative strategies almost exclusively with a contemporary moment of literary production and thus uses its values and critical codes as the yardstick for measuring the failings and achievements of nineteenth-century texts. These codes constitute the "key words," to borrow from Raymond Williams, the generic vocabulary of critical terms for literary study on African American women: COLOR, CLASS, STEREOTYPE, and SEXUALITY. These key concepts converge in easily the most studied issue in the recent past: the representation of "black womanhood," especially the mulatta.*

Critics have long been locked in a fierce struggle over just how to read the representation of the middle-class mulatta in turn-of-the-century fiction by black women, over just how to resolve the range of cultural tensions around race and gender/race and class attached to this figure. Their debates have been fueled by a fundamental question: Does the mulatta figure serve or subvert dominant ideologies of race and gender?

Influenced by Alice Walker's engaging discussion of race and color in nineteenth-century fiction by black women ("If the Present Looks Like the Past"), I concluded that the "past" should look like the "present." In other words, in all matters central to the literary representation of black womanhood, Iola Leroy *should resemble* The Color Purple, *a strategy destined to overlook the possible ways in which Walker's ideologies of race, gender, sexuality, and class, which she locates in a literary utopia, might not only be open to some dispute, but might also be seen as the contemporary counterpart of the idealism associated strongly with her nineteenth-century precursors.*

While many share Walker's concern to explain the pervasiveness of the mulatta in nineteenth-century black fiction, they have gone astray in reading this figure as an unequivocal capitulation to dominant beliefs in the "rightness" and superiority of whiteness. Hazel Carby offers a more constructive and complicated conceptualization of the function of the mulatta in black women's fiction of the era. Against the popular critical perspective that the mulatta functions as a "gesture of acquiescence to a racist social order" and is thus "politically unacceptable," Carby argues that the mulatta acts as a "mediating device." As such, she continues, the mulatta enabled an exploration of both the sexual and social relations between the races, relations proscribed under Jim Crow laws and customs.

Carby's rereading of the mulatta enables a reconsideration of sexuality in Iola Leroy. *In reading both* The Color Purple *and* Iola Leroy, *I proceeded from a reification of "sexuality." I resorted to the modern tendency to view sexual expression as inherently liberating, rather than governed by relations of power in a steadily changing and complicated cultural field. Such a reification is most glaring in my treatment of* Iola Leroy *and probably results from providing an overly "literary" context for evaluating Harper's work, work that was a vital part of what Hazel Carby terms an "autonomous black feminist movement" that exploded in the 1890s. That wider political context enabled Harper to achieve the popular success as a writer that she might not have otherwise.*

If the context for reading Harper's work is enlarged to take the goals and strengths of this movement into account, then my reading of how and why sexuality functions as it does in Iola Leroy *must be completely rethought. Appropriating standard opinions of nineteenth-century fiction, I argued that in order to counter the widespread assumption that black women were sexually immoral, nineteenth-century black women "wanted to be remembered as upholders of puritan morality," hence, much of their work involved "encourag[ing] . . . masses of black women to accept the sexual morality of the Victorian bourgeoisie." However valid such an explanation might be, removed from historical context, even a reconstructed context, it oversimplifies the complex ways racialist (and racist) ideologies shaped and continue to shape black women's sexual choices. The sexual habits of turn-of-the-century women appear considerably less "prudish" when we consider the sexual dimensions in constructions of race that operated, then and now, to separate "good" sexual practices from "bad" and to construct black sexuality as the deviant alternative to more culturally prescribed sexual norms. The alleged sexuality of black women, defined against the so-called purity of white women, was the fulcrum on which racialist sexual ideologies turned. This discursive construction found practical enforcement and consequences in the uncontainable rush of lynchings—sexually motivated weapons of terrorist control—that swept across the South during the 1890s.*

If we take this context into account, then, for black women to defend themselves at the level of discourse against racist allegations of their sexual immorality, did not "represent some misguided bow to outmoded Victorian sexuality," as Elizabeth Ammons is correct to note. Rather, their self-defense "represented an essential part of their life-and-death struggle as women against lynching in the U.S." As Ammons goes on to say, black women's sexual history "did not consist of the right to be more sexual. It consisted of the right to be less sexual, the right even to be unsexual." Therefore, Ammons concludes, "Harper's heroine is characterized as a moral paragon—linked to an elevated Victorian image of womanhood—to demonstrate the vicious untruth of the "wanton theory underlying rape-lynch mythology."

Foregrounding this rape-lynch mythology further strengthens the thematic connections I tried to press between Walker and Harper. One could argue that The Color Purple *self-consciously re-enacts a form of rape in a significant feature of its plotting: stolen letters. As Ruth Perry suggests, "reading the letters written and intended for other eyes is the most reprehensible invasion of privacy and consciousness in epistolary fiction. These are overtones of sexual invasion—of mind rape—in the intercepting or "violating" of another's words. This experience is suggestive for the audience as well since they are reading letters not intended for public consumption. The most unholy thing in these books is uninvited access to another's inner life." Perry goes on to describe the marketing of such letters by booksellers who "advertised the fact that a set of letters had not been intended for publication because privacy, like virginity, invites violation."*

The ever-present threat of violation served Frances E. W. Harper's construction of a counter-mythology through representing marriage as a social program geared toward black self-determination. According to twentieth-century feminist reading strategies, marriage is an unambiguous capitulation to the status quo—meaning the oppression of women—but in a persuasive argument, Claudia Tate suggests a way to recuperate marriage for more transgressive ends and aims. She argues that a masculinist discourse of unconditional freedom (and here she might have added a feminist discourse as well), construes marriage as freedom's antithesis. This reading formation has dominated criticism of African American culture in the twentieth century and explains why contemporary readers construe marriage as a loss of freedom.

Against the hegemony of these reading formations, Tate proposes that nineteenth-century novels by black women be read with the understanding that "exercising the civil right to marry . . . was as important to the newly freed black population as exercising" the right to vote. For black people of that era, she continues, "to vote and to marry . . . were two civic responsibilities that nineteenth-century black people elected to perform: they were twin indexes for measuring how black people collectively valued their civil liberties." Thus, for the women writers who represented that group experience, "marriage and family life were not the culminating points of a woman's life but the pinnacle of a people's new beginning." The value of Tate's reconsideration of these nineteenth-century writers lies precisely in its attempt to historicize their narrative choices and to read their plots according to the specific contours of racial formation pervasive in their time.

These recent reevaluations of nineteenth-century fiction by black women have done much to reorient our thinking about the most vexing aspects of their work. Recuperating the figure of the mulatta as a component of a larger interventionist strategy disturbs many of the critical complacencies surrounding this perennial subject of critical controversy. But however welcome such recuperations might be, they still leave some matters yet unsettled. That Emma Dunham Kelley, Frances E. W. Harper, and their contemporaries, despite their best intentions and political motivations, could both fight and reproduce dominant racialist ideologies around color cannot be denied. Color-based social stratification within the race was real. Though not the only basis for divisions in black communities, color-consciousness was real and pervasive and found subtle, perhaps unconscious, expression in strategies of nineteenth-century black fiction and overt expression in the structures of everyday life that affected those who wrote it. To acknowledge this is not to detract from the power these writers command as cultural critics, but rather, to caution ourselves against the limits and dangers of hyper-idealization and -correctness. Lacking a critical vocabulary that could encompass these nineteenth-century writers, we have erred outlandishly in trying to fit them into a twentieth-century world picture. In our zeal to correct that error, we have remade these writers into aesthetic ideals and granted them an artistic and political self-consciousness that re-homogenizes them, even as it insists on their "difference." We have made our corrections by drawing on the necessary discipline of "historicism" and contextualism, but one that frequently and falsely implies a notion of both history and of context in need of its own corrections. We assume that our twentieth-century world picture is itself clear of the film and residues of "history," and that context can be retrieved as a whole cloth. As Jonathan Culler argues, "the notion of context frequently oversimplifies rather than enriches discussion" and overlooks the workings of semiotics, which render contexts in equal need of elucidation. Or as Dominick LaCapra puts it, "contexts are [not] ipso facto explanatory," nor do they "escape involvement in a relational network." In other words, what we know of context we have made. But to make this observation is not, in the final analysis, to invalidate our recent efforts to reconstruct the pieces of a nineteenth-century past; it simply requires that we be alert to the "new" critical complacencies they might engender.

CARLA KAPLAN

"Somebody I Can Talk To": Teaching Feminism Through The Color Purple

> "us talk and talk . . ."
> —Alice Walker,
> The Color Purple

"She Tell Lies"

In *The Color Purple*, Alice Walker gives us a heroine, like the others I've discussed, whose being in some way hinges on her ability to narrate her life story and to find an audience fit to hear and understand it. Where the other texts I've discussed use tropes of discursive and social exchange to critique the liberal premise that anyone can participate as an equal in the cultural conversation, Walker gives us a heroine whose story works transformative magic, putting all of its listeners—including the reader—on the same footing and thereby representing exchange as just the equalizing and fair social machinery it represents itself to be.

If *Their Eyes Were Watching God* can only imagine a satisfying discursive exchange within a dyadic, female, identificatory, homogeneous, and private public sphere (the back porch), Alice Walker's *The Color Purple* is prepared to celebrate the utopian possibilities of discourse, community, and social exchange without the reserve and distrust exhibited by the other texts I've

From *The Erotics of Talk: Women's Writing and Feminist Paradigms* by Carla Kaplan. © 1996 Carla Kaplan.

discussed. Those texts distrust the transformational effects of narratives written from the social margins to be read by those in positions of relatively greater power even as they attempt to generate just such effects. *The Color Purple*, by contrast, suggests that there is no need for skepticism or withdrawal, since simply through the intersubjective exchange created when we speak to one another it is in our power to create a perfect (or nearly perfect) world which realizes the values of intimacy we prize in the private sphere. This perfect world is, ultimately, in fact, the private sphere writ large. In Walker's hands, the trope of an erotics of talk becomes the model for the way things finally are in Celie's transfigured, ideal, familiar, feminist world.

What are we to make of this? In a sense, Walker offers just the happy ending which feminist criticism has sought to read into many fables of women's talk: making the mad narrator of "The Yellow Wallpaper" or the women readers of "The Blank Page" and "A Jury of Her Peers" heroic rescuers in an enterprise of recuperative reading, imagining successful contracts for Linda Brent, projecting ourselves as the ideal listener/lover Jane and Janie long for. In Michael Awkward's words, *The Color Purple*'s story is "the achievement of (comm)unity." Here at last the imperatives of a politics of voice and an erotics of talk are no longer at odds. By speaking out, Celie transfigures her world. In her new community, anyone can talk, everyone listens; talk is, indeed, the "language game" of justice in which, as Lyotard puts it, "one speaks as a listener."

Given its instructive, inspiring story of an oppressed, abused, isolated woman who learns to fight back, speak for herself, defend other women, "git man off her eyeball," and make her way in a racist, patriarchal world that would deny her subjectivity, agency, and pleasure, it is hardly surprising that Walker's *The Color Purple* "took the feminist world by storm." Or that it has been taken up as a "feminist fable." Or that Celie has become a "role model for contemporary feminists," "an example of woman's oppression and liberation," a symbolic "'Everywoman'" in both her reduction to object and her struggles to become a speaking subject.

Although *The Color Purple* has occasioned heated debates over black cultural representation and white patronage, a debate that is sometimes reminiscent of the fiery polemics of the twenties, Jacqueline Bobo, in her interviews with African American women about their responses to the novel, reported "overwhelmingly positive reactions." Even Trudier Harris, who joined a number of black male critics in faulting the novel for a "reaffirmation of many old stereotypes" and for giving "validity to all the white racist's notions of pathology in black communities," celebrates Walker's depiction of "a woman who struggles through adversity to assert herself against almost impossible odds."

Whereas many black feminist critics stress the racial specificity of Walker's portrayal, reading the novel as an allegory of "the process and problematics of writing *for the black woman*," white feminist critics have often universalized the novel as a "paradigm of change," rejoicing in how "Celie wrests language from those who would persecute and silence her." A novel like *The Color Purple*, Alison Light writes, "can be popular with a whole range of women readers, cutting across the specificity of its black history, in its concern with family, emotionality, sexual relations, and fantasy life."

There are good reasons for this novel's privileged status as a pedagogical and political model. Celie ruptures the patriarchal injunction to silence "'You better not never tell nobody but God. It'd kill your mammy.'" And she keeps faith with her own perception, in spite of the way others try to invalidate it: "'She tell lies,'" "Pa" tells Mr. _____ as he hands her over to him, just as Jane is branded a "liar" when she is passed between Mrs. Reed and Mr. Brocklehurst. Celie refuses to accept that her own view is a "lie."

Alice Walker is a writer working within the recuperative, archeological tradition of feminist criticism; she has dedicated herself to uncovering the voices of women she calls "Crazy Saints . . . our mothers and grandmothers . . . who died with their real gifts stifled within them." "I'm always trying to give voice to specific people," Walker writes. *The Color Purple* was written, Walker remarked in a *Newsweek* interview, so that "people can hear Celie's voice." Walker wants us to understand such recuperation as an act of self-preservation. "The life we save," she asserts, "is our own." Without freeing earlier artists "from their neglect and the oppression of silence forced upon them because they were black and they were women," the contemporary African American woman writer, Walker believes, will be condemned to similar silence and neglect. "We are a people. A people do not throw their geniuses away. And if they are thrown away, it is our duty as artists and as witnesses for the future to collect them again for the sake of our children, and, if necessary, bone by bone."

The fictional act of recovering Celie's narrative grounds *The Color Purple* in the politics of voice and recuperation I have discussed earlier. Celie, as Linda Abbandonato writes, is "an 'invisible woman' . . . traditionally silenced and effaced in fiction; and by centering on her, Walker replots the heroine's text." Walker, Linda Kauffman writes, "views history from the bottom up and reconstructs it to reflect the voices of the oppressed, the disenfranchised, the silenced." Celie herself models this archeological enterprise by recuperating Nettie's buried voice; with Shug's help she saves Nettie's story, shares it, puts it in order.

Also clearly grounded in the topos of an erotics of talk, the novel has Celie long for an ideal listener, someone who will listen to her story, sympathize with it, understand it (and her), and respond accordingly. Walker makes explicit what *Jane Eyre* and *Their Eyes Were Watching God* imply: Celie's ideal listener—a woman—is also her ideal lover, and vice versa. Shug and Celie, as Henry Louis Gates, Jr., puts it, are "literal 'kissin-friends.'"

In fact, *The Color Purple* "signifies" upon Hurston's novel by rejecting its ethics of disengagement, even as it builds on its aesthetic of reciprocity by providing Celie with a nearly endless supply of desirable, conversational partners. Contesting one's community, Walker implies, can transform it. Even Mr. _____ in the end becomes "somebody I can talk to," Celie says. This transformation, and the theory of narrative exchange it articulates, will be the focus of much of what follows.

Exchange is at the heart of our self-understandings as autonomous *and* social beings, as Seyla Benhabib has argued. The normative ideals of bourgeois society—the right of all to freedom, equality, property—are expressed in social relations of exchange between citizens, who are equal in their abstract right to voluntarily dispose of what belongs to them. "Social relations of exchange in the marketplace actualize the norms of equality, freedom, and property."

On the face of it, Celie's exclusion from language—"you better not never tell"—holds this normative self-understanding up to the scrutiny of actual social relations, calling into question the very ideal of exchange as an equalizing norm. "When the *norms* of bourgeois society are compared with the *actuality* of the social relations in which they are embodied, the discrepancy between ideal and actuality becomes apparent." The dimension of the novel which makes this discrepancy apparent is its rehearsal of failed exchanges: between Celie and various members of her community, between Nettie and Celie, between Nettie (and company) and the Africans, between Africans and European imperialists, between southern American blacks and whites, between men and women. These failed exchanges suggest not only that ideals and actualities do not mesh, but more important that the ideals represented by social exchange are, in fact, effaced by the practice of exchange itself. In short, under conditions of radical inequality, exchange relations benefit the advantaged. Exchange, by itself, is not a medium for redistributing social and symbolic resources but, Walker suggests, for recirculating them back to their original proprietors. The novel's most interesting moments of social critique, in my view, are all refracted through such failed exchanges, failed communications. It is when, suddenly, such failures as Mr. _____'s inability to listen become successes that I would question the way exchange is operating in this novel and, in turn, the sort of model *The Color Purple* offers for either liberation or, read allegorically, criticism.

"You Got to Fight"

It would be hard to disagree with Gates's assessment that *The Color Purple* is an exemplary text of "voice." It does not merely represent a new version of Hurston's Janie on a quest for voice. It also polemicizes *against* black female texts like *Incidents in the Life of a Slave Girl* and *Their Eyes Were Watching God* which express ambivalence about the effectivity—and desirability—of discursive contestation. It seems to suggest that however delegitimated one's discursive position may be, self-isolation is not a viable, moral position. It both valorizes "voice" in the sentimentalizing terms I have criticized and seems, until the end, to question that very sentimentalization.

Walker, in fact, does not really represent Celie as "finding" a voice. Even in her most oppressed state, she is able to express herself by writing. It is the process of developing that voice, orienting it toward her different audiences, that is really at stake. Above all, Celie needs to learn to use her voice to resist oppression. She must be convinced that resistance and contestation are not incompatible with fulfillment and satisfaction. Making this convincing, as we shall see, proves a very difficult task.

Numerous times, other women tell Celie that she must learn to fight back. "You got to fight. You got to fight," Nettie tells Celie when she sees how Mr. _____'s children ride roughshod over her. "You've got to fight," Nettie writes. "I don't know how to fight. All I know how to do is stay alive," Celie replies. Having internalized the patriarchal warning that the wages of rebellion are death, Celie believes that resistance and survival are necessarily at odds. "It's like seeing you buried," Nettie writes, hoping to free Celie's voice.

Celie's next letter reopens the same debate. "You got to fight them, Celie, she [Mr. _____'s sister, Kate] say. I can't do it for you. You got to fight them for yourself." "I don't say nothing," Celie says, "I think about Nettie, dead. She fight, she run away. What good it do? I don't fight, I stay where I'm told. But I'm alive." Celie, it is important to note, is not entirely misguided. Resistance and rebellion *are* costly. And just as Nettie's resistance has caused her absence, so Kate is kicked out of Mr. _____'s house and hence out of Celie's life for trying to speak on Celie's behalf and protest her mistreatment by Mr. _____ and his sons.

But Celie also misreads this lesson. Her inability to associate fighting *with* survival is, it is implied, tied to her mistaken faith in authoritative narratives, her failure as an "overreader," to return to the problematic explored in Chapter One. As Mr. _____ drags Nettie away, Celie enjoins her to "write" (just as Nettie has been enjoining Celie to "fight"). "Nothing but death can keep me from it," Nettie promises. Never again hearing from

Nettie, Celie presumes that she is dead. Celie does not know how to "overread": filling in gaps, reading between the lines, learning to hear the "voice" of silence, madness, babbling, muttering, or screaming—women's "self-talk." Before Celie can learn to "fight," she must identify her models and resources by learning—like Walker "reading" the hundred-year-old quilt of an anonymous black woman in Alabama, like the protagonist of "The Yellow Wallpaper" reading the "sub-pattern" of "bars" and "the woman behind it . . . as plain as can be," like the "old and young nuns, with the Mother Abbess herself" reading the "blank page" of the anonymous, missing princess, like Mrs. Peters and Mrs. Hale, reading the uneven stitches of Mrs. Foster's quilt block, or like Nettie trying to get Corrine to read Celie's story in a quilt—to recognize the alternative texts that code and preserve women's stories of resistance. Only after Celie has discovered Nettie's hidden letters and learned, therefore, that there *are* hidden, unofficial, even silent stories to be recuperated from behind the official— and false—narratives that obscure them does she begin to "fight back" with her own self-narrations.

Walker makes *The Color Purple*'s project a panegyric to the therapeutic and transformational potential of telling counternarratives: the unofficial histories of the private or intimate sphere over and against official histories of the public sphere. It is "a historical novel" that "starts not with the taking of lands, or the births, battles, and deaths of Great Men, but with one woman asking another for her underwear." In place of the so-called "antinarrativism" often assumed to be the inevitable outcome of poststructural skepticism about "historical unities, subjects and totalizations," Walker champions what one critic has recently called the "tactical value of narrative" in the "struggle against dominant culture," its ability to represent what Toni Morrison calls "discredited" and Michel Foucault "unauthorized" forms of knowledge.

In this context, Steven Spielberg and screenwriter Menno Meyjes were right to make cinematic hay out of what are relatively brief mentions of literacy and education in the novel. Through a dramatic tracing-paper flutter of hand-lettered signifieds—"apples," "iron," "kettle," "eggs," "shelf," "honey," "jar," "window," "hair," "arm," "sleeve," "stocking," and, of course, "sky" (which Celie finds on the floor long after Nettie is gone)— the film depicts the importance of narrative mastery. Insofar as a coherent sense of self depends upon becoming the "author of a coherent life-story," Celie's very being depends upon her access to narrative and her ability to construct a counternarrative that (re)tells the story of her own life over and against the disembodied patriarchal injunction to self-silencing which speaks first in the novel and the misrepresentations—"she tell lies"—that those in power promote.

Celie's pointed inability to do this opens the novel, much as negation and dissatisfaction open *Jane Eyre* and *Their Eyes Were Watching God*. Self-description becomes self-erasure in her aborted effort to proclaim herself a good girl. "~~I am.~~" "Not only am I not a good girl, but I am not." "I do not exist." "I am no one." By coaching her to "fight," other women prompt Celie to develop narratives that can assert both her "goodness" and her being, a provocation Celie finally answers when she articulates the exploitation at the heart of family romance: "You was all rotten children, I say. You made my life a hell on earth. And your daddy here ain't dead horse's shit." Her tongue-lashing ends with the crucial replacement of "I'm here" for her earlier self-erasure "~~I am.~~"

Telling a counternarrative, it would seem, heals Celie's fragmented self and enables her coherent self-assertion. This power of renaming is repeated several times. Sexual desire seems foreclosed for Celie, who experiences sex as pure objectification and humiliation: "he get up on you, heist your nightgown round your waist, plunge in. . . . Never ast me how I feel, nothing. Just do his business, get off, go to sleep." But by renaming Celie "still a virgin," Shug unsutures sexuality and abuse. She calls it not it, we might say, echoing the pun exchanged by Mrs. Hale and Mrs. Peters in "A Jury of Her Peers." Shug uncovers Celie's buried desire as Celie is later to uncover Nettie's buried voice, designating her as alive not dead, present not absent. It is a short step from here to uncovering a buried voice by renaming it. "Squeak, Mary Agnes, what difference do it make?" Harpo asks. "It make a lot, say Squeak. When I was Mary Agnes I could sing in public."

This privileging of counternarratives shapes the novel's form. Interweaving the historical narratives of Africa and Georgia is a way of countering the official, racist, pathologizing representations of slavery and black southern life with an unofficial and variegated history of poor, rural, post-Reconstruction small-town life, an unofficial history of African American resistance and entrepreneurship, as well as with the often repressed story of black African participation in the slave trade. A web of contestations emerges. *American blacks versus Africans*. "No one else in this village wants to hear about slavery. They acknowledge no responsibility whatsoever"; "the Africans don't even *see* us. They don't even recognize us as the brothers and sisters they sold." *European and American imperialism versus black African culture*: "the things they have brought back! . . . jewels, furniture, fur carpets, swords, clothing, even *tombs*." *Black African men versus black African women*: "the Olinka don't believe in educating girls." *The European rubber industry versus African roofleaf. Black versus white missionaries* (who show no real interest in Africans). *Straight white male Englishmen versus an (implicitly) lesbian white Englishwoman writer*: "she wanted to write books. Her family was against it. They hoped she'd marry. Me *marry!* she hooted." *The North* (where Nettie travels prior to leaving for Africa) *versus the South*. This web of contestations, formally at least, suggests a heterogeneous speech community and the importance of speaking across it. It suggests the importance of contestation and argument.

The question of what counts not merely as true but also *as* narration takes shape in myriad jokes over mainstream white *history* ("I learned all about Columbus in first grade, but look like he the first thing I forgot"); *journalism* ("The news always sound crazy. People fussing and fighting and pointing fingers at other people, and never even looking for no peace. People insane, say Shug. Crazy as betsy bugs"); and *national identity* ("white people busy celebrating they independence from England July 4th, say Harpo, so . . . us can spend the day celebrating each other").

The question of what counts is also particularly sharp when Celie learns her own buried family history: her successful father was lynched for his store and her grieving mother was driven insane and taken advantage of by a "stranger." While these parents are buried in unmarked graves and Celie has no record of their lives, the record of "Pa's" (that is, the stranger's) life both mirrors and mocks hegemonic modes of memorialization. As Celie enters the graveyard where "Pa" is buried she sees "something like a short skyscraper . . . sure enough it's got Alphonso's name on it. Got a lot of other stuff on it too. Member of this and that. Leading businessman and farmer. Upright husband and father. Kind to the poor and helpless." The counternarratives that connect Columbus to cucumbers and newspapers to science fiction, that render national celebrations ludicrous and reduce the memory of Alphonse to a lying concrete phallus, are given both a therapeutic and a revolutionary force. They can heal communities and contest hegemony. Or so the novel *seems* to insist.

"I Was Dying to Tell"

As much as Celie must learn to "fight back," winning battles isn't really what Celie's war is all about. For Celie to become a "dignified" subject and enter into the public sphere as an agent to be reckoned with, she must not only find her voice, she must exercise it with someone besides herself, must avoid seeming to engage in what Goffman calls "self talk" or "muttering." As Molly Hite writes, "the drama of Celie's epistolary self-creation revolves around the discovery of a female audience that finally fulfills the ideal of co-respondence. . . . The process of finding her speaking voice is a process of finding her audience."

Unlike Hurston's Janie, for Celie, finding a listener and finding her voice are inextricably related, just as believing one has an ideal and sympathetic listener may give one the courage to fight back against others. Only when her sister-in-law Kate tells her, "'You deserve more than this,'" does she begin to consider, "Maybe so. I think." Becoming Nettie's ideal listener and saving her letters from oblivion teaches Celie about how good listeners help others to survive, how social and personal identities are constructed by our relations with others and their recognitions of us. When Celie finally does talk back to Mr. _____, saying "I'm pore, I'm black, I may be ugly and can't cook . . . but I'm here," her "voice" speaks to "everything listening." Without "everything listening," everything's "hungry listening," we might say, her response would not have been possible. Without a sympathetic audience, such as Shug, Celie might never have been able to go from her first self-effacing statement "I am" to her later declaration, "I'm here."

But there is also a tension between these two imperatives. "Finding a voice" means one thing, for example, when the audience to be addressed is a group of hostile "others": the courthouse Janie faces, Minnie Foster will face, or Linda Brent might have faced had she either been caught or had tried to press her legal "rights" to her children. It means another thing altogether when the audience to be addressed is Pheoby, Shug Avery, Mrs. Peters and Mrs. Hale, the woman in the wallpaper, or Diana and Mary Rivers.

Earlier I suggested that Walker "signifies" on Hurston's text by imagining a much wider and much more successful field of discursive contestation for Celie. Celie does "fight"—even with God ("us fight")—in ways that Janie resists. *The Color Purple* could, in fact, be read as re-staging Hurston's courtroom scene in *Their Eyes Were Watching God*, a revision in which the "accused" defends herself, in her own voice, in front of all of her different constituencies. Walker not only "signifies" on Hurston's politics of voice, suggesting that Janie—and perhaps Hurston as well—"got to fight." She also sends Celie out on Janie's quest for a "bee for her blossom," a search for the "creaming," "frothing," delight of "self revelation."

Nettie's letters to Celie and Celie's letters to God dramatize their unmet needs for the conditions enabling such "creaming" and "frothing." "I remember one time you said your life made you feel so ashamed you couldn't even talk about it to God, you had to write it, bad as you thought your writing was. Well, now I know what you meant," Nettie writes from Africa, where she suffers from having "hardly anybody to talk to, just in friendship." Nettie, like Celie before she meets Shug, like Jane in *Jane Eyre*, like Janie before Pheoby, is "dying to tell" her story but has no one to tell it to.

The epistolary form is particularly well suited for dramatizing this. While epistolary narratives may well embody a "desire for exchange," Linda Kauffman points out that they are more likely to depict that desire as a thwarted one: "letters are repeatedly lost, withheld, seized, misdirected, or misplaced. . . . An addressee who is absent, silent, or incapable of replying is one of the distinguishing characteristics of epistolarity." Failed exchange, Kauffman argues, is "endemic" to the form.

Many critics have argued that Nettie's letters are digressive and boring compared with Celie's. But they play a vital role in developing the novel's initial skepticism about the utopian possibilities of discursive and social exchange. Nettie's letters dramatize the problematic of failed exchange.

Nettie writes often about communicative and intersubjective failure, describing the "indifference," for example, with which the Africans greet the black missionaries who've come to "help" them. "Sometimes I feel our position is like that of flies on an elephant's hide," she confides to Celie. "They never even listen to how we've suffered. And if they listen they say stupid things." She describes the men's indifference to women: "there is a way that the men speak to women that reminds me too much of Pa. *They listen just long enough to issue instructions*," Nettie writes. She describes Corrine's indifference to the truth about who Adam and Olivia's mother is: "Oh Celie, unbelief is a terrible thing."

It is not only in personal relations that Nettie witnesses failed exchange. The social relations she takes note of all have to do with failures of exchange as well. The chief of the Olinka, for example, engages in what Nettie describes as a "pathetic exchange." He tries to explain to the white governor of the English rubber company that their road and rubber trees are wiping out their livelihood. But the Olinka not only lose their village, they end up paying rent to farm there and taxes to use their own water.

Nettie not only describes failed exchanges, she also fantasizes about exchange. "I imagine that you really do get my letters and that you are writing me back: Dear Nettie, this is what life is like for me," she writes.

There is a lesson for Celie in all of these failed exchanges between people of different social status and power. These failures lead those on the losing end of bad transactions to call for revolt. They imply that Celie ought to do so as well. As a consequence of their chief's "pathetic exchange" with the white men, the Olinka conclude that it's a waste of breath to argue with men who can't—or won't—listen. "We will fight the white man," they declare. Samuel, a voice of rationality and caution, finally comes to the same conclusion: "He said the only thing for us to do if we wanted to remain in Africa, was join the Mbeles [the resistance fighters] and encourage all the Olinka to do the same."

Celie, like Nettie, lacks an appropriate audience. Her letters parallel Nettie's by documenting failed exchanges, chiefly in the private, domestic sphere. God, Celie decides, is just like the other men she has known. "The God I been praying and writing to is a man," she says, "and act just like all the other mens I know. Trifling, forgitful, and lowdown. *If he ever listened to poor colored women the world would be a different place, I can tell you. . . . just sit up there glorying in being deef*" (emphasis mine). Shug points out to Celie that there is no point in being angry at God for not listening, because there was no point ever expecting that he could. "You mad cause he don't seem to listen to your prayers. Humph! Do the mayor listen to anything colored say? Ask Sofia." "I don't have to ast Sofia. I know white people never listen to colored, period. If they do, they only listen long enough to be able to tell you what to do," Celie replies.

Celie not only lacks a listener, she is, like the Olinka, on the losing end of discursive, economic, and social systems of exchange. Speaking across differences of gender and race proves as vexed for her as it is for them: "I don't have nothing to offer and I feels poor." In the white man's store, which has replaced the store of Celie's lynched father, Corrine is made to buy 40 cents' worth of thread in "bout the right color" that she does not want. This scene, omitted entirely in the movie, portrays the women's inability to participate as equals in a system of exchange based on prerogatives of status and race from which they are, by definition, excluded. As simple an act as buying fabric and thread becomes humiliating.

Celie's first positive exchange with another woman immediately follows this scene and in a sense compensates for it. Celie sees Corrine at a loss for a safe place to wait for her husband's return and realizes that she does have something to offer: a seat in her wagon. In return, Corrine thanks her for her "'*Horse*pitality'" "'I git it and laugh,'" Celie says, "it feel like to split my face."

Celie is not the only character to experience difficult or imbalanced exchanges. We see this again and again with the black women in the novel. Addie Beasley, for example, the schoolteacher, tries to argue "Pa" out of his decision to take the girls out of school, but when he brings Celie out and parades her pregnancy, Addie Beasley "stop talking and go." A similar failed exchange occurs when Mr. _____'s sisters, Carrie and Kate, argue over his first wife, Annie Julia. Kate tries to defend her, pointing out that Mr. _____ "just brought her here, dropped her . . . nobody to talk to, nobody to visit." But Carrie remains unmoved. When Kate argues with Mr. _____ she is thrown out of the house. When Sofia fights with Harpo, they separate. She is subsequently jailed for "sassing" the mayor and his wife.

The failed exchanges I am rehearsing here are part of the novel's formal as well as thematic structure. Although Walker interweaves the narratives of

Africa and Georgia by paralleling certain of Nettie and Celie's experiences—
falling in love, growing up, raising other people's children, and so on—the
two narrative strains nonetheless operate at a considerable distance from one
another. They are never, in short, *about* each other. Although they are
implicitly joined by a history of slavery and by a problematic of failed
exchanges, nothing that happens in Milledgeville, Georgia, is shown to bear
on Africa, and nothing that happens in Africa is shown to bear on Georgia.
There is no trace of a pan-Africanist sensibility among Harpo and his juke
joint friends, for example. None of the forms of vernacular expression which
are prized in the novel is tied back to the African cultures in which it may
have originated. These stories never really speak *to* each other. It is as if they
never quite learn one another's tongue.

But this paradigm of failed exchange does not apply across the board.
Walker attributes it most often to the public, heterogeneous sphere. In the
world of romance and female friendship (which for Walker are on the
"lesbian continuum" Adrienne Rich has described), exchange is a far less
problematic, far more pleasurable proposition. As the story develops,
characters increasingly find ideal interlocutors with whom they can "change
words" as an erotics of talk.

The relationship between Celie and Shug, for example, turns around
talk. At Christmas, for example, Celie relates that "me and Shug cook, talk,
clean the house, talk, fix up the tree, talk, wake up in the morning, talk." "I
talk so much my voice start to go." "Shug talk and talk." The romance
between Samuel and Nettie also turns on talk. Samuel satisfies Nettie's need
for a listener: "[He] asked me to tell him about you," Nettie writes, "and the
words poured out like water. I was dying to tell someone about us." Their
courtship, like Jane and Rochester's or Janie and Tea Cake's, is a "simple
conversation." Tashi and Adam also court through seductive talk, a bantering
reminiscent, in fact, of Rochester and Jane. "I wish you could have seen
[Adam and Tashi] as they staggered into the compound," Nettie writes to
Celie, "filthy as hogs, hair as wild as could be. Sleepy. Exhausted. Smelly.
God knows. *But still arguing*" (emphasis mine).

How is this discursive pleasure and free exchange related to the need to
"fight back" in the public sphere? Does the one develop from the other? Do
they flow in both directions? What allows for shifts between them?

Walker's economy is in fact a one-way street. Whereas Walker's private
sphere of intimate, reciprocal values can ultimately transform the public
sphere of debate and contestation, there is no exchange of discursive form in
the other direction. On the contrary. The erotics of talk that shapes the
novel's romances, including the "romance" between Celie and Nettie, does
not grow out of situations where characters have learned to use their voices

to "fight back." In each of these instances, an erotics of talk is made possible only once the speakers turn their backs (give up, in effect) on arguing with their oppressors and begin to speak to one another instead. Turning away from Mr. _____ allows Celie both to "change words" with Shug and to foster an alternative economy. Similarly, Samuel and Nettie are able to realize their conversational romance only after they first give up on fighting the Europeans and prepare to leave Africa altogether. Tashi and Adam emerge from the forest as sweethearts precisely at the moment that Adam takes Tashi away from the fighting Mbeles.

What are we to make of these apparent renunciations of rebellion in a novel which, as I have argued, seems to take issue with Hurston's *Their Eyes Were Watching God* precisely for Janie's refusal to "fight back" with her voice? Is Walker, like Hurston, endorsing a strategy of "feather bed resistance"? Is she suggesting, as Janie does, that "fighting back" against oppression just "'tain't worth de trouble'"?

No character in *The Color Purple* is more known for her rebellious, contestatory voice and for "fighting back" than Sofia. Sofia even walks like a soldier. "Look like the army change direction, and she heading off to catch up." Sofia's willingness to fight is her signature trait. She simply cannot resist contestation, whether it is telling Mr. _____ that she's not in trouble, "big though," or whether it is telling the mayor's wife "Hell no" she didn't want to be her maid, a rebuff that takes twelve years off Sofia's life and reminds us of the costs of resistance. What is it, exactly, that drives Sofia to fight? Is it, like Mrs. Farrinder, the love of conflict for its own sake? What is she fighting? Sofia is fighting conflict itself: "All my life I had to fight. I had to fight my daddy. I had to fight my brothers. I had to fight my cousins and my uncles. A girl child ain't safe in a family of men. But I never thought I'd have to fight in my own house," she says sadly.

Sofia separates a politics of voice and an erotics of talk. She articulates the strand of the narrative logic that I have been tracing in descriptions of failed exchange. This strand of the narrative demonstrates that those at the bottom of the social order cannot transfigure the world simply by speaking their minds or, even more benignly, by telling their stories and sharing their painful experiences. All the more surprising, then, that what happens in the conclusion is exactly the reverse. The utopian conclusion of the novel argues that those whose lives are "oppressed almost beyond recognition" can transfigure the world purely through the power of their voices, even when they have ceased to engage their oppressors at all.

The Color Purple has often been celebrated precisely for the force of its narrative dialectic of psychological cure and social transformation. Among feminists it is often venerated, as in Christine Froula's treatment of the novel, as a "radical cure of the hysterical cultural text that entangles both women and men," celebrated for its representation of a "hero . . . who recreates the universe by telling her story to the world."

The Color Purple is a disarmingly complex novel, a novel in many ways at war with its own narrative logic. On the one hand, Walker creates an almost formulaic and sentimentalizing construction of the rebellious and curative voice of the disempowered. Yet, until the conclusion, *The Color Purple* not only deploys its own ambivalence about narrative's healing and transformational power, it affords us a "cautionary tale" about what happens when we assume that Celie's rebellious voice has the power to "liberate speaker and auditor alike." For much of the novel, Walker works, I want to continue to demonstrate, with a productive tension between a politics of voice and an erotics of talk, with the necessary back and forth between them. Her conclusion, however, collapses the very tension that has given the novel its energy.

"Somebody I Can Talk To"

Although it takes both Jane and Janie nearly their whole lives to find one ideal listener, Celie seems to spend her life in constant conversation. Nearly everyone becomes her "co-respondent," as we see in the utopic family reunion that closes both the novel and the film. Many critics have remarked that Mr. _____'s transformation strains readerly credulity, but it is not only Mr. _____ who is magically transformed. Transformation is the rule of a world in which anyone may become "somebody I can talk to."

Spielberg, Molly Hite notes, played on this transformational emphasis by making Mr. _____'s "change of heart the turning-point of the action" and adding what Hite rightly calls a "textually gratuitous daddy" for Shug. Shug's filmic daddy will not speak or listen to her. But eventually he is converted, like Mr. _____, into someone she can talk to and take comfort in. Spielberg gets the narrative logic right: anyone can be transformed into an ideal listener. (Counter)narratives create the transformations they desire.

Stepto argues that African American writers, motivated by their distrust of literate culture and mainstream audiences, attempt to create that sense of direct and immediate exchange which, according to Benjamin, is lost to modernity. African American storytelling, Stepto argues, attempts to recreate telling and hearing as a social transaction, to constitute the reader as "a hearer, with all that that implies in terms of . . . the *responsibilities* of listenership." This is a matter of active transformation and change. Responsible hearers engage in what I have described as acts of collaboration which answer the "prompting" of the text.

Mr. _____'s "collaboration" is particularly notable. "When you talk to him now he really listen," Celie writes. He attempts to "do right" by Celie by locating Nettie, Samuel, Adam, Olivia, and Tashi and securing their return to America. Not only can Mr. _____ now understand how Celie feels and thinks, not only does he become her audience for transmitting the tales of Africa she has learned from Nettie, but he even enters into Celie's alternative economy by becoming a maker of shirts to go with her "folkspants" and by joining the "ethic of care" that predominates in Celie's female community. Sewing while he listens, Mr. _____ pauses to "look at the different color thread us got," differentiating himself from the men in the store who force Corrine to buy thread in "bout" the right color, as if such "trifles," as the men in "A Jury of Her Peers" might say, don't matter. In his sewing, Mr. _____ demonstrates his ability to listen to people's needs: "Got to have pockets, he say. Got to have loose sleeves. And definitely you not spose to wear it with no tie. Folks wearing ties look like they being lynch." Mr. _____ learns to identify with others.

This is not the only male transformation in the novel. Harpo, who originally wanted to beat Sofia into submission, becomes the primary caretaker of their (or rather Sofia's) daughter Henrietta. In place of criticizing Sofia, he offers verbal and practical support: "I loves every judgment you ever made," he tells her. Like Mr. _____, Harpo participates in an alternative economy: promoting the vernacular culture of African American music through his juke joint "way back" in the woods.

It is not only black men who can change and be good friends to black women, Walker implies. White women can learn to hear also, *if* they are "told off." When Eleanor Jane reappears at the end of the novel she is all talk, in the worst sense. She pesters Sofia to say that Reynolds Stanley Earl, her son, is "sweet," "the smartest baby you ever saw," "*innocent*," "cute," and that Sofia "just love him." "You know how some whitefolks is," Celie adds in her letter to Nettie, "they gon harass a blessing from you if it kill." But Sofia, clearly fed up with being "harass[ed]" to say what she doesn't believe, finally lets Eleanor Jane have it:

> No ma'am, say Sofia. I do not love Reynolds Stanley Earl. Now. That's what you been trying to find out ever since he was born. And now you know. . . . [He] head straight for Sofia's stack of ironed clothes and pull it down on his head. . . . He can't even walk and already he in my house messing it up. Did I ast him to come? Do I care whether he sweet or not? Will it make any difference in the way he grow up to treat me what I think? . . . I don't feel nothing about him at all. I don't love him,

I don't hate him. I just wish he couldn't run loose all the time messing up folks stuff.

I just don't understand, say Miss Eleanor Jane. All the other colored women I know love children. The way you feel is something unnatural.

I love children, say Sofia. But all the colored women that say they love yours is lying. They don't love Reynolds Stanley any more than I do. But if you so badly raise as to ast 'em, what you expect them to say? Some colored people so scared of whitefolks they claim to love the cotton gin. . . . I got my own troubles and when Reynolds Stanley grow up, he's gon be one of them.

We know that Eleanor Jane is transformed when, a few pages later, we learn that she has gone to her mother to ask why Sofia "come to work for them" in the first place. Because she really listens to the answer, Eleanor Jane turns her back on the white world and comes to work for Sofia, disproving Celie's earlier hypothesis that "white people never listen to colored, period. If they do, they only listen long enough to be able to tell you what to do." Like Mr. _____ and Harpo, Eleanor Jane has learned to identify with black women.

Transforming Mr. _____, Harpo, and Eleanor Jane into good listeners allows Walker a double articulation. First, that "the reader" is a fiction. There is no neutral audience. Instead, multiple factors, such as race and gender, condition how different readers will respond to different narratives and inflect whether or not they will be likely to understand them. Second, by transforming all these bad listeners into good ones, Walker suggests, as I have stated, that everyone can become "somebody I can talk to."

Well, perhaps not everyone. It is one thing, after all, to convert black men and white women and another thing altogether to convert white men. Or is it? "Colored don't count to those people," as Celie well knows. And the world white men create just seems silly and bizarre to black folk. When it isn't gendered, racial foolishness—"white women . . . laughing, holding they beads out on one finger, dancing on top of motorcars. Jumping into fountains"—it's gendered, racial violence: a white sheriff who rapes Squeak, a white mayor who beats and imprisons Sofia, a white man's war that nearly kills Nettie, Samuel, Adam, Olivia, and Tashi.

Even white men, however, end up transformed by The Color Purple's vision. Many critics argue that Celie throws over her "big and old and tall and graybearded and white" God and replaces him with a sense of spirit, commonality, and moral goodness. But the change in Celie's God is exactly like the other transformations I've discussed. Celie tells God off for lynching her parents, giving her a rapist for a stepfather, making her life, as she says, "a hell on earth": "you must be sleep," she tells him. Celie asserts that the world would be different if God listened to poor colored women. And within a very few pages the world is a very different place for Celie. "I am so happy," she tells Nettie. "I got love, I got work, I got money, friends and time." God is now listening, as becomes clear in Celie's last letter. She includes God once again in her address, verifying that he too, at last, has become somebody Celie "can talk to." "*Dear God.* Dear stars, dear trees, dear sky, dear peoples. Dear everything. *Dear God.*"

So what is wrong with this? Why shouldn't Walker give us a vision in which even the worst, most recalcitrant antagonist is converted and transformed by the power of a poor black woman's voice? Who is to say that she's wrong?

The Color Purple is built on a fundamental contradiction. The very logic of discursive transformation which the conclusion affirms has been undermined and exposed as illusory—or, at best, contingent—throughout the story. Only by effacing difference altogether and creating as her utopia a homogeneous world where everyone speaks the same language, where everyone, symbolically speaking, has their tongue in everyone else's mouth, can Walker reconcile this contradiction. When critics celebrate the novel's affirmation of "voice," taking for granted that it establishes a "collaborative" dialogue with us, they only obscure this contradiction between its two competing logics.

"We Get Real Quiet and Listen"

Not all listeners are the same; a novel has to register that difference and devise a strategy of response. According to Goffman, there are three potential sorts of listeners: those who *over*hear, those who are "ratified participants but are not specifically addressed by the speaker," and those who are "ratified participants who *are* addressed." Only Nettie and God are ever officially "ratified" as the designated recipients of Celie's story. Although they are addressed directly, Celie never really expects a response from either of them, although she *desires* a response from both. Shug, on the other hand, is not addressed directly, but she is very much a "ratified" participant, and a response is certainly expected and desired of her, as it is of participants such as Sofia and Squeak, who are never even addressed. Harpo and Mr. _____, on the other hand, are never addressed directly, no response is expected of them, but they are ratified participants nonetheless. Deborah McDowell has argued that Celie's audience (and Walker's) is clearly intended to be other African American women and that everyone else is in the unratified position

Goffman describes as "overhearing," a position, McDowell argues, reinforced by "the act of reading letters that are written and intended for other eyes." *The Color Purple* is thus a paradigmatic text of "private narrative fiction," addressing itself to "a private readership, or one within that cultural matrix. . . . The qualitative differences between the letters to God and those to Nettie imply a causal connection between a receptive audience (imaged as one with 'kinship' ties to the writer) and the emergence of a forceful, authoritative, and self-validating narrative voice."

McDowell raises an intriguing question. Is Walker structuring a gap between some readers and the more "ratified" listeners so as to make a point about who is or is not able to engender the "voice" of this text? And if so, are critics, like Froula, who take for granted their own "ratified" positions, simply missing the point of what, for McDowell, is a conception of gender particularized by both gender and race? McDowell, I believe, would suggest that they are. But this is a generous reading of the novel's logic. Walker's arrangement of listeners, addressed and ratified, fictive and real, ultimately has the effect of making everyone into "ratified participants who *are* addressed, that is, oriented to by the speaker in a manner to suggest that his [sic] words are particularly for them, and that some answer is therefore anticipated from them." By transforming all listeners, ratified and nonratified, receptive and nonreceptive, into allegories of an intersubjective, discursive ideal, Walker dehistoricizes and departicularizes what sets different social groups apart. Even the particularity of black women is distilled down to an Archimedean magic: the most oppressed black woman has the power (and perhaps the responsibility?) to revolutionize everyone else.

McDowell also suggests that Walker represents a receptive audience as one with "'kinship' ties to the writer." It is the meaning of that symbolic kinship that needs to be taken into account. Where Brontë and Hurston both contrast the difficulty of converting adversaries with the pleasure of conversing with friends, Walker tries to reconcile the two by making all adversaries over into friends. *The Color Purple* attempts to dissolve the tension between a contestatory discursive ethos and an erotic discursive aesthetic through the same strategy Brontë and Hurston use to heighten it.

A complex logic of sameness undergirds the novel's resolution of its contradictory attitudes toward both narrative exchange and "kinship." As Keith Byerman puts it, the novel resolves its tensions "by making all males female (or at least androgynous), all destroyers creators, and all difference sameness." It reduces sexuality and desire to familial affection and identification, thus erasing the relationship between the public and private spheres that much of the narrative has been at such pains to create.

Mr. _____ does not merely become a good listener. He becomes someone increasingly *like* Celie herself: a good housekeeper, a designer of folkshirts, a nurturing member of a principally female and decidedly domestic world. *The Color Purple* expands the discursive horizons of *Their Eyes Were Watching God*, in other words, not by making it possible for Janie to talk to "Mouth-Almighty" but by converting "Mouth-Almighty" into a sea of Pheobys. The political implications of this "signifying" revision are complex. Reconciling Celie to her community as Hurston will not do for Janie or Brontë for Jane (who lives in the very private sphere of Ferndean, tucked back in the woods, away from everyone and everything else) works not finally by making the public sphere accountable to the practices and values of the private sphere, but by making the public sphere an image of that most private sphere of all: the family. The world transformed is nothing more than a romantic image of an extended family. The public sphere against which the values of this novel have strained and contested simply and suddenly evaporates.

Here too Spielberg and Meyjes alter the novel in a way that goes to the heart of its narrative logic. In the novel, the song that Shug sings for Celie, called simply "Celie's song," has no lyrics. "It all about some no count man doing her wrong again," Celie remarks. But in the film version, "Miss Celie's Blues" is given the following lyrics:

> Sister, you been on my mind
> *Oh Sister, we're two of a kind*
> Oh Sister, I'm keeping my eye on you.
> I bet you think I don't know nothing
> but singing the blues,
> Oh sister,
> have I got news for you
> I'm something,
> I hope you think you're something too. (emphasis mine).

This song fits a scenario in which sisterhood, as a metaphor for both safety and similarity, comes increasingly to dominate and shape all other forms of social relation, at the expense of *both* difference and eros. Shug and Celie "sleep like sisters" more than they sleep like lovers. This logic of "sisterhood" or kinship solves the novel's narrative problems, particularly the tension around talk's uses and its limits.

The problem with making everyone a symbolic sister is that it begs the very question it seeks to address. When Brontë and Hurston tie the possibilities of discursive effectivity and pleasure to a (perhaps essentialistic) notion of kinship, their position is that difference is not easily breached. But when Walker uses kinship as the key to transforming bad listeners into good ones, she suggests not that we can speak across differences but more precisely that talk (alone) can meld difference into sameness. Bad listeners cannot "hear" because they are too different. But if only sameness or "kinship" can transform them, then difference remains at best problematic and at worse unbridgeable. Where Walker gives us a story that is sensitive to difference, the underlying structure of that story remains wedded to a normative investment in identicality and sameness.

If all bad listeners can be converted into "kin" simply by being "told off," what a wonderfully changed world results simply from exchanging our stories and talking to each other. This is purely poetic justice. It is utopianism with a vengeance. Or rather, it is utopianism without vengeance, without its admission that it presents its idylls *because* they are unrealizable, without its acknowledgment that to do so is both to step outside of and to peer critically into the world and conventions of realism. As Benhabib puts it in her important discussion of utopianism, the critical force of the utopian is its ability to "project beyond the limits of the present," not to apologize for the present by making it out to be much more pleasant than it is. It would be unfair to say that Walker simply affirms the social world. But her conclusion, having built all its premises around opposition to the social world, suddenly forgets about the social world altogether.

Although Walker provides compelling representations of failed exchanges and suggests the larger political issues they entail, she ultimately vitiates her own critique by exempting storytelling, narrative, and talk, treating them as capable of transcending the social relations from which they emerge, by attempting to explain how everyone can change. Transforming everyone in the novel into an ideal listener makes this novel, to borrow a phrase of Walker's, a "cautionary tale."

The transformed world which closes this novel is a premodern and sentimentalizing answer to the problematic of exchange relations the novel itself addresses, often quite compellingly. It is utopian in that it is a world in which there is nothing left to protest or "fight." But it is also a world in which difference, desire, and, ultimately, exchange itself, have been effaced. Walker's utopia is static. Her homogeneous, ideal community is sterile—and strikingly un-erotic. By providing aesthetic solutions to the very problems that the other texts I've discussed portray as aesthetically irresolvable, Walker undermines her own aesthetic and political project.

Mr. _____'s transformation into a competent, perhaps even ideal, interlocutor is evidence of what one critic has appropriately labeled the novel's "passionate hopefulness." This is the same passionate hopefulness that we have seen in feminist readings of "The Blank Page," "A Jury of Her Peers," "The Yellow Wallpaper," *Incidents in the Life of a Slave Girl, Jane Eyre,* and *Their Eyes Were Watching God,* particularly regarding the possibilities for "dialogue" between the feminist critic and her texts and the possibilities for a woman's tongue being both political weapon and source of pleasure. In its working out of this double—and sometimes contrary—desire, *The Color Purple* is a particularly apt text with which to conclude this study of feminist criticism's political investment in recovering women's voices and in the difficult and not always progressive pleasures such recovery may provide. If I am right that feminist criticism has often asked that its classic texts hold up a positive and affirming mirror of its own critical enterprise, Walker's *The Color Purple* reflects just such acts of mirroring. Self-consciously recuperative, rebellious, and transformative, it fulfills those desires for recognition and reciprocity often experienced as foreclosed by racist, patriarchal, capitalist society. Walker's dramatization of failed communication turns out to be just a foil for her ultimate romance with communication. Or to put it another way, all of her insights into social wrongs are righted by her romance with transformation itself.

In faulting Walker for appealing to nostalgic forms of community and for failing, in a sense, to be utopian *enough*, I recognize the peculiarity of suggesting that *The Color Purple*—of all books—fails its own utopian project. What could be more utopian, after all, than a novel which transforms an impoverished, abused woman of color into a successful, propertied entrepreneur, delighting in her own sexuality, enmeshed in a supportive, loving, multigenerational community of men and women, connected to a nurturing, extended, even transnational family, a story which either buries her abusers or transforms them into pleasant, helpful, supportive, conversational friends?

A useful vocabulary for assessing Walker's utopianism is provided by the distinction Benhabib makes between two visions which she differentiates as the "politics of fulfillment" and the "politics of transfiguration." A "politics of fulfillment" asks bourgeois civil society to make good on its own promises. It corresponds to a politics of voice in that it can be grasped, as Paul Gilroy has observed, "through what is said, shouted, screamed, or sung." Benhabib's "politics of transfiguration," on the other hand, corresponds to an erotics of talk. It represents those forms of friendship, intimacy, and recognition that appear unrealizable under the conditions and apparent trajectory of modern bourgeois civil society. Through it emerge, in Benhabib's words, "qualitatively new needs, social relations, and modes of association." Despite the apparent tension between these two conceptions, as Benhabib shows, no truly useful social vision—literary or critical—can fail to do justice to them both. We must maintain this tension if we are to "understand the dreams of the present [by] also showing that these dreams cannot become a reality in the present." Maintaining this tension may mean leaving certain things unexplained and unresolved, refusing to close gaps that cannot be healed textually.

For Mr. _____ and the other bad listeners to be converted into "somebody I can talk to," the transformational effect of counternarratives has to be presupposed as an intrinsic feature of discursive exchange. But to suggest that ideal understanding or perfect exchange may always already be immanent in the communicative act is a form of wish fulfillment. A world of perfect, immanent understanding and homogeneous sisterhood, moreover, means that even exchange itself is no longer necessary. Why communicate experiences, after all, that everyone else has already had, that everyone else already understands just as we would like them to? Walker's ideal world is both private and miniaturized. Her utopian resolution simply could not obtain in a variegated, complex, larger society—the very society that this utopian resolution at some level must seek to address.

If we imagine ourselves, as empathetic "sisters," to participate only in a text's erotics of talk, to "fulfill" the text rather than being "told off" and truly transfigured by it, then to whom is its contestatory, transfiguring, and oppositional message addressed? Is "the subversive voice we find representative of the age," one that does not criticize us but merely lets us participate in criticizing others? And who and where are they? Doesn't keeping faith with the project of enabling the self-articulations of concrete others demand that we avoid assuming that our position as somebody the text can talk to, somebody who fulfills *its* erotics of talk, can simply be taken for granted?

The Color Purple, unlike the other texts I have looked at, invites us to take that for granted. Instead of reminding us that we are likely to be neither Nettie or Shug, that we may be only eavesdropping (not "ratified"), it reassures us that everyone ("dear everything") is welcome. This alone, perhaps, may not account for the novel's enormous popularity and for the fact that it has so often been used as an exemplary model of feminism. But I am suggesting that our most successful counternarratives, those we read and those we write ourselves, will energize us toward the transfigurations and transformations yet to come, not merely reassure us about the fulfillments we have already enjoyed.

The family picnic at the close of the novel resonates with all of my earliest memories of consciousness-raising: a familiar, familial space, cleared—putatively at least—of uncomfortable difference and contestation.

A "safe" space to eat (although not barbecue, usually), trade our stories, heal the wounds of a culture that told us we had no one to talk to, that accused us of "muttering" when we did—at last—find our voices. I miss the safety of that space. And when I read *The Color Purple* I am grateful to Walker for recreating it for me. But I am also on my guard against such seductive—and sexy—pleasures. It is not only, as Helena Michie has argued, that the discourse of the family and of sisterhood has too often collapsed into a "therapeutic idiom . . . as if all female difference is something that needs to be gotten over, grown out of," it is also that I have learned, even as I continue to seek its comforts, that feminism's "family home"—the space of safety, homogeneity, familiarity, and sameness, a community intent on identification and self-affirmation to the exclusion of difference, desire, and critique—can also be, in Adrienne Rich's words, a "dangerous place."

YVONNE JOHNSON

Alice Walker's The Color Purple

Zora Neale Hurston and Harriet Jacobs can be considered public poets because they identify at least a portion of their narratives as autobiographical and address them to the reading public. Alice Walker, on the other hand, is what Richard Hugo terms a "private" poet.

Readers cannot hear the autobiographical voice in Walker's *The Color Purple* (1982) as easily as they hear the voice in Hurston's *Dust Tracks on a Road* and *Their Eyes Were Watching God* or Jacob's *Incidents in the Life of a Slave Girl.* On the other hand, Walker has written extensively about her characters, their lives, and the act of creating them. Because she has written about her life, her opinions, and her writing, the authorial voice is identifiable in *The Color Purple.* Walker herself says that she allows her characters "to *speak* through me." Walker explains that she was forced to leave New York while writing *The Color Purple* because her characters were constantly complaining about the city. She tried to write in San Francisco, but was finally forced to move to northern California to a place that "looked a lot like the town in Georgia most of them were from, only it was more beautiful and the local swimming hole was not segregated."

Like Jacobs's Edenton, North Carolina and Hurston's Eatonville, Florida the setting for Walker's novel is near Eatonton, Georgia, the rural area where she was raised. Walker, in a manner similar to Hurston's, draws

From *The Voice of African American Women: The Use of Narrative and Authorial Voice in the Works of Harriet Jacobs, Zora Neale Hurston, and Alice Walker* by Yvonne Johnson. © 1998 Peter Lang Publishing.

the imagery, characterizations and language for her novel from her childhood home. Walker's parents worked as sharecroppers in rural Georgia and family and friends serve as starting points for many of her narratives. She describes how she discovered the germ of the story that became *The Color Purple*:

> I was hiking through the woods with my sister, Ruth, talking about a lovers' triangle of which we both knew. She said: 'And you know, one day The Wife asked The Other Woman for a pair of her drawers.' Instantly the missing piece of the story I was mentally writing—about two women who felt married to the same man—fell into place.

Walker's novel grew, then, from this family story. It diverged from this "germ" of her story and incorporated other stories and personalities, but throughout *The Color Purple* the reader can discern the authorial voice.

One way the reader can locate Walker's authorial voice in *The Color Purple* is by identifying her obsessions. Walker is obviously committed to exposing the oppression of black women. As she writes, "I am committed to exploring the oppressions, the insanities, the loyalties, and the triumphs of black women." Walker's voice explores women's roles within the patriarchal system, emphasizing their desires for freedom, spirituality and creativity. According to Mary Helen Washington, Walker is especially preoccupied with the subject of the psychic and physical oppression of women. Washington writes of an interview with Walker: "Ms. Walker spoke of her own awareness of and experiences with brutality and violence in the lives of black women, many of whom she had known as a girl growing up in Eatonton, Georgia, some in her own family."

In a later publication, Walker discusses the impact of patriarchal violence within her own family. When she was seven years old, her brother shot her in the eye with an air rifle, and the copper pellet used in the rifle destroyed the pupil of her eye. For many years afterward, Walker considered herself disfigured and devalued. Walker's parents, who bought guns for their sons, referred to the event as "Alice's accident," but as an adult, Walker describes her blinding as a "patriarchal wound." Celie, the protagonist of *The Color Purple*, is psychically and sexually abused by the man she believes is her father. Celie states: "He never have a kine word to say to me. Just say You gonna do what your mammy wouldn't." After giving birth to two children by this man, Celie is traded like chattel to the man she calls "Mister." When Celie is summoned by her "Pa" her future husband, who has accepted the cow and linens that come with her, "look me up and down." Harriet Jacobs recounts a similar image in *Incidents* when Dr. Flint decided to sell her grandmother, Aunt Marthy. "When the day of sale came, she took her place among the chattels, and at the first call she sprang upon the auction-block." Both Celie and Aunt Marthy are victims of a patriarchal system that reduces them to the status of property

Walker focuses on the issue of the powerlessness of Southern black women throughout her novels, short stories and essays. Within the patriarchal system, women are objectified and often regarded as less than human. In *The Color Purple*, Sofia complains that all Harpo wants is obedience from her. "He don't want a wife, he want a dog." In Walker's short story "Roselily" the protagonist finds herself in the midst of a wedding ceremony in which she is being married to a Black Muslim. Like Celie she has little choice in the matter and feels "something . . . behind her eyes. She thinks of the something as a rat trapped, cornered, scurrying to and fro in her head, peering through the windows of her eyes." Many of the women in Walker's stories feel helpless and trapped by either husbands or fathers, or both. The images of entrapment. and powerlessness are also very much a part of the narratives of Harriet Jacobs and Zora Neale Hurston.

The powerlessness Walker's women feel is often reaffirmed by the physical abuse they endure in their marriages. Many of the women in Walker's stories have been silenced by abuse. According to Belenky and others, "The actions of these women are in the form of unquestioned submission to the immediate commands of authorities." When Celie's stepfather tells her to "never tell nobody but God" after he has raped and abused her, Celie obeys by writing her story in a series of letters to God. When her husband beats her, Celie survives by refusing to feel. "I make myself wood." Mem Copeland, in *The Third Life of Grange Copeland*, is another of Walker's powerless, silent women. She endures "many years of Saturday-night beatings" and although she makes an attempt to better her condition and that of her children, she is permanently silenced by her shotgun-wielding husband. The imagery for this murder came from an experience Walker had as a child. According to Washington, "a friend's father killed his wife, and Walker, a curious child, saw the mother's body laid out on a slab in the funeral home." The image of this body stayed with Walker. As an adult she remembered the woman "lying on the slab with half her head shot off, and on her feet were those shoes that I describe—hole in the bottom, and she had stuffed paper in them." This very imagery is used to describe Mem Copeland's body as it lay on the walk outside her house.

Violence directed toward women is prefigured in earlier texts by African American women. Harriet Jacobs is not only beaten by her master but is also threatened by "death, and worse than death." Hurston's protagonist, Janie, is beaten by all three of her husbands, and Hurston herself admits that her husband, A. W. Price, used physical violence against her. Physical violence is a real presence in all of the narratives under consideration, but only in *The Color Purple*, as Celie stands over Mr. _____ with a razor in her hand, does the author confront her own potential for violence and transcends it.

In *The Color Purple*, Mister's first wife, Annie Julia, is subjected to insult and injury by both Mister and his lover, Shug. Annie Julia takes a lover who also abuses her and finally kills her in front of her son, Harpo. Harpo cradles his dying mother's head in his arms. Walker undoubtedly drew from family stories as she created the murder of Annie Julia and its effect upon Harpo. In her essay entitled "Father," Walker describes her father's childhood. "His mother had been murdered, by a man who claimed to love her, when he was eleven. His father, to put it very politely, drank and terrorized his children." In Walker's short story, "The Child Who Favored Daughter" the father cuts off his daughter's breasts because she is dating a white boy. The daughter is silenced by her father, a man whose soul is so disfigured by racism that he cannot endure a disobedient daughter who has become a "white man's slut." Walker states in an interview that she has always wanted to explore relationships between men and women to know why "women are always condemned for doing what men do as an expression of their masculinity." The powerlessness of women is only a part of Walker's concern with familial relations.

At the heart of these relations, and related to women's lack of power, is Walker's concern with the overall effects of sexism. After describing how her father "expected his sons to have sex with women," Walker says she "was relieved to know his sexist behavior was not something uniquely his own, but, rather, all imitation of the behavior of the society around us." Sexist behavior on the part of men is a recurring image in Walker's novels. In *The Third Life of Grange Copeland* Brownfield tells Mem that nobody will hire her because she is "'a snaggle-toothed old *plow* mule.'" He tells her to "'look in the glass sometime. You ain't just ugly and beat-up looking, you's old!'" Societal attitudes in the United States cause both men and women to focus on women's bodies and outward appearance.

Walker's concern for women is global. In *The Color Purple*, Nettie, Celie's sister, discovers that the Olinka people of Africa think very little of women who are not connected to men through marriage. In this society women have status only as mothers. When Nettie states that she is not the mother of anybody's children but is still something, she is told: "'You are not much.'" Walker expands her concern for African women in her novel, *Possessing the Secret of Joy*, and in her documentary film and publication, *Warrior Marks*. In *Possessing the Secret of Joy*, Walker tackles the issue of female circumcision, which she calls the "sexual blinding" of women. Her protagonist, Evelyn Johnson, explains that she had herself circumcised in order "to be accepted as a real woman" by the Olinka people and that no man "would even think of marrying a woman who was not circumcised." Walker has devoted her most recent years to fighting for women throughout the world, for those "survivors and champions" who refuse to become victims of sexist traditions.

In *The Color Purple*, when Sofia's mother dies, Harpo argues that she and her sisters should not be pall bearers. "Women weaker, he say. People think they weaker, say they weaker, anyhow. Women spose to take it easy. Cry if you want to. Not try to take over." Of course, Mister makes what is perhaps the most sexist statement in *The Color Purple*. When Shug announces that Celie is going to Memphis with her, Mister tells Celie that she is worthless. "You black, you pore, you ugly, you a woman. Goddam, he say, you nothing at all." Walker explains why she is so concerned with such sexism in her essay entitled "Looking to the Side, and Back." "It was at the Radcliffe symposium that I saw that black women are more loyal to black men than they are to themselves, a dangerous state of affairs that has its logical end in self-destruction." Walker advocates a sisterhood of black women, really all women, who will support each other in resisting patriarchy.

The patriarchal system objectifies women. Since many of Walker's short stories and novels are women-centered or womanist, she often focuses on the objectification of women. Many of her heroines either become or are introduced to the reader as active, speaking subjects. Celie is introduced as a woman who first writes, and then speaks herself into existence. Through her letters she moves from oral silence to speaking subject, or as she says "into creation." She announces: "I'm pore, I'm black, I may be ugly and can't cook . . . But I'm here." In her short story "Coming Apart," Walker confronts the issue of pornography and the objectification of black women. The husband, who has been addicted to pornographic photos, realizes, through the active insistence of his mate, that he thinks of his wife as "*still* black, whereas he feels himself to have moved to some other plane." This man sees women as objects and himself as the subject. His objectification of women extends to his wife. This husband, much as Mister in *The Color Purple*, realizes that "to make love to his wife as she really is, as who she really is—indeed, to make love to any other human being as they really are—will require a soulrending look into himself."

Susanne Kappeler contends that the subject-object dichotomy, the root of pornography, prevents effective communication between men and women. "He is a pure subject in relation to an object, which means that he is not engaging in exchange or communication with that objectified person, who by definition, cannot take the role of a subject." She identifies the oppression of white women and the "double oppression" of black women as cultural constructs, a "convenient excuse for the establishment of oppressive social systems." In a similar manner, Walker concludes that "the more ancient roots of modern pornography are to be found in the almost always pornographic treatment of black women, who, from the moment they entered slavery, even in their own homelands, were subjected to rape as the 'logical' convergence of sex and violence. Conquest, in short." Harriet Jacobs's narrative gives testimony to the sexual assaults experienced by slave women, and adds historical validity to Walker's statement. Conquest, oppression and accompanying violence toward objectified humans are the historical accomplishments of the individualized subject.

The patriarchal system itself enslaves and degrades women, for it institutionalizes and valorizes the subject-object dichotomy. Woman, according to Simone de Beauvoir, "is defined and differentiated with reference to man and not he with reference to her; she is the incidental, the inessential as opposed to the essential. He is the Subject, he is the Absolute—she is the Other." In *The Color Purple*, Celie, with Shug's help, succeeds in freeing herself, (de)objectifying herself, from this system which is characterized by interlocking dualisms. The women in this novel form a community that resists patriarchal control. According to Bettye Parker-Smith, "They are sisters in body as well as in spirit and the spirit *cannot* be broken." Walker is not advocating the destruction of men themselves, but of a system that robs both men and women of their humanity. According to Barbara Christian, Walker "sees the possibility of empowerment for black women if they create a community of sisters that can alter the present-day unnatural definitions of woman and man." At the end of *The Color Purple*, Celie and Mister actually become rather close friends. Because of her love for Shug, Celie is able to move toward an understanding of the man she only knew as "Mister" for many years.

Walker describes the patriarchal system as "the enemy within . . . that has kept women virtual slaves throughout memory." She actually moves beyond the restoration of Celie's voice to approve the destruction of "the patriarchal marriage plot that sanctions violence against women." In *The Temple of My Familiar*, Walker openly prescribes the abolition of such marriage. The protagonist, Suwelo, explains why he and Fanny decided to divorce. Couples, though living together, often individuate and eventually separate from each other. "There is no longer a spiritual or even an authentic physical connection. Instead, they are connected by house payments, a car, children, political expediency, whatever. The divorce was merely our first shedding of any nonintrinsic relatedness." While Fanny believed that marriage did not fit anyone, Suwelo was not so sure, "being a man within a patriarchal system." Fanny is connected to *The Color Purple*. She is Olivia's daughter, and remembers fondly the relationship between Shug and her grandmother, Celie. She is another expression of the resistance to the patriarchal system presented in *The Color Purple*. A recurring motif within almost all of Walker's texts is identified by Rafe in *The Temple of My Familiar*: "Ruling over other people automatically cuts you off from life." Walker advocates alternative relationships for men and women, situations in which women do not see themselves solely in relation to black men. The men and women in both *The Color Purple* and *The Temple of My Familiar* make significant progress toward intersubjectivity, where neither is objectified and both are free to express themselves as creative subjects. Walker signifies upon Hurston's texts as she moves her protagonists into intersubjective relationships. Although Janie and Tea Cake initially move toward intersubjectivity in *Their Eyes Were Watching God*, they are ultimately unable to resolve the conflicts within their relationship.

Walker advocates freedom of expression for women. In her essay "In the Closet of the Soul," she argues for sexual freedom. "Women loving women, and expressing it 'publicly,' if they so choose, is part and parcel of what freedom for women means, just as this is what it means for anyone else." Walker believes that a person who is not free to express his or her love is enslaved, just as anyone who would prohibit expression of love has a "slaveholder's mentality." When Celie is beaten by her stepfather because he says she has winked at a boy, she writes: "I don't even look at mens. That's the truth. I look at women, tho, cause I'm not scared of them." Celie is attracted to Shug. "First time I got the full sight of Shug Avery, I thought I had turned into a man." The two women live together for awhile until Shug meets a young man and falls in love with him. Celie is heartbroken and returns home. During this period of her life Celie and Mister become friends and he proposes marriage "in the spirit as well as in the flesh." Celie, however, is not attracted to men, they are all "frogs" to her. She also allows Shug to follow her own feelings. "Just cause I love her don't take away none of her rights."

According to Barbara Christian, "Walker in *The Color Purple* does for the sexual relationships between black women what Hurston in *Their Eyes Were Watching God* did for sexual relationships between black women and men." While Jacobs, as a slave woman, is unable to portray intersubjective sexual relationships, both Hurston and Walker create female subjects who assert their sexual and emotional independence. In her essay "Breaking Chains and Encouraging Life," Walker encourages black women writers and nonwriters to affirm the rights of black lesbian women by declaring, "*We are all lesbians.*" Adrienne Rich describes the power of women in similar terms. She states:

> I believe it is the lesbian in every woman who is compelled by female energy, who gravitates toward strong women, who seeks a literature that will express that energy and strength. It is the lesbian in us who drives us to feel imaginatively, render in language, grasp, the full connection between woman and woman.

The love between Shug and Celie is intersubjective because both women are free to love and each is a speaking subject. Walker brings the two women back together in *The Temple of My Familiar* as they live out their lives together in the house that Celie inherited from her father. And, Walker, who describes herself as a "homospiritual" would probably agree with Rich that primarily women-oriented women are, in a larger sense, lesbians.

Walker calls these woman-oriented women, "womanists" rather than feminists. Some of these women are heterosexual, such as the protagonist of the short story, "Coming Apart," who thinks of herself as a womanist. Walker states: "A womanist is a feminist, only more common. (The author of this piece is a womanist)." Walker defends black women who love other women, because she believes they also "have concern, in a culture that oppresses all black people (and this would go back very far), for their fathers, brothers, and sons, no matter how they feel about them as males." Walker often portrays such women as living apart from men. In *The Color Purple*, Celie and Shug live apart from men for awhile, and at the end, Celie chooses to live in her own house. In *The Temple of My Familiar*, Miss Lizzie tells Suwelo about the peaceful foundation of her many lives. She remembers the very small people she lived with, where "the children live with the mothers and the aunts; our fathers and uncles are nearby, and we visit and are visited by them, but we live with the women." Such sex-segregated living arrangements have historic precedents in seventeenth- and eighteenth-century West African traditions. As Deborah Gray White writes, "West African women usually did not raise small children with the help of their husbands, but raised them alone or with the assistance of other women."

In *The Color Purple* Mister tells Celie that he loves Shug because she is so honest and upright. "Shug act more manly than most men." Celie on the other hand, thinks not. "What Shug got is womanly it seem like to me." Walker warns black women not to "dissociate themselves from the women's movement," for fear of abandoning "their responsibilities to women throughout the world." Walker's womanly, "womanist," authorial voice advocates healing wounds and opening communication between men and women within the African American community. Zora Neale Hurston earlier proposed bridging the communication chasm between African American men and women in her discourse between Janie and Tea Cake. Walker forcefully reiterates Hurston's proposal throughout her novels and short stories.

The themes of forgiveness and reconciliation are prominent in Walker's writing. In *The Temple of My Familiar* Walker's character-actors work toward forgiveness of each other. Fanny writes to Suwelo: "Forgiveness is the true foundation of health and happiness, just as it is for any lasting progress. Without forgiveness there is no forgetfulness of evil; without forgetfulness there still remains the threat of violence." In *The Color Purple*, Celie forgives Mister. She realizes that she no longer hates him. She cannot hate him because he loves Shug and because "look like he trying to make something out of himself. I mean when you talk to him now he really listen."

While Walker affirms her belief in intersubjective relationships for men and women, her attitude toward women's bodies and pregnancy is somewhat ambivalent. According to Sabine Bröck and Anne Konen, "In Walker's underlying concept of sexuality . . . the female body is regarded as woman's enemy, a trap; a girl's first menstruation is consequently described as an initiation into the terrors of patriarchal society." Many of the images of women's bodies and sexuality in Walker's novels and short stories are presented in less than positive terms. In *The Color Purple* pregnancy is presented as a trap. Celie worries that her stepfather will sexually abuse her sister Nettie, so she urges her to marry Mister. "I say Marry him, Nettie, and try to have one good year out your life. After that, I know she be big." Pregnancy ends Celie's dreams for independence; she can only hope that her sister can escape through education. In the first years of the twentieth century, many African Americans hoped that education would bring them independence. While obtaining a higher education was difficult for men, many African American women found the pursuit of education almost impossible. "Speeches and articles abound citing black women as the nurturers and the guardians of—not the thinkers or leaders of the race." Women's dreams were certainly limited by the demands of motherhood. Similarly, in *The Third Life of Grange Copeland* Mem is brought back to "lowness" through the "weakness" of her womb. "The two pregnancies he forced on her in the new house, although they did not bear live fruit, almost completely destroyed what was left of her health."

Walker's attitude toward women's bodies and pregnancy is prefigured by both Hurston and Jacobs. Zora Neale Hurston's protagonist, Janie, is also entrapped by her sexuality. When her grandmother realizes that Janie has reached adolescence, she marries her to Logan Killicks. Janie's mother, like

Mem Copeland, is brought to "lowness" through the "weakness" of her womb. Leafy is raped by her teacher, and her life falls apart after the birth of Janie. Harriet Jacobs takes a white lover as a grand show of choice, but the two children that are produced from their relationship not only anger her master, Dr. Flint, but also keep Jacobs in Edenton, trapped in the garret of her grandmother's house.

Walker's images of entrapment not only reflect an obsession of many African American women but also may well be autobiographical. Walker explores the alternative to pregnancy in her short story "The Abortion." Her protagonist agonizes that she is "Still not in control of her sensuality, and only through violence and with money (for the flight, for the operation itself) in control of her body." As a young woman, Walker returned to complete her last year of college after a summer in Africa "healthy and brown" and pregnant. She states that she "felt at the mercy of everything, including my own body." After coping with an abortion on her own she states that she "began to understand how alone woman is, because of her body." In her essay "One Child of One's Own," Walker discusses the conflict that many artists and writers face when contemplating parenthood. She states: "For me, there has been conflict, struggle, occasional defeat—not only in affirming the life of my own child (children) at all costs, but also in seeing in that affirmation a fond acceptance and confirmation of myself in a world that would deny me the untrampled blossoming of my own existence." Because of her need to write, to create, she made the decision to have only one child. "'With more than one you're a sitting duck.'" Walker is passionately committed to the blossoming of the lives of women.

Despite Walker's ambivalent attitude toward women's bodies and sexuality, she is a committed mother. The joys and trials of motherhood, especially for the African American woman, is an ever present part of her writing. In her essay on "Writing the Color Purple," she discusses her feelings when she learned that her daughter would be living with her for two years: "Could I handle it?" She discovered that not only could she handle it, but "My characters adored her." *The Color Purple* opens with the birth of Celie's second child. Both her children are taken from her, but she thinks of herself as their mother, and is finally reunited with them at the end of the novel. Meridian, the protagonist of the novel *Meridian*, gives her child up for adoption in order to receive a scholarship that will enable her to attend college. Meridian is haunted by the guilt that she feels regarding this child. Shug, in *The Color Purple* also gives up her children; this time to her parents to raise. Shug, like Meridian feels guilty because she has given up her children, but later is reconciled with at least one of them.

The importance of motherhood and modeling within the African

American community is further demonstrated in Walker's search for what she terms a literary "foremother." She finds this foremother in Zora Neale Hurston and describes her search in her essays "In Search of Our Mothers' Gardens" and "Looking for Zora." In her essays on Hurston, Walker describes how she first heard the names of now famous black women writers "appended, like verbal footnotes, to the illustrious all-male list that paralleled them." She relates her need for a literary foremother and explains how her discovery of Hurston fulfilled that need. Walker states that were she condemned to a desert island for life, she would take with her Hurston's *Mules and Men* and *Their Eyes Were Watching God*. Of *Their Eyes* she emphatically states: "*There is no book more important to me than this one.*" According to Molly Hite, both Walker and Hurston turn their attention to conventionally marginal protagonists in order to let those characters assert their voices "in a world full of speechmakers." Hurston and Walker create women who unexpectedly transform themselves from objects into speaking subjects within the African American community. These creations of Walker and Hurston emerge from their narratives as independent, empowered beings who take charge of their own lives. Walker describes how she traveled to Florida, representing herself as Hurston's niece in order to gain information about her and locate her grave. Hite argues that Walker recreates her relationship with Hurston "as a reciprocal and interactive one," and that Walker "dramatizes Hurston's literary role as the undoer of inessential and divisive hierarchies" by casting Hurston in the role of Shug in *The Color Purple*.

While Walker emphasizes the intersection of racism and sexism throughout her writings, her focus, like Hurston's, is on relationships within the African American community. In an interview with Claudia Tate, Walker states: "Twentieth-century black women writers all seem to be much more interested in the black community, in intimate relationships, with the white world as a *backdrop*, which is certainly the appropriate perspective, in my view." The white community exists on the fringes of consciousness in Walker's characters much as it does in Hurston's characters, but its oppression, the oppression expressed through patriarchy, reaches into the black community. Both Walker and Hurston explore the indirect effects that racism has on their protagonists.

In Hurston's *Their Eyes Were Watching God*, Mis' Turner, a light-skinned African American states emphatically that she cannot understand why Janie is married to dark-skinned Tea Cake. "'Ah jus' couldn't see mahself married to no black man. It's too many black folks already. We oughta lighten up de race.'" In *The Color Purple*, Sofia is sent to prison for slugging the white mayor of the town. She is beaten and abused and her spirit is broken. She tells Celie that in order to survive, "Every time they ast me to do something, Miss Celie, I act like I'm you. I jump right up and do just what they say." This is a mirror image of the relationship Celie has with Mister, an image that folds back in upon itself in the patriarchal system. Walker brings the system full circle in *The Color Purple* when Celie tells "Mr. _____" what Nettie wrote to her about the Olinka people. It seems that the Olinka's historical knowledge extended to the time beyond the Biblical Adam; therefore, they explained to Nettie that Adam was not the first man, that white people had been born to the Olinka peoples and "they throwed out the white Olinka peoples for how they look. They want everybody to be just alike." The essence of patriarchy in all cultures seems to be the need to assign status based on difference.

In Eurocentric cultures, those who are different, those who are seen as the Other, are dark-skinned people. In *The Third Life of Grange Copeland*, Brownfield wonders at the white man who is able to "turn his father into something that might as well have been a pebble or a post or a piece of dirt," but after he becomes a victim of racism himself, he reproaches his wife with her color. "He liked to sling the perfection of white women at her because color was something she could not change and as his own colored skin annoyed him he meant for hers to humble her." Brownfield is passing on to his wife the oppression and abuse that white society has exerted on him and his father before him. The reader can see most clearly in this novel the guilt that black women often feel for the emasculation of black men. "Black women not only digest the hurt and pain, they feel it their duty to become a repository of the Black man's rage." In *The Color Purple* the author offers an alternative. Celie, Harpo, Mary Agnes, Mister and Shug realize they must get Sofia out of jail, that she will die if she remains in prison. They plot together, Mary Agnes agrees to seduce the jailer, and they successfully manipulate the racist system that threatens Sofia's life. Throughout *The Color Purple*, the authorial voice speaks for subverting a system that promotes both racism and sexism.

Walker does encourage black men and women to support each other, and she disparages the incipient racism so often found within the African American community itself, especially the significance attached to skin color. There are numerous references to skin color in *The Color Purple*. Harpo tells Celie that Sofia is "bright." Celie asks him if he means "smart," and he replies "Naw Bright *skin*. She smart too though, I think." Obviously, the color of Sofia's skin is more important to Harpo than her intelligence. Mister's father comes to visit when he hears that Shug is staying at his son's house. He proceeds to insult Shug by telling his son that "she black as tar, she nappy headed." Finally, Nettie tells Celie that Tashi has real misgivings about leaving Africa for America. Tashi has read magazines from the United States and "it was very clear to her that black people did not truly admire blackskinned black people like herself, and especially did not admire blackskinned black women." Walker responds to novels of the nineteenth century that portray African American protagonists with fair skin. She argues that, "black men could be depicted as literally black and still be considered men (since dark is masculine to the Euro-American mind), the blackskinned woman, being dark and female, must perforce be whitened, since 'fairness' was and is the standard of Euro-American femininity." Walker believes that the fairskinned African Americans will disappear as blacks, that they will "pass" into white America with little connection to their heritage. She calls for attention to this situation, for "it is the whole family, rather than the dark or the light, that must be affirmed. Light- and white-skinned black women will lose their only link to rebellion against white America if they cut themselves off from the black woman."

Walker recalls her father's "colorism." "He *did* fall in love with my mother partly because she was so light; he never denied it." Walker's women are often dark-skinned African Americans, and they are direct links to the community of their heritage. Walker states: "What the black Southern writer inherits as a natural right is a sense of *community*." Both Walker and the women she creates advocate a removal of the hypocrisy that preaches "Black is Beautiful" while operating within a Eurocentric patriarchy that, while objectifying women, sets its own standards of beauty. Both Harriet Jacobs and Hurston's Janie Woods are light-skinned women with European features, women whose appearance makes them more acceptable within their respective communities. Walker revises their images of beauty as well as the writing of other African American women who glorify the light-skinned mulatta as a part of the countermyth.

Walker is obsessed with spirituality, her own as well as her characters'. Celie writes her letters to God because she is too ashamed to speak aloud what has happened to her. During her life with Mister, she consoles herself with thoughts such as "This life soon be over. Heaven last all ways." Once she gains her voice, however, her image of God begins to change. Shug assures her that God loves sex, and that God is not white but is in everything. Walker states that she is constantly involved, internally, with religious questions, that she does not believe in God, but sees God in nature. "The world is God. Man is God. So is a leaf or a snake. . . ." Celie expresses this view of God as she addresses her last letter. "Dear God. Dear stars, dear trees, dear sky, dear peoples. Dear Everything. Dear God." The authorial voice is perhaps most evident in *The Color Purple* when Shug states: "I think it pisses God off if you walk by the color purple in a field somewhere and don't notice it." Although Shug refuses to be bound down, according to Catherine Keller, "she does not give up on religion as attunement to the interconnected whole of things." Shug, with her female sense of being part of everything, tells Celie: "One day when I was sitting quiet and feeling like a motherless chile, which I was, it come to me: that feeling of being part of everything, not separate at all. I knew that if I cut a tree, my arm would bleed." According to Keller, this is a clear case of "oceanic feeling," of feeling connected to all of life, to all of creation. The connectivity of women is an underlying theme in both *The Color Purple* and *The Temple of My Familiar*. Celie's connection to the whole of things is prefigured in Hurston's *Their Eyes Were Watching God*. When the wind that accompanies the hurricane threatens destruction,

> Janie and Tea Cake sat in company with the others in other shanties, their eyes straining against crude walls and their souls asking if He meant to measure their puny might against His. They seemed to be staring at the dark, but their eyes were watching God.

This view of God and religion is expanded in *The Temple of My Familiar*. Olivia tells Fanny that her father Samuel eventually ceased believing in Christianity because he saw it "as a religion of conquest and domination inflicted on other peoples." In this sequel to *The Color Purple* Celie and Shug form a religious community they call a "band," and Rafe remembers "that women were called *first* and this calling was something men took away from them." Shug even writes her own beatitudes or "helps" produced as "The Gospel According to Shug." Walker stresses interconnectivity in her poem, "Let us be intimate with/ ancestral ghosts/ and music/ of the undead." In *The Temple of My Familiar* Walker's protagonists relate to each other, to creation, and to lives lived in the past. According to Keller, "we never begin from scratch, but with deep and difficult accumulations of past history." Walker encourages her readers to keep alive the "voices of the ancestors." She believes that one of the manifestations of heaven on earth is "that where there is spiritual union with other people, the love one feels for them keeps the circle unbroken and the bond between us and them strong, whether they are dead or alive."

In a sense, the reader of *The Color Purple* is hearing the voices of the ancestors through the authorial voice. Celie, the protagonist, speaks in a turn of the century black rural dialect that "transforms illiterate speech into something that is, at times, very beautiful, as well as effective in conveying her sense of her world." In a real sense Celie's speech itself is authorial, for according to Walker, she "speaks in the voice and uses the language of my step-grandmother, Rachel." Walker realizes that language defines one's world, it constructs reality, and in the case of Celie, it reveals her inner core. Walker, recognizing the intransparency of language, states: "Celie is created out of language. Her being is affirmed by the language in which she is revealed." The use of an authentic, but individualized idiom by Celie does not allow readers to distance themselves, nor does it allow the narrator or author to do so. Further, Celie's language validates her existence, and causes the reader to actually see and feel her world. Walker defends the description of Celie's rape. She says that she "found it almost impossible to let her say what had happened to her as *she* perceived it, without euphemizing it a little. The author herself found that once the lie that rape is pleasant was stripped away, it was difficult to deal with the "positive horror" of the many children "who have been sexually abused and who have never been permitted their own language to tell about it." The use of the protagonist's language to graphically describe sexual violence is an unusual occurrence in African American women's literature. According to Joe Weixlmann, "a history of experiencing sexuality in combination with violence (like rape, enforced pregnancies) influenced Black women's attitudes towards sex," and before the late sixties made them rather hesitant to deal with sexual subjects.

Barbara Christian states that the "most obvious" recurrent theme in the works of Alice Walker is her "attention to the black woman as creator." This is certainly the case in *The Color Purple*. Michael Awkward describes Celie's creative spirit as "muzzled," a spirit that exists in an environment where men try to "silence and control women." Celie is an intelligent, creative woman who has been denied the formal education she desired. Besides the writing of her letters, Celie also discovers that she has a talent for designing pants, and her pants, in addition to her letters, become the symbols of her liberation. She calls her creations "Folkpants" and turns her talent into a successful business venture. In Walker's short story, "Really, Doesn't Crime Pay?," her protagonist is a female writer who gives her stories to a young man who then proceeds to steal her ideas and publish them in his own name. This woman is married to a man who does not understand her artistic talent and tries to buy her with a house and other material possessions. The woman is frustrated with her life and her husband, but decides not to kill herself. She does, however, try to kill her husband; unfortunately, the chain saw wakes him up. In desperation, after her stay in the hospital, she decides that when she is ready, she will leave his house. Walker's short story is written with grim humor, but in her essay "In Search of Our Mothers' Gardens," she is very serious. She speaks for the African American grandmothers and mothers who had no opportunity to express their creativity. "They were Creators, who lived lives of spiritual waste, because they were so rich in spirituality—which is the basis of Art—that the strain of enduring their unused and unwanted talent drove them insane." Walker also celebrates those women who expressed their creativity in the making of quilts, or those who, like her mother, "adorned with flowers whatever shabby house we were forced to live in." These women obviously had a need to express their creativity and had little opportunity for doing so. Thus, the everyday, often taken-for-granted household items like quilts and flowers became outlets for their artistic drive, and it is this artistic drive and creativity that they have passed to their daughters and granddaughters. Walker compares the structure of her writing to that of a crazy quilt: "A crazy-quilt story is one that can jump back and forth in time, work on many different levels, and one that can include myth." Even items of clothing became a mode for expressing the artistic as well as the symbolic. Deborah McDowell states: "The use of 'clothing as iconography' is central to writings by Black women." Alice Walker is no exception. In *The Color Purple* Mister's sister, Kate, takes Celie to buy fabric to make a dress. Celie wants purple fabric, but there is no purple. Her second choice is red, but Kate says, "Naw, he won't want to pay for red. Too happy lookin." Celie is thrilled at the prospect of a dress. "I can't remember being the first one in my own dress." When Mister rescues a very ill Shug and brings her to stay at his house, one of the first things Celie notices is her clothing. "She got on a red wool dress and chestful of black beads. A shiny black hat with what look like chickinhawk feathers curve down side one cheek, and she carrying a little snakeskin bag, match her shoes. She look like she ain't long for this world but dressed well for the next." Clothing is important for expressing not only the psychological state of these women, but in *The Color Purple*, the creation of clothing becomes an artistic as well as liberating expression for Celie. Celie is rejecting her past as well as the traditional role of woman that she was forced to play.

In Walker's novel, *Meridian*, her protagonist Meridian's clothing is also symbolic. "Meridian's railroad cap and dungarees . . . are emblems of her rejection of conventional notions of womanhood." The notion of clothing as iconography may well have been passed to Walker by her "foremother" Zora Neale Hurston, for Janie Crawford's clothing is a symbol of her liberation as well. Just as Meridian's cap and dungarees are symbols of her liberation, Janie removes her "head-rag" and lets her hair flow freely down her back after Joe Starks's death. The removal of the "head-rag" symbolizes Janie's freedom in much the same way that Meridian's clothing is a symbol of her freedom from patriarchal oppression. When Janie returns to Eatonville as a single independent woman, she is wearing "overhalls," a rejection of the "silken ruffles" that Starks required her to wear.

While clothing is used ultimately to symbolize freedom for the female protagonists in both Hurston's and Walker's novels, Harriet Jacobs uses it as a symbol of oppression in her slave narrative. She recounts an incident that occurred after her daughter was baptized. Her father's old mistress "clasped a gold chain around my baby's neck." Jacobs recognizes that the woman wished her well, but says, "I did not like the emblem," for she saw it as a symbol of her enslaved condition. In another even more ironic instance, Dr. Flint proposes to give Jacobs's Brent her freedom by setting her up with a cottage of her own and providing her with light labor, "such as sewing for my family." Although Jacobs does not use clothing to symbolize her freedom from oppression, clothing is used as iconography in the narratives of Jacobs, Hurston, and Walker.

A final theme that recurs in Walker's novels, as well as the novels of other African American women writers, is the theme of (the) journey. "One of the central images in Black literature is the Black man on the move—on trains, in cars, on the road." While women have been traditionally portrayed as remaining at home, African American women present the motif of journey for their speaking subjects, whether the journey is inward or external. Harriet Jacobs, in *Incidents in the Life of a Slave Girl*, journeys from the plantation back to Edenton, from North Carolina to New York City and Boston, and from Boston to England and back. Janie Crawford, in Hurston's *Their Eyes Were Watching God*, journeys from her West Florida home to Eatonville, from Eatonville to the Florida Everglades, the Muck, and back to Eatonville. Hurston revises Jacobs's narrative by relating Janie's journeys to her psychological development, her sense of self. Walker signifies upon the journeys in both of these earlier texts in her novel, *The Color Purple*. Celie's journey is totally psychological. Celie "journeys" from a seemingly silent object to speaking subject. Meridian's journey is both external, as she travels about the South, and internal, as she tries to answer the question, "Could she kill?" Suwelo and Fanny both engage in journeys in *The Temple of My Familiar*. The motif of the journey may well derive from the slave narratives, but African American women writers in the twentieth century have transformed their protagonist's lives through such journeys. Just as Walker has traveled throughout the world and delved into her past for the women and men she has written about, the journeys of her creations are symbolic of the self knowledge acquired by all of Walker's women. The journeys are expressions of the search for the African American woman's spirit; a spirit that has not been destroyed by racism and sexism.

Geoffrey Wagner describes the letters written by Cecile in *Les Liaisons dangereuses* as "dramatic soliloquies, intimate revelations of herself, which she can only really recognize when they are written out." These letters are a kind of "emotional diary, or couch confession to oneself." Celie's letters in *The Color Purple* serve much the same function, for in the only statement in the novel that is not incorporated into a letter, Celie's stepfather tells her, "You better not never tell nobody but God. It'd kill your mammy." Thus begin Celie's letters addressed "Dear God," and asking in the first letter for help in "letting me know what is happening to me." These are letters that function in the double discourse of reviving an epistolary style that Laclos originally used to give voice to women, and in appropriating and revising that style to give voice to a semi-literate African American woman who lived in the rural South at the turn of the century. Celie writes herself into existence through her letters while she simultaneously offers an explication of the culture in which she lives. She records the intersection of racism and sexism within the patriarchal system. More important, she also records the discourse of a community of women within the larger community. According to Lauren Berlant, Celie's narrative resists patriarchal, political language in favor of "a mode of aesthetic" representation. "These discursive modes are not 'naturally' separate, but *The Color Purple* deliberately fashions such a separation in its attempt to represent a national culture that operates according to 'womanist' values rather than patriarchal forms." Celie's discourse offers the portrait of a person and a community made whole, as well as the possibilities of community and wholeness, "the spirit of everyday life relations," that women who support each other can affect.

There are two semi-public narrators of *The Color Purple*. Celie is the primary narrator who finds her sister's letters and presents them to the reader approximately half-way through her epistolary narrative. Like the narrator of *Incidents in the Life of a Slave Girl*, Celie is an autodiegetic narrator. As an autodiegetic narrator she is the focus or "star" of the narrative, not merely a bystander or "walk-on" character. Celie cannot be considered a completely public narrator because, with the exception of the first line of the narrative in which her stepfather tells her not to tell anyone but God, the remainder of her story is in the form of letters written either to God or her sister, Nettie. While Nettie's story diverges from Celie's, Celie's is the first voice the reader encounters and her journey toward self-knowledge is the primary focus of the text. Michael Awkward refers to the "dual narrative voices of *The Color Purple*" which "become unified in much the same manner that the scraps of well-worn cloth are combined into a magnificent quilt." Celie incorporates two letters into her narrative; one from her sister which she includes in a letter to God, and one from Shug which she presents in a letter to her sister, Nettie.

In addition to the two public narrators, there are two private narrators in *The Color Purple*. Just as Janie, as a private narrator, is given a brief opportunity to tell her story to Pheoby in *Their Eyes Were Watching God*, Celie allows both Squeak and Sofia to tell their experiences and observations in two of her letters to God. While these letters are private discourse and are not presented to the public by an external editor, they assume the form of a journal or diary that presents Celie's consciousness in a manner which can be read by the public. It is also worth noting that Celie maintains textual control of the letters throughout her narrative.

Janet Gurkin Altman states: "the paradox of epistolarity is that the very consistency of epistolary meaning is the interplay within a specific set of polar inconsistencies." For instance, the letter format has the "power to suggest both presence and absence, to decrease and increase distance." Celie obviously needs to distance herself from the rape and childbirth experiences that occasion her letters. Her first fifty-one letters are addressed to God. The letters are ordered chronologically for the most part, and they are unsigned. They are undated and since they obviously were not meant to be read by anyone but Celie, they read more like journal entries than letters. *The Color Purple*, however, is not a diary novel. The diary novel does not contain the desire for exchange; however, the reader is aware from her very first letters that Celie *does* desire exchange. Celie addresses her letters to very specific narratees. The very structure of the epistolary novel relies on what Altman calls a "notion of reciprocity" or exchange between the writer and addressee. According to Michael Awkward, "If Altman's assertions are correct, then the epistolary narrative form, because of its intrinsic insistence upon active exchange between writer and reader, is a potentially ideal medium through which Afro-American writers can render the quintessential black verbal behavior of call-and-response." This is the supreme irony of *The Color Purple*; it is written in a form that expects a response, yet there is no possibility of response nor do the protagonists expect one. The responses are contained within the textual interchange, and focus on the discursive interchange of the women of the novel. The discourse between Celie and Shug is recorded in Celie's letters and demonstrates not only Celie's development of self, but the affection that is growing between the two women. These discursive responses are eventually extended to the entire community of women within *The Color Purple* as they learn to encourage and support each other's development.

Celie's letters range in length from two short paragraphs near the beginning of the novel, to several pages as Celie's life and voice begin to unfold. The reader of her letters is immediately struck by Celie's powerlessness. She has no oral voice; she exists only in her letters which simultaneously suggest both the presence and absence of her voice. The first letters serve to emphasize the isolation of Celie, a young girl who is a victim of incest, victimized by her stepfather and the patriarchal system. These letters, unlike Celie's later letters, do not contain an "acute sense of audience." The letters do, however, serve a cathartic function for Celie; they enable her to distance herself from her trauma, and they also enable her to approach her trauma and herself in order that she may understand what has happened and who she is. The letters also serve to draw the reader into the narrative. According to Gates, the epistolary "form allows for a maximum of identification with a character, precisely because the devices of empathy and distance, standard in third-person narration, no longer obtain." The reader is certainly aware of the intersubjective communication brought about by the epistolary form in *The Color Purple*. The careful reader is also aware of a community of discourse, a subversive addition to the usual intersubjectivity, for the women in this novel are speaking subjects who constitute their own separate discourse that is found in the humor, the pathos, and the support that they give one another.

Epistolary discourse is broken into discrete units, in which "writer and reader share neither time nor space." This lack of shared time and space allows the writer to "measure and correct his words, to polish his style." In addition, since the letter is a tangible document, there are nonverbal signs that send messages about the writer and her message. The reader of *The Color Purple* is made aware of such a message in the second sentence of Celie's first letter to God. Celie tells God that she is fourteen years old. She begins her second sentence with the words "I am" but draws a line through the words and substitutes "I have always been a good girl." The reader is immediately aware of a change in her self-perception because of the line drawn through these words. The reader is also made aware of the self-reflexive nature of the document and the process of editing. For instance, Celie never calls her husband by his first name. She is not even aware of his name until she hears Shug call him Albert. Because of the nature of the epistolary form, this name appears as "Mister _____," and serves to make the reader aware not only of the distance that exists between Celie and her husband, but also of the position of servitude in which Celie is placed.

Not only does *The Color Purple* make use of the epistolary form to communicate with the reader, but Celie approaches the addressee as well as the reader through her use of language and speech patterns. She presents, in a rather informal manner, the conversations and conversational patterns of the other characters in the novel. According to Sara Mills, "the novel is less like a series of letters, but rather like a series of conversations." In addition to African American dialect, the speech patterns of the characters, their voices, are presented throughout the novel. These voices, translated by Celie, are presented in direct discourse that is punctuated only with "I say," or "he or she say." The informal, conversational tone of Celie's letters makes for intimacy between writer, addressee and reader. In addition, Celie "uses certain words such as 'titties,' 'thing,' 'pussy,' which would normally only be used in intimate settings or in jokes." The effect of this word usage is not only to provide an intimate glimpse of Celie's mind, but to assure that the reader will travel with Celie. In fact, the reader of *The Color Purple*, more than most epistolary novels, has a voyeuristic sense of reading messages and hearing voices that were not meant for public consumption.

Altman suggests that "even spelling can be part of the message." This is certainly the case in *The Color Purple*, for Celie writes as she speaks, in dialect. For example, Celie spells kind as 'kine,' and ask as 'ast.' "As written dialogue, epistolary discourse is obsessed with its oral model." Most of Celie's letters are written in present tense. One reason for this, according to Walker, is a conscious effort to preserve the "'elders' language (and it is truly astonishing how much of their language is present tense, which seems almost a message to us to remember that the lives they lived are always current, not simply historical), for it can be a light held close to them and their times, that illuminates them clearly." While Harriet Jacobs's appeal to the women of the North in *Incidents* is expressed in carefully worded standard English, Celie's letters are given power by the use of dialect.

There are two other reasons for the use of the present tense in this novel. The epistolary form itself requires the spontaneity of oral expression. For example, in her third letter to God, Celie writes of her stepfather: "He act like he can't stand me no more. Say I'm evil an always up to no good." This use of the present tense brings an immediacy to the text; the reader senses an attempt to bring past and present, absence and presence together. It is, of course, impossible to unite these opposites, for epistolary language itself is "the language of absence," and only unites through the imagination. The use of the present tense in unstructured letter chapters also provides a connection to the reader. According to Sara Mills, "The events are not narrated in the conventional way of situating the narrator at a particular point in time describing the events in chronological order: here the narrator is situated at the same point in time as the events—they are described as they happened with the lack of hindsight and foreshadowing which letters or a diary would have." Since Celie seemingly has the same knowledge as the reader, readers have both a sense of immediacy as they read as well as empathy for the narrator.

Despite the sense of immediacy brought about by the use of the present tense in this novel, epistolary discourse is marked by a time lag between action and narration; the narrator is recording events in the past which are to be read later by the addressee. This discourse is also marked by gaps and blank spaces between letters. "Yet it is also a language of gap closing, of writing to the moment, of speaking to the addressee as if he were present." Celie's first eight letters cover a period of approximately six years. She states that she is fourteen in the first letter, and her Pa puts her age at "near twenty" in the seventh letter. After stating her age, however, "Pa" immediately tells "Mister _____" that, "She tell lies," so it is difficult to ascertain her age or passage of time even in this letter. Celie has been silenced by the prohibition of the father, the prohibition that prefaces her letters. According to Belenky and others, silent women have "little inkling of their intellectual powers." They are women who "see blind obedience to authorities as being of utmost importance for keeping out of trouble and insuring their own survival." Celie is aware that she must obey in order to survive.

Even in her first letters, however, Celie indicates that she may develop the capacity to move beyond her silence. Christine Froula calls attention to the passage in which Nettie has been trying to explain the shape of the globe. "She try to tell me something bout the ground not being flat. I just say, Yeah, like I know it. I never tell her how flat it look to me." This passage shows the reader the pathos of Celie's situation. It also indicates what will eventually be the source of Celie's strength, her ability to retain a sense of herself and her world. According to Froula, "Celie's eventual emergence from silence, ignorance, and misery depends upon her fidelity to the way things look to her." Since the letters are undated, the reader cannot ascertain exactly how much time has passed between letters, but the very fact that they are undated is a form of authorial intrusion. The use of the present tense and lack of dating in Celie's letters is an indication of the rural South as it still exists for African Americans. These first letters also lengthen from two paragraphs to three pages. The very length of the letters indicates the growth of Celie's intellectual as well as emotional abilities.

Celie's consciousness grows as she interacts with other women in her life. On such an occasion, Celie breaks into laughter, but her laughter is silenced when "Mister _____" growls, "What you setting here laughing like a fool fer?" Celie's status is returned to that of an object by this remark. According to Lauren Berlant, however, "her split face" refers "to an object posed, but not yet constituted, the split face that produces plurivocal discourse, not a muted utterance from a victimized shadow." The shared humor of the women and the subsequent anger that Celie feels toward "Mr. _____" foreshadow the voice that is to emerge. The wordplay and humor between these women, a kind of signifyin(g), binds them in community against sexism, much as it brings the larger African American community together against racism.

While Celie is unable to fight "Mr. _____" verbally, the subversive,

ironic humor and parody that she shares with Nettie are early indications of
Celie's growing consciousness and voice. Celie and Nettie are acting in a
"womanist" manner because their humor is audacious and outrageous, and
somewhat self-assured. Their behavior is reminiscent of Zora Neale
Hurston's description of herself as a young girl. Hurston would sit on the
gate-post of her yard and ask for rides from white travelers. She would often
ride a short distance and then walk back home, always without the
knowledge or permission of her parents. She states:

> "When they found out about it later, I usually got a whipping.
> My grandmother worried about my forward ways a great deal.
> She had known slavery and to her my brazenness was
> unthinkable."

Hurston undoubtedly prefigured the "womanist" behavior of Walker's
protagonists.

Celie's growing sense of self enables her to take her first action against
the oppression of patriarchy. She is told to get Old "Mr. _____" a glass of
water. She obeys but then spits in his water. Celie has become a "silent
revolutionary," a woman who does not yet have the power to verbally express
herself, but whose knowledge of herself is growing. Celie rebels, on behalf of
Shug, the woman who is to become her mother, her friend, and her lover.
Nettie's letters prove to be an important aspect of *The Color Purple*. Awkward
argues that one of the central themes of the novel concerns "male efforts to
dominate and silence women," and that "Nettie's letters prove both in their
content and in their manipulation essential factors in the author's
delineation." Shug and Celie recover the letters that "Mr. _____" has
hidden and put them in order by their postmarks. Letters fifty-two through
fifty-eight are letters from Nettie to Celie. Like Celie's letters, they are
undated; unlike Celie's letters, they are signed. Both women are writing their
letters to potentially unresponsive addressees, but neither of their (written)
voices can be silenced by patriarchy. The letters which Celie reads serve
another function. John F. Callahan, in reference to African American call-
and-response patterns, argues: "To know and use your voice you need to hear
and read and interpret other voices, other stories." The letters Celie receives
from Nettie, then, are as important to her acquisition of self and voice as the
discourse she shares with Shug and Sofia.

Nettie's letters are an embedded discourse within *The Color Purple*.
Celie arranges the letters and includes them in her narrative but presumably
does not edit or revise them. Nettie, then, becomes the second semi-public

narrator of *The Color Purple*. The fifty-fifth letter in Celie's collection is the third letter in her arrangement of letters from Nettie. This is the first letter written from Africa. This letter is something of an anomaly, for although the letters are all undated, this letter does not fit into the rather rough time frame of the others. Nettie describes seeing Sofia after she was released from prison; however, this would have made Nettie middle-aged, and Adam and Olivia near adulthood. Sofia did not marry Harpo until five years after Celie married "Mr. _____." Sofia and Harpo had five children before she left him, and has a total of six when she reappears at Harpo's jukejoint. After she hits the mayor of the town, she spends three years in jail before Squeak is able to trick the sheriff into releasing Sofia into the custody of the mayor's wife. At least fifteen years have elapsed. If Nettie had seen Sofia in the capacity of the mayor's wife's maid, Celie's children would have been nearly twenty years old. Also, it is hard to imagine that Celie and Nettie would not have contacted each other had Nettie remained in their hometown for fifteen to twenty years. Nettie tells Celie how she is being educated by Samuel and Corrine and how much she is reading and learning every day. She also sends words that are meant to encourage her sister: "Oh, Celie, there are colored people in the world who want us to know! Want us to grow and see the light!" Nettie's letters not only enlarge the scope of Celie's world, they also reflect the authorial voice. The reader is aware that Nettie's impressions of Africa are drawn from the author's aforementioned visit.

The image of women bonding through work is one that is repeated throughout the novel. Sofia and Celie make a quilt together after Sofia confronts Celie for telling Harpo to beat her. This bonding becomes cross-sexual after "Mr. _____," initially devastated by Celie's departure, learns how to communicate intersubjectively. Near the end of the narrative, Celie and Albert actually make pants together as a symbol of their friendship. By this time "Mr. _____" has become Albert and has abandoned the role of the patriarch whose "law was unspoken, his ways immutable, and his words so close to the patriarchal script that he didn't have to finish his sentences."

Keller describes Shug's statement of interconnectedness as "a clear case of oceanic feeling," that prevents her from giving up "on religion as attunement to the interconnected whole of things." The narrative voice in Celie's last letters is also connected to the authorial voice. In her essay "Everything Is a Human Being," Alice Walker states: "we must begin to develop the consciousness that everything has equal rights because existence itself is equal." The spiritual essence of both narrative and authorial voices are interconnected in the narrative itself. The last letter that Celie writes is addressed to "Dear God. Dear stars, dear trees, dear sky, dear peoples. Dear Everything. Dear God." Celie writes a letter of celebration and thanksgiving for the return of her sister and children. This letter represents the (re)creation of Celie's world, and brings the narrative to the present, as much as an epistolary form can.

In her chapter on the epistolary essay, Anne Herrmann asks:

> What happens when women resort to the epistolary not for an amorous but for a dissident discourse; when they no longer seek to retrieve a male lover unchanged but seek to change the exclusionary practices of a male-dominated culture; when the letter no longer finds its inscription in a repetitive structure of desire but in a unique opportunity to advocate social change?

The answer to Herrmann's question can be found in *The Color Purple*. Celie's first letters are written to a God that is patriarchal and Eurocentric by definition. As her self-knowledge and confidence develops she addresses her letters to her sister. The letter that signifies her wholeness, interconnectivity, and peace is the final one which is addressed to "Everything." The protagonists of this narrative bridge the chasm that is produced by an androcentric culture by finding within themselves the interconnectedness that enables them not only to relate to one another but to the whole of creation. Gates considers Walker's use of the epistolary form "the most stunning instance of revision in the tradition of the black novel." Walker's use of the epistolary form is indeed a stunning revision within the African American literary canon. In addition to its contribution to African American literature, however, *The Color Purple* is a brilliant revision, or (re)voicing of the epistolary form itself. The reader can see and hear the merging of separate texts and separate voices, in the letters of two sisters and in the narrative and authorial voices, into an interconnected and unified whole.

Chronology

1944   Walker is born on February 9, in Eatonton, Georgia, the eighth and last child of Willie Lee and Minnie (Grant) Walker, both sharecroppers.

1952   Walker is shot accidentally with a BB gun and blinded in one eye. Scar tissue covers that eye and she becomes withdrawn.

1958   The scar tissue is removed from Walker's eye.

1961–63   Walker attends Spelman College in Atlanta Georgia and becomes involved with the civil rights movement.

1964   Walker travels to Africa and begins writing the poems that will later appear as *Once*. She also transfers to Sarah Lawrence College in New York.

1965   Walker receives BA degree from Sarah Lawrence College.

1965–68   Walker works in the welfare department in New York City and becomes deeply involved in the civil rights movement. She returns to the South to participate in voter registration drives and campaigns for welfare rights and Head Start. In 1966 she becomes the Breadloaf Writer's Conference Scholar, and in 1967 she receives both the Merrill Writing Fellowship and a McDowell Colony Fellowship.

1967   Walker marries Melvyn Roseman Leventhal, a civil rights lawyer, and later has one daughter, Rebecca.

1968   Her book of poetry, *Once*, written in the aftermath of a traumatic abortion in college, is published. She becomes a writer-in-residence and teacher of black studies at Jackson State University, Mississippi. The following year she teaches at Tougalou College.

1970   Walker's first novel, *The Third Life of George Copeland*, is published

1971   Walker receives a Radcliffe Institute Fellowship from Harvard University and the following year teaches at Wellesley College.

1973   *In Love and Trouble: Stories of Black Women*, is published as well as *Revolutionary Petunias*, a book of poetry. Walker finds and marks Zora Neale Hurston's burial site in Forte Fierce, Florida. She also receives the Lillian Smith Award.

1974   Walker publishes *Langston Hughes*, a biography for young people, and receives the National Institute of Arts and Letters Award for *In Love and Trouble*.

1976   *Meridian*, a second novel, is published. She and Leventhal divorce.

1977   Walker receives a Guggenheim Fellowship.

1979   *Good Night Willie Lee, I'll See You in the Morning*, a collection of poems, is published. Walker edits *I Love Myself When I Am Laughing . . . And Then Again When I Am Looking Mean and Impressive: A Zora Neale Hurston Reader*. She moves to California to begin work on *The Color Purple*.

1981   *You Can't Keep a Good Woman Down*, a book of stories, is published.

1982   *The Color Purple*, a novel, is published, receiving nominations for numerous awards including the National Book Critics Circle Award. Walker is named distinguished writer in Afro-American Studies at Berkeley. She teaches at Brandeis University as the Fannie Hurst Professor of Literature.

1983   Walker wins the Pulitzer Prize and the American Book Award for *The Color Purple* and publishes *In Search of Our Mother's Gardens: Womanist Prose*, a collection of essays.

1984   *Horses Make a Landscape Look More Beautiful*, a volume of poetry, is published.

1985   *The Color Purple* is adapted for film, directed by Steven Spielberg and stars Whoopi Goldberg as Celie.

1988   *Living by the Word: Selected Writings, 1973–1987* is published.

1989   *The Temple of My Familiar,* a novel, is published.

1991   *Her Blue Body, Everything We Knew: Earthling Poems 1965–1990 Complete* is published.

1992   *Possessing the Secret of Joy,* a novel, is published.

1993   *Warrior Marks: Female Genital Mutilation and the Sexual Blinding of Women* is published as a companion volume to the documentary *Warrior Marks,* directed by Pratibha Parmar and produced by Walker.

1996   *The Same River Twice: Honoring the Difficult,* a book of essays, is published.

1997   *Anything We Love Can Be Saved,* a collection of essays, is published.

1998   *By the Light of My Father's Smile,* a novel, is published.

Contributors

HAROLD BLOOM is Sterling Professor of the Humanities at Yale University and Henry W. and Albert A. Berg Professor of English at the New York University Graduate School. He is the author of over 20 books, including *The Anxiety of Influence* (1973), which sets forth Professor Bloom's provocative theory of the literary relationships between the great writers and their predecessors. His most recent book, *Shakespeare: The Invention of the Human* (1998), was a finalist for the 1998 National Book Award. Professor Bloom is a 1985 MacArthur Foundation Award recipient, served as the Charles Eliot Norton Professor of Poetry at Harvard University in 1987–88, and has received honorary degrees from the universities of Rome and Bologna. In 1999, Professor Bloom received the prestigious American Academy of Arts and Letters Gold Medal for Criticism.

TUZYLINE JITA ALLAN teaches in the English Department at Baruch College (CUNY) and is co-editor of *Literature Around the Globe*. She has written extensively on twentieth-century women writers.

LAUREN BERLANT is an associate professor of English at the University of Chicago. She is the author of *The Anatomy of National Fantasy: Hawthorne, Utopia, and Everyday Life*.

HENRY LOUIS GATES JR. is the W. E. B. Du Bois Professor of the Humanities at Harvard University and the chair of the Afro-American Studies Department at Harvard. His books include *Figures in Black, The Signifying Monkey*, and *Loose Canons: Notes on the Culture Wars*.

MOLLY HITE is a member of the English departmant faculty at Cornell University. She is the author of *Ideas of Order in the Novels of Thomas Pynchon*, published by Ohio State University Press in 1983.

BELL HOOKS is professor of English and Afro-American at Yale University. Her books include *Ain't I a Woman: Black Women and Feminism* and *Black Feminist Theory: From Margin to Center.*

YVONNE JOHNSON is Associate Professor of History at Central Missouri State University in Warrensburg, Missouri. She received her doctorate from University of Texas at Dallas.

CARLA KAPLAN is Assistant Professor of English at Yale University and has collaborated with Henry Louis Gates Jr. and Elizabeth Laura Adams on *Dark Symphony and Other Works.*

TAMAR KATZ teaches English at Brown University. She has written about the works of Alice Walker and Virginia Woolf.

DEBORAH McDOWELL is Professor of English at the University of Virginia. She is coeditor, with Arnold Rampersad, of *Slavery and the Literary Imagination* and the author of essays on a range of African American texts.

DIANE GABRIELSEN SCHOLL is Associate Professor of English at Luther College, and has published articles on the works of George Herbert and Emily Dickinson.

LINDA SELZER teaches at Pennsylvania State University where she is a member of the American literature, African American literature, and American Studies programs.

CAROLYN WILLIAMS is associate professor of English at Boston University. She has written feminist essays on Charlotte Brontë, George Meredith, and Virginia Woolf. Her book on Walter Pater's aesthetic historicism, *Transfigured World*, was published in 1989.

Bibliography

Alps, Sandra. "Concepts of Self-Hood in *Their Eyes Were Watching God* and *The Color Purple*." *Pacific Review* 4 (Spring 1986): 106–12.

Awkward, Michael. *Inspiring Influences: Tradition, Revision and Afro-American Women's Novels*. New York: Columbia University Press, 1991.

Babb, Valerie. "*The Color Purple*: Writing to Undo What Writing Has Done." *Phylon* 47 (June 1986): 107–16

Banks, Erma Davis, and Keith Byerman. *Alice Walker: An Annotated Bibliography 1968–86*. New York: Garland, 1989.

Barksdale, Richard K. "Castration Symbolism in Recent Black American Fiction." *CLA Journal* 29 (June 1986): 400–13.

Bloom, Harold, ed. *Alice Walker*. New York: Chelsea House, 1989.

Bob, Jacqueline, "*The Color Purple*: Black Women as Cultural Readers." In *Female Spectators: Looking at Film and Television*, edited with an introduction by E. Deidre Pribram. London: Verso, 1988.

Brock, Sabine and Anne Koenen. "Alice Walker in Search of Zora Neale Hurston: Rediscovering a Black Female Tradition." In *History and Tradition in Afro-American Culture*, edited by Gunter H. Leenz. Frankfurt: Campus, 1984.

Butler-Evans, Elliot. *Race, Gender, and Desire: Narrative Strategies in the Fiction of Toni Cade Bambara, Toni Morrison and Alice Walker*. Philadephia: Temple University Press, 1989.

Byerman, Keith. "Desire and Alice Walker: The Quest for a Womanist Narrative." *Callaloo* 12 (Spring 1989): 343–45.

Chambers, Kimberly. "Right on Time: History and Religion in Alice Walker's *The Color Purple*." *CLA Journal* 31 (September 1987): 44–62.

Cheung, King-Kok. "'Don't Tell': Imposed Silences in *The Color Purple* and *The Woman Warrior*." *PMLA* 103 (March 1988): 162–74.

Christian, Barbara. "The Contrary Black Women of Alice Walker." *Black Scholar* 12 (March–April 1981): 21–30, 70–71.

———. "Alice Walker: The Black Woman Artist as Wayward." In *Black Women Writers (1950–1980): A Critical Evaluation*, edited by Mari Evans. Garden City, NY: Anchor-Doubleday, 1984.

———. "No More Buried Loves: The Theme of Lesbianism in Lorde, Naylor, Shange, Walker." *Feminist Issues* 5 (Spring 1985): 3–20.

Coleman, Viralene J. "Miss Celie's Song." *Publications of the Arkansas Philological Association* 11 (Spring 1985): 27–34.

Collins, Gina Michelle. "*The Color Purple*: What Feminsim Can Learn From a Southern Tradition." In Southern *Literature and Literary Theory*, edited by Jefferson Humphries. Athens: Universtiy of Georgia Press, 1990.

Davis, Jane. "*The Color Purple*: A Spiritual Descendant of Hurston's *Their Eyes Were Watching God.*" *Griot* 6 (Summer 1987): 317–31.

Dreifus, Claudia. "Alice Walker: Writing to Save My Life" (interview). *The Progressive* 53 (August 1989) 29–32.

Duckworth, Victoria. "The Redemptive Impulse: Wise Blood and *The Color Purple.*" *The Flannery O'Connor Bulletin* 15 (1986): 51–56.

DuPlessis, Rachel Blau. *Writing Beyond the Ending: Narrative Strategies of Twentieth-Century Women Writers*. Bloomington: Indiana University Press, 1985.

Early, Gerald. "*The Color Purple* as Everybody's Protest Art." *Antioch Review* 44 (Summer 1986): 261–75.

El Saffer, Ruth. "Alice Walker's *The Color Purple.*" *International Fiction Review* 12 (Winter 1985): 11–17.

Fannin, Alice. "A Sense of Wonder: The Pattern for Psychic Survival in *Their Eyes Were Watching God* and *The Color Purple.*" *The Zora Neale Hurston Forum* 1 (Fall 1986).

Fifer, Elizabeth. "The Dialect and Letter of *The Color Purple*." In *Contemporary American Women Writers: Narrative Strategies*, edited by Catherine Rainwater and William J. Scheick. Lexington: University Press of Kentucky, 1985.

Freeman, Alama S. "Zora Neale Hurston and Alice Walker: A Spiritual Kinship." *SAGE* 2 (Spring 1985): 37–40.

Heirs, John T. "Creation Theology in Alice Walker's *The Color Purple*." *Notes on Contemporary Literature* 14 (September 1984): 2–3.

Henderson, Mae G. "*The Color Purple*: Revisions and Redefinitions." *SAGE* 2 (Spring 1985): 14–18.

Hite, Molly. *The Other Side of the Story: Structures and Strategies of Contemporary Feminist Narrative*. Ithaca, N.Y.: Cornell University Press, 1989.

Hudson-Weem, Clenora. "The Tripartite Plight of African-American Women as Reflected in the Novels of Hurston and Walker." *Journal of Black Studies* 20 (Dec. 1989): 192–207.

Inge, Tonette Bond, ed. *Southern Women Writers: The New Generation*. Tuscaloosa: University of Alabama Press, 1990.

Irwin, Edward E. "Freedoms as Value in Three Popular Southern Novels," *Proteus* 6 (Spring 1989): 37–41.

Jump, Harriet Devine, ed. *Diverse Voices: Essays on Twentieth-Century Writers in English*. New York: St. Martin's Press, 1991.

Juneja, Om P. "The Purple Colour of Walker Women: Their Journey from Slavery to Liberation." *The Literary Criterion* 25 (1990): 66–76.

Kelly, Lori Duin. "Theology and Androgony: The Role of Religion in *The Color Purple.*" *Notes on Contemporary Literature* 18 (March 1988): 7–8.

McDowell, Deborah E. *"The Changing Same': Black Women's Literature, Criticism, and Theory.* Bloomington: Indiana University Press, 1995.

Pickney, Darryl. "Black Victims, Black Villains." *The New York Review of Books* (January 29, 1987): 17–20.

Proudfit, Charles L. "Celie's Search for Identity: A Psychoanalytic Developmental Reading of Alice Walker's *The Color Purple.*" *Contemporary Literature* 32 (Spring 1991): 112–37.

Robinson, Daniel. "Problems in Form: Alice Walker's *The Color Purple.*" *Notes on Contemporary Literature* 16 (January 1986): 2.

Ross, Daniel M. "Celie in the Looking Glass: The Desire for Selfhood in *The Color Purple.*" *Modern Fiction Studies* 34 (Spring 1988): 69–84.

Saunders, James Robert. "Womanism as the Key to Understanding Zora Neale Hurston's *Their Eyes Were Watching God* and Alice Walker's *The Color Purple.*" *The Hollins Critic* 25 (October 1988): 1–11.

Scholl, Diane Gabrielsen. "With Ears to Hear and Eyes to See: Alice Walker's Parable *The Color Purple.*" *Christianity and Literature* 40 (Spring 1991): 255–66.

Shelton, F. W. "Alienation and Integration in Alice Walker's *The Color Purple.*" *CLA Journal* 28 (June 1985): 382–92.

Stade, George. "Womanist Fiction and Male Characters." *Partisan Review* 52 (1985): 265–70.

Tavormina, M. Teresa. "Dressing the Spirit: Clothworking and Language in *The Color Purple.*" *Journal of Narrative Technique* 16 (Fall 1986): 220–30.

Tucker, Lindsey. "Alice Walker's *The Color Purple*: Emergent Woman, Emergent Text." *Black American Literature Forum* 22 (Spring 1988): 81–95.

Walsh, Margaret. "The Enchanted World of *The Color Purple.*" *The Southern Quarterly* 25 (Winter 1987): 89–101.

Williams, Carolyn. "'Trying to Do Without God': The Revision of Epistolary Address in *The Color Purple.*" In *Writing the Female Voice: Essays on Epistolary Literature,* edited by Elizabeth Goldsmith. Boston: Northeastern University Press, 1989.

Acknowledgments

"Race, Gender, and Nation in *The Color Purple*" by Lauren Berlant. In *Critical Inquiry* 14, no. 4 (Summer 1988). © 1988 University of Chicago. Reprinted by permission.

"Color Me Zora: Alice Walker's (Re) Writing of the Speakerly Text" by Henry Louis Gates Jr. In *The Signifying Monkey: A Theory of Afro-American Literary Criticism* by Henry Louis Gates Jr. © 1988 Henry Louis Gates Jr. Reprinted by permission.

"Writing the Subject: Reading *The Color Purple*" by bell hooks. In *Alice Walker*, edited by Harold Bloom. © 1988 bell hooks. Reprinted by permission.

"Show Me How to Do Like You": Didacticism and the Epistolary Form in *The Color Purple*" by Tamar Katz. In *Alice Walker*, edited by Harold Bloom. © 1988 Tamar Katz. Reprinted by permission.

"'Trying To Do Without God': The Revision of Epistolary Address in *The Color Purple*" by Carolyn Williams. In *Writing the Female Voice: Essays in Epistolary Literature*, edited by Elizabeth C. Goldsmith. © 1989 Elizabeth C. Goldsmith. Reprinted by permission.

"Romance, Marginality, Matrilineage: *The Color Purple*" by Molly Hite. In *The Other Side of the Story: Structures and Strategies of Contemporary Feminist Narrative* by Molly Hite. © 1989 Cornell University. Reprinted by permission.

"With Ears to Hear and Eyes to See: Alice Walker's Parable *The Color Purple*" by Diane Gabrielsen Scholl. In *Christianity and Literature* 40, no. 3 (Spring 1991). © 1991 Conference on Christianity and Literature. Reprinted by permission.

"*The Color Purple*: A Study of Walker's Womanist Gospel" by Tuzyline Jita Allan. In *Womanist and Feminist Aesthetics: A Comparative Review* by Tuzyline Jita Allan. © 1995 Tuzyline Jita Allan. Reprinted by permission.

"Race and Domesticity in *The Color Purple*" by Linda Selzer. In *African American Review* 29, no. 1 (Spring 1995). © 1995 Indiana State University. Reprinted by permission.

"'The Changing Same': Generational Connections and Black Women Novelists—*Iola Leroy* and *The Color Purple*." In *"The Changing Same": Black Women's Literature, Criticism, and Theory* by Deborah E. McDowell. © 1995 Deborah E. McDowell. Reprinted by permission.

"'Somebody I Can Talk To': Teaching Feminism Through *The Color Purple*" by Carla Kaplan. In *The Erotics of Talk: Women's Writing and Feminist Paradigms* by Carla Kaplan. © 1996 Carla Kaplan. Reprinted by permission.

"Alice Walker's *The Color Purple*" by Yvonne Johnson. In *The Voice of African American Women: The Use of Narrative and Authorial Voice in the Works of Harriet Jacobs, Zora Neale Hurston, and Alice Walker* by Yvonne Johnson. © 1998 Peter Lang Publishing. Reprinted by permission.

Index